The 12th Man

The 12th Man
A journey into the mind of a die-hard football fan

Published by The Conrad Press in the United Kingdom 2021

Tel: +44(0)1227 472 874
www.theconradpress.com
info@theconradpress.com

ISBN 978-1-913567-58-3

Typesetting and Cover Design by:
Charlotte Mouncey, www.bookstyle.co.uk

The Conrad Press logo was designed by Maria Priestley.

Printed and bound in Great Britain by Clays Ltd, Elcograf S.p.A.

The 12th Man

A journey into the mind of a die-hard football fan

Steven Dawson

Preface

I saw an advert a few years back that depicted life in England without football. The general premise was that upon encountering one another, men would attempt to start a conversation, only to realise that they had absolutely nothing to say in the absence of their sole common interest. I'm sure it will have rung true with every male sports fan in the country.

Although there are some huge fans out there that are women, of whom I know a couple, the sport-related question that I've heard asked more than any other during my life is *why are men so obsessed with sport?*. I've asked myself multiple times over the years, and it wasn't until recently that I managed to conjure any kind of explanation.

When it comes to being a British male, few things make you more 'normal' than being a sports fan. Furthermore, I'd say that it's the only interest that I've ever come across that seems incapable of becoming abnormal, irrespective of how much you do it. In other words, it's the only interest that remains socially acceptable when it becomes an obsession.

I have many highly intelligent and intuitive friends and family members, but none of them questioned my obsession with sport. They didn't voice concerns about the obscene amount that I watched, even though they did about other behaviours of mine. Had they raised it with me, it's unlikely that I've listened anyway.

It took me writing a full first draft of this book for me

to realise that my sports fandom had been unhealthy. I'd set out writing intending to answer that question, *why are men so obsessed with sport?*, which I believed I could achieve through an exploration of the male psyche by reflecting on personal sporting experiences. I hadn't anticipated that reflecting on personal sporting experiences would not only lead me deep into the *male* psyche, but also my *own* psyche.

Without even realising that I was doing it, I delved into both the conscious and subconscious elements of my mind and discovered things about my sports fandom that I couldn't even have imagined. It was as though I'd taken a microscope to my memories, as I made sense of how the obsession started, the reasons that I watched so much sport, and why there was a lot more to my sport-related behaviour than I'd ever considered.

Getting to the roots of my obsession was a very challenging process, so I hope this book can provide a breakthrough not only for sports fans but for anybody who has ever questioned their actions and behaviours.

The First Half

1

Nature, nurture and Leeds United

There can be no doubting that I was dealt a good hand at birth. I was born healthy, male, white, into a middle-class family, with two loving, attentive parents, in one of the richest countries in the world. Never likely to be prejudiced against, while having a hell of a lot going in my favour, you'd think that something dramatic would have to happen for me to find life a struggle.

I'm now thirty-three, I still have four grandparents, I've never experienced grief, and I have warm, loving relationships across my entire family and my vast friendship group. I can have next to no complaints about the environment in which I've existed.

If we clutched at straws, we might point to the fact that my parents split up when I was nine, that I'm a middle child, or that I went to a state school when both my brother and my sister attended private school. However, my parents' break-up only served to bring me closer to each of them individually, there are few people I love more in the world than my brothers and sister, and it was my decision, at six years old, to stay at state school, even though my parents had planned for me to follow my brother to private school. Overall, my *nurture* has been almost perfect.

So what about my *nature*? Well, I'm quite a lot brighter than the average person, I'm a natural sportsman, which goes a long way as a boy, and although I'm no David Beckham, I'd class myself as a decent-looking bloke too.

For the downsides, I could argue that I'm disadvantaged at 5'6" tall, that I don't have the best fine motor skills, or that I have quite a slow metabolism, but once again, I'd be clutching at straws. I got a good deal in terms of my *nature* on the surface of things too; *on the surface.*

Of what my friends and family have seen, there's been minimal conflict in my life. I moved from nursery, to primary school, to high school, to sixth-form college, to university, to full-time work, with a few travelling trips amid all this, with consummate ease.

However, as I'm sure is the case with vast swathes of people across the world, there's been a hell of a lot occurring psychologically and emotionally, which appears to have been the case from long before my earliest childhood memories.

My mum has always taken a lot of pleasure in telling me about what I was like as a young child. There doesn't seem to be an end to the number of stories that she can tell, but there are always two that stand out.

The first is of a two-year-old me running to the toilet at nursery to fetch tissues for my best friend, who I'd known since I was just a few months old. My friend had started to cry as he'd realised that his mum was about to leave him for the day, and my instinctive response was to bring him tissues to help him dry his eyes. What an adorable child, I'm sure you're thinking.

The second story is of my mum telling me that it was time to leave a playground in the park, also as a two-year-old. After refusing to acknowledge this, I was given a 'count to three', after which she told me that I would be in severe trouble should I not obey. When I refused to comply after that, my mum had to physically drag me away from the slides, which caused me to throw an extraordinary tantrum. I flailed my arms wildly, repeatedly banged my head on the concrete, and screamed at a decibel level that few fully grown adults are capable of producing. Not such an adorable child.

If these were one-off events, or if they'd occurred at an older age, it could be argued that I was conscious of my actions and that it wasn't merely my *natural* response to each situation. However, my mum recalls that I fetched a tissue for my friend *every* time that he started to cry. The occasion at the playground was by no means an isolated one either, with every caregiver that I've ever had able to recall identical behaviours in either the same or a similar situation. This conflicted nature was a sign of things to come, although I experienced little of it in my early primary school years.

An obvious advantage for me at primary school was my intelligence. Schoolwork wasn't a challenge, and I was close to the top of the class, whether I tried or not. However, being able to apply my intellect to social situations was particularly valuable, and made becoming popular a breeze for me.

An even more significant advantage that I benefitted from was my natural co-ordination and sporting aptitude, as the prestige that comes with being in the football team is immense for boys in their early school years. Still, more importantly, it provides a better platform for developing close friendships than any other activity.

With sporting genes coming down from the paternal side of my family, and my dad and my older brother having had me out in the garden kicking a ball pretty much from the minute that I'd learned to stand, getting into the side wasn't even an afterthought for me. I was guaranteed a place from the very first training session, and once you're immersed in it, you don't even consider what it must be like for the lads that have to deal with a rejection from something that they're desperate to be a part of, at such a tender age. It's brutal when you think about it.

In the short-term, the role that my dad played in developing my football *playing* skills was undoubtedly the most impactful for me. However, there can be no questioning which aspect of his fatherhood had the most substantial impact in the long-term.

I became a Leeds United fan long before I attended my first match. It wasn't because I had a couple of Leeds United shirts, or because I'd told my friends from school that I supported this football team. There's a realistic chance that it was floating around in my subconscious before I could even talk.

Another story that my mum has often recalled is of my dad telling my brother and me that we love Leeds United during our infancy. I think it was something along the lines of 'you love Leeds United, yes you do, yes you do', in the familiar baby-talk voice. This continued into our early childhood, and I have clear memories of nodding my head in agreement as he said this to me. No reason was given, asking why was futile, we just loved Leeds United.

Further to that, he also insisted that we hated a team called Manchester United, or 'Scum' as he'd sometimes say, usually in an aggressive, but friendly tone of voice. I managed to put two and two together by aligning the name Leeds United with my home city. I was clueless as to what my connection with Manchester United was, but I was happy to accept that I hated them.

When I first visited Elland Road in April 1993, I had no idea who the opposing team, Crystal Palace, were. I can't actually recall anything from the game; I just know that I was there as I kept my ticket for years after. In August 1993, I'd never heard of Norwich City when they were the visitors; they were nothing more than 'the yellow team' as far as I was concerned. On my third outing at Elland Road, I knew *exactly* who our opponents were.

Although I can remember exact details of our 4-0 defeat to Norwich, in particular Jeremy Goss' stunning volley, it wasn't until Scum came to town in the spring of '94 that I truly enjoyed what football fans call *a matchday experience*.

I didn't even know that I had a ticket until I got home from school on Wednesday 27th April 1994. My old man was incredibly excited to tell me that we were going to the game, which I later realised was because of our opponents, and it gave me the first buzz of pre-match anticipation that I'd ever had. Knowing that I was going to watch Leeds United vs Manchester United at Elland Road was enough in itself of course, but I couldn't help but be thrilled by the notion that I'd be staying up until at least 10 pm on a school night too.

After dinner, my dad and I got wrapped up warm in our jackets, scarves and hats, and headed off into the night. With my brother and I having to alternate for when we went to watch Leeds, I felt the polar opposite to how I'd felt just a few weeks earlier when it had been he and my dad that had set off to watch us draw 1-1 with Newcastle United. It was devastation that night, but it was elation on this night.

Although I was giddy on the drive to the ground, that's not one of the archetypal elements of the matchday experience that I recall with particular joy from that night. My dad handing me my ticket to pass to the guy at the turnstile isn't one either, nor the first view of the pristine green pitch as I entered the stadium and made my way up the steps. They were all great, but two specific moments define that occasion for me.

We used to park at the top of a massive mound to the south of the stadium called Beeston Hill, from which you can get a spectacular view of the ground. I'd not experienced an over-awing sense of wonder before the Norwich game, but I can specifically remember feeling blown away upon my first sight of the stadium that night.

In the fading evening light, I was amazed to see some bright lights shining from the roofs of each of the stadium's stands. My dad told me that these were called floodlights and that they were on because the game would be finishing after dark. This might not have been so special to many kids of that age, but to me, this night-game experience was like being transported to a different world. Add to that the view that I had of thousands of people all heading in one direction below me, and I was totally overawed.

With the first moment having occurred outside of the ground, the second moment came inside, just before kick-off. After we'd taken our seats, I can remember looking around the stadium, across all four of the north, west, south, and east stands and being staggered by how many people there were, in such close proximity. Then, as the teams emerged from the tunnel, the noise that the 40,000-plus capacity crowd generated is something that I'll never forget.

My recollection is of feeling an overwhelming surge of adrenaline, unlike anything that I'd experienced before. It was magical, and it wasn't until very recently that I could come up with a reason as to why.

Even at seven years old, I experienced a feeling of being a small part of something so much bigger that night. I was just a little droplet amid this sea of people and noise, and I loved it. I couldn't comprehend this at the time, of course, particularly bearing in mind how little you understand about the magnitude of the world and the universe at that age. The feeling was there, though, it just took decades for me to understand it.

Sadly, we went on to lose the game 2-0, with a flying twenty-year-old winger by the name of Ryan Giggs grabbing Scum's second goal, but probably for the only time in my life in which Manchester United have beaten Leeds United, that didn't matter. I'd fallen in love with the concept of going to watch football and spent the late journey home unable to contain my excitement for whenever my next visit to Elland Road would be. Funnily enough, my fourth visit was also a night game.

That summer, my dad or my brother must have taught me about the concept of a season in football. By the time August came around, 'last season' had gone, and we were now in a 'new season', labelled the 1994/95 FA Premiership. I don't think I quite understood what it meant, but what I did know was that both my dad and my brother seemed more excited than they had been the previous April as all three of us prepared to go and see the season's first home game against Arsenal.

When I asked my dad why all three of us were going, he told me that he'd bought three of what were called 'season tickets', which meant that all of us would be going to every game that season. It was truly wonderful news to receive, and I was particularly excited to learn that I even had my own booklet of tickets. Each one was to be ripped out when attending its corresponding match, and after I'd ripped out my Arsenal ticket to hand to the man at the turnstile on Tuesday 23rd August 1994, I counted the number that I had left in my booklet. There were twenty, which meant that I would be going to twenty-one matches in total that season, I can't put into words how happy that made me. Note to football fans reading this, 1994/95 was the last season in which the Premiership contained twenty-two teams.

With Leeds having failed to score in any of my first three outings, I thought that I was on the way to making that four out of four as the clock reached eighty-nine minutes that night. At that point, I think I'd started to wonder why my dad had so often told me that we loved Leeds United; we never won any matches, and we never scored any goals. By way of this, I figured that my school team were far better than my home-town Premiership football team. However, as the Arsenal game entered its last minute, there was a dramatic intervention by a young substitute.

My favourite players at the time were Gary McAllister and Gary Speed, and I knew the name of every other player that had played for Leeds during my time as a fan up to that point. I have no shame in admitting that I'd not even heard of Noel Whelan before that night, but I don't think I'll forget his name for as long as I'm alive.

The ball broke towards a back-to-goal Whelan about forty yards out from Arsenal goalkeeper David Seaman's net. With his first touch, he spun away from his defender, leaving him now facing goal about thirty-five yards out. He was slightly to the right of the centre of the pitch, with our highest up attacking players bunched comfortably outside of their penalty box, meaning that a cross wasn't on at the time. Bearing in mind how far out he was, and the fact that a goalkeeper of Seaman's quality was in between the Arsenal sticks, by no means would there have been anybody inside Elland Road that would have thought that a shot was on.

Most likely guided by the exuberance of his youth, the nineteen-year-old Whelan got the ball out of his feet with his second touch, before hitting a fairly modest strike towards goal. It wasn't a great hit, but it was on target and looked as though it was going to bounce awkwardly in front of Seaman. Moments after it did just that, there was absolute chaos inside Elland Road.

To this day, I don't remember getting up there, but the next thing I knew after the ball squirmed past Seaman and hit the back of the net, I was standing on my seat, jumping up and down, and screaming my head off. It was ecstasy, euphoria, perfection, and was so worth my two-year, or 360-minute wait to see Leeds United score a goal.

It wasn't just any goal either; it was one to put us 1-0 up, in the 90th minute, against a giant of a club like Arsenal, in our first home game of the season. I may have fallen in love with going to watch football in April 1994 during the match against Manchester United, but I fell in love with Leeds United after Noel Whelan's strike against Arsenal in August 1994.

We held out to win the match, and as we left the ground, my dad said to me, 'you enjoyed that goal, didn't you?'. I don't think he realised at the time that I'd not seen us score a goal before, whereas my brother had, but even with that in mind, I think he was surprised by just how strong a reaction it had induced in me. It was a long way beyond a normal response, and as big as the goal was, neither of us quite knew why. What I think he did realise was that he'd created a monster of a Leeds United fan.

Maybe he should have expected that having indoctrinated me from infancy, and by no means am I implying that this is a bad thing, I remain eternally grateful for it to this day. I guess the point is that I may always have been bound to turn out a certain way as a result of my *nature*, but there can be no guaranteeing that I'd have become the Leeds United fan that I became that day had my father's *nurture* not created that monster.

2

Ego and England

Any real football fan will know that scoring a goal to put your team 3-1 up, in a match that eventually finishes 3-2, does not constitute scoring the winning goal. In theory, it could be classed as the winning goal, but you've only truly scored the winning goal if your strike is the one that puts your team into the lead.

When I was nine years old, I scored a goal to put our school football team into a 3-1 lead in a cup final that eventually finished 3-2. Scoring a goal in a cup final, and the crucial goal as it was, should have been enough for me to have basked in glory for months afterwards, but apparently, it wasn't. I referred to my strike as the 'winning goal' any time a conversation about the final came up, even though I knew that it wasn't.

Don't get me wrong, winning that final was probably the best feeling that I'd had in my life up to that point. However, my desire to try and further promote myself by making that claim tells me that I had an inner drive to be seen as particularly special.

As much as I will be assassinating my character on a personal level in this book, I believe that this is a male trait in general. I don't think I've met a bloke in my life that doesn't display some kind of behaviour that conveys an attempt to self-promote, which most likely stems from an innate desire to be the alpha male.

We can't deny our biology; we are animals at the end of the day, and I see this trait as being the one that most obviously aligns male humans with other mammals in the animal kingdom. I could relate this to my nurture; being regularly put in my place by my older brother could have created a particular yearning for superiority, but I still believe that my general male nature characterised this behaviour.

I believe that women have an innate desire to feel special too, but are more subtle in the way that they seek that approval. Men are naturally more overt in their expression, but a lack of awareness or confidence as to how to assert oneself can elicit some very unusual behaviours. I was a massive culprit of this en route to becoming a fan of the England national football team.

After getting my season ticket for Leeds United before the start of Year Three, I was extremely fortunate to have it for three consecutive years from then. I can remember telling the kids in class about it, and I often gained adulation on Fridays for the fact that I'd be going to watch Leeds United that weekend. There was a very positive kind of jealousy that others expressed towards me as a result, and I revelled in the status that came with it.

Sometimes, if my brother couldn't go to a game, my dad would allow me to invite one of my classmates, which enhanced that status even more. Not only did I go to the games, I sometimes had the power to be able to take other kids with me, almost all of whom had never been to Elland Road in their lives.

It's pretty pathetic to feel good about that sort of thing at nine years old, but I'd venture that most men still get a buzz from being put on a pedestal at forty! As a result of this perceived pedestal of mine, the furore that surrounded Euro '96 yielded arguably the most bizarre decision of my life to date.

Not only did I believe myself to have some kind of higher social standing as a result of my season ticket, but I was also by far the biggest Leeds United, and football fan, in my class. Quite simply, I knew the most about it, and I was the one that people would come to if they had questions about Leeds or anything else football-supporting related.

The problem for me when Euro '96 came around was that I'd never really watched England play, and could barely class myself as a fan. Suddenly, we were doing projects in class about the tournament, and plenty of the other boys were talking about how exciting it was. Some had England shirts, others were discussing individual players, and all of a sudden, I wasn't the 'alpha' football fan any more. If you think that's embarrassing, it's nothing in comparison to the behaviour that followed.

In the summer of 1995, we'd taken our first family holiday abroad to Menorca in Spain. I'd found the concept of flying somewhere on an aeroplane to be utterly remarkable, and it left me feeling a connection with Spain that I'd not felt with any of the home-based holiday destinations I'd visited as a child. However, by no means was I so connected with the country that their football team warranted my support.

Out of pure resentment for the positive attention that England were getting, I informed my class that I supported Spain immediately before the tournament. I reasoned that I 'always go on holiday there', even though I'd only been once, and my loyalty has long been with their national team. I was delighted with the response that I received.

Not only did my classmates make quite a big deal out of it, but there were also teachers and kids from other classes asking me about it too. There was plenty of friendly banter coming my way, and in my head, I'd managed to deflect attention away from England, and back on to me. It's laughable upon reflection.

The funny thing was that after the tournament started, nobody in class seemed to care. There was no knowledge about how it was unfolding, no discussion of England's matches, and even when my home nation knocked out my supposedly beloved Spain at the quarter-final stage, only my teacher made a friendly joke about it.

I can even remember watching England vs Germany in the semi-final and willing an England victory. Once the furore surrounding the national team had settled down, I must have perceived that there was no longer a threat to my football fandom, opening up an innate desire to support England as a result. Ultimately, my dad hadn't indoctrinated me to become an England fan from a young age, which meant that I didn't care when they lost on penalties.

Ironically, having actively avoided supporting England because of my bizarre classroom politics, it was in a classroom at the same school that I became an England fan a couple of years later.

In October 1997, in the early stages of my final year at primary school, I'd gone to my lifelong friend Linley's house with my dad one Saturday evening. I'd not known why I was going at the time, but after getting there, I was informed that we'd be watching Italy vs England in the football.

Having not even thought about my apparent supporting

of Spain for nearly eighteen months by this point, I almost made a fatal error of announcing to Linley's dad that I was an honorary Spaniard. Fortunately, all that came out when he asked me whether I was looking forward to the game was that I didn't care about England. Knowing what a massive Leeds fan that I was, he took serious offence to me not feeling the same way about England, and proceeded to give me an emotive fifteen-minute lecture on the history of the English national team, and what it means to support England.

With my father having expressed little passion for England, it took the passion of a friend's father for me to start feeling a genuine connection with them. I'd become an ardent fan of watching football matches in general by this point, not just those involving Leeds United, which left me interested enough to enjoy the spectacle for what it was. When my friend's dad explained that England would qualify for the World Cup in France the following summer should they earn a draw in Italy, I was invested. By the end of the most dramatic 0-0 I've ever watched, England were no longer *they* to me, they were *we*.

Despite my apparent newfound fandom of England, almost an entire domestic season had elapsed before I engaged with *us* again. I had undoubtedly switched allegiances from Spain/No National Team to England that night at my friend's house, but I probably hadn't become a fully-fledged fan. That happened in the reception classroom of my primary school on Monday 15th June 1998.

A few days before this, I'd gone back to Linley's house after school to find that a live football match was on TV. It was a Thursday, it was about 4 pm, and Brazil and Scotland were facing off against each other right there and then; there was something beautifully baffling about football being on during the day, on a school day.

Back to Monday 15th, and if I had been aware that England were playing that day, then I'd forgotten about it by 1.25 pm. With our class having just returned from our lunch break, my teacher called my friend Tom and me outside while the rest of the kids took their seats. A few of our peers grinned at us as we exited the room, clearly assuming the worst, just as Tom and I were.

Throughout Year Six, I'd not had a great relationship with my teacher, almost entirely because I was bright, while also being a little shit. I liked to push the boundaries, would often talk back unnecessarily, while also completing my work with relative ease. I think my previous teachers had chosen to overlook this for the most part as they knew that I was a good kid, but this teacher hadn't and had regularly kicked me out of class for my misbehaviour. I assumed that I was in the bad books once again, as Tom and I learned that we would be going down to Reception.

She sent us on our way without accompaniment, with some of the lads in class still sniggering at us as we headed off. Tom and I mused about what we might have done as we headed down the hall past all of our previous classrooms, before eventually reaching our destination.

As we arrived, the young kids were all gathered in one corner of the room, having a story read to them by Reception's teaching assistant. The teacher herself was standing in the opposite corner, playing around with a television, with two seats set up right in front of it. After seeing us walk in, she then beckoned us over, gave us a friendly welcome, before asking us to take a seat in front of the TV.

Tom and I somehow remained clueless as to what was going on until the picture appeared and turned most of the screen green. My eyes lit up as the reality hit home, and I felt my first sense of overwhelming patriotism as I heard the start of the national anthem.

The two of us jumped up and down in celebration as we acknowledged that we'd been sent down to Reception to watch England's first game of France '98 against Tunisia. Neither of us had a clue what we'd done to deserve it, as Tom wasn't popular with our class teacher either, but we'd been selected to take an afternoon away from schoolwork to watch a game of football. It was total euphoria.

Tom wasn't the biggest football fan in the world but was undoubtedly the best player in our year group. He'd just started playing for Leeds United Boys, and I think he'd been selected by the teacher to go down and watch the football on account of her understanding of his love for *playing* football. However, I knew for a fact that my teacher knew how much I loved *watching* football, and she must have selected me for that reason. The feeling of being a special football fan may have escaped me during the last international football tournament, but my teacher had made me feel more special than ever for it at this one.

My love for the England national team was born that day circumstantially. I'm convinced that I'd have gone on to support us at some point had it not been then, but it was the unique nature of being taken out of class to watch a football match that cemented an attachment.

When Alan Shearer headed us into the lead just before

half-time, I jumped up and down and screamed with utter joy. It felt amazing to be celebrating a live England goal, at a major international tournament, from within a primary school classroom. I can't deny that the feeling was enhanced by getting a lighthearted telling off from the class' teachers for our over-zealous reaction.

We stayed there for the entire match, with many other school teachers and kids coming to join us to watch the finale when school finished with ten minutes remaining. When Paul Scholes rattled in England's second to secure victory in the last minute, I went so wild that one of the teachers even said, 'You sure know how to celebrate a goal don't you?', in the aftermath. It was almost a carbon copy of my dad's comment after my maiden moment of delirium at Elland Road.

I guess the reality of all this is that I can't guarantee that I'd have become the England fan that I am today had I not felt so special to have been watching that game during a day at school. I'm sure I would have, but I genuinely believe that the joy that feeling special gave me was undoubtedly the critical contributor to me becoming attached to England.

There can be no doubting that this attachment was instanta-neously deep-rooted. A couple of weeks later, I cried my eyes out when Argentina knocked us out of the World Cup on penalties. It had only been a few months earlier that I'd wept my first sporting tears as a result of Leeds getting knocked out of the 1997/98 FA Cup at the quarter-final stage by Wolverhampton Wanderers. I was far too young to understand why I was so upset, but I did know that nothing in my life had even come close to make me feel as strongly as sport did.

I'd not expected to leave primary school with any fond

memories of my year six class teacher, but that gesture defined my opinion of her. Ultimately, my school experience up to that point had been defined by how often I would feel special, which wasn't to continue.

3

Self-esteem and Alan Smith

Maybe I'm being narrow-minded, but I don't think any eleven-year-old child can mentally prepare themselves for high school. Personally, I spent seven years at primary school in a small, homely environment that I became more and more familiar with as the years passed by. Then, by the time I reached my final year, I was at the head of the school, commanding all the respect, while having nothing to fear. Then, I finished, enjoyed six weeks of freedom, before being thrown in to a polar opposite situation. Sound familiar?

My transition involved moving from a year group of twenty-five kids, to one of 270, from a general school population of about 150, to one of 1500, and from a catchment area of exclusively affluent, middle-class suburbs, to one that encompassed the entirety of Leeds. I hadn't planned for any of this, of course, so I got an almighty shock in my first week.

I can remember entering the school grounds on my first day, and feeling like it would take me an eternity just to walk from one side to the other. The place was enormous, with one of the buildings alone seemingly four or five times bigger than the entirety of my primary school. The whole complex was like a maze, and one I had to navigate amid the presence of what appeared to be an infinite number of people.

I'd always been quite a small kid, but I'd never felt intimidated as a result of my height. With our primary school classes having largely been kept apart by the school's layout, I'd not really spent much time around older kids, and there's only so tall that any child can grow up to the age of eleven. Here, I felt like I was walking among giants.

Having spent my final year of primary school feeling like a bit of a big shot, it was clear from the get-go that I would be nothing of the sort in high school. The days of strutting around my little kingdom were gone, I was now a lost puppy, sent out in to the wild to try and survive among a jungle of hardened, embattled creatures.

The good news was that there were essentially 269 other lost puppies, which made making friends an easy process. I met some kids from similar backgrounds, and others from completely different ones, but felt comfortable to befriend anyone. Once it became clear that there were others in it with me, I quickly adapted to the reality that school was now a place at which I was insignificant.

Although I could deal with losing my social standing, I found it a bit more difficult to do without the things that I'd come to depend on for self-esteem. Having always enjoyed being one of those at the top of the class, it was soon apparent that there were a number of kids at high school on a different level to me intelligence-wise. Furthermore, although I made the cut for the school football squad, the ability level was much higher than it had been at primary school. With there being some quicker, more agile, and stronger players trying out, I was forced to move back from my favoured midfield position in to defence to ensure that I was picked to play. The most difficult thing was that only two games were organised for us in the first two months, meaning that I was barely getting the buzz of playing football at all.

As much as my perceived personal struggles were impacting upon my mood state, I at least knew that it was within my control to do something about it. I could always work harder in lessons if I wanted to get to the top of the class, practice more at football if I wanted to regain my midfield spot, or go and join a team outside of school if I wanted to play more. However, one other area of my life, over which I had no control, had also come to majorly impact my mood.

When my parents separated just before my final year at primary school, I was actually happy that it happened. There'd been quite a bit of conflict between them for a while, and as I'd seen a couple of friends go through routine parental separations, I was happy to accept it in the knowledge that it was for the best. Although we had the inconvenience of alternating between my mum's house and my dad's flat each weekend, I really didn't see my life as having been impacted negatively at all.

However, with all that was going on, and my sister to consider too, I'd not foreseen that my dad would have to give up our Leeds United season tickets after he moved out.

Since witnessing that Noel Whelan goal against Arsenal in August 1994, supporting my football club had become by far my most important interest. Although the team had experienced mixed results during my three years of having a season ticket, matchday was the undoubted highlight of my week. Even when we were playing away from home, I couldn't wait to listen on the radio, or tune in to Sky Sports if we were fortunate enough to be on TV.

I'd started out as a fan with Howard Wilkinson as our manager. Wilkinson had led us to the top-tier title in 1991/92, the last season before it became the Premiership, and also the last season before I started supporting Leeds. However, between then and 1996, performances steadily declined, and he was eventually replaced by the highly-regarded George Graham early on in the 1996/97 campaign.

Graham had won multiple trophies at Arsenal before coming to Leeds, and hopes had been high that he would bring that kind of success with him. He was known for creating solid, organised teams, and he used the remainder of the 1996/97 season to do just that with us. By the season's end, we'd conceded only thirty-eight goals from our thirty-eight games, although we finished in the bottom half of the table on account of only scoring twenty-eight. I sometimes wonder whether the fifteen goals we scored in nineteen home games was the actual reason for my dad giving up our season tickets, but the lack of entertainment hadn't bothered me; I just loved going to games.

Although I didn't have a season ticket during my final year of primary school, that didn't deter my fandom. If anything, it only served to increase my love for my team, as I listened to every match of the 1997/98 season on the radio, home and away, without fail. If I was at my mum's, my brother and I would listen in from the back room, while also having the Ceefax Premiership score updates on a continuous loop on the TV. If we were at my dad's, I'd plug some headphones in to his hi-fi system while my sister watched the telly, with my wild emotional responses indicating what was happening in the matches to my dad and my brother.

The hard yards that had been put in at the back during the 1996/97 campaign paid off in 1997/98. While maintaining our defensive solidity, we improved massively in the forward department to over double our goals tally from the previous campaign. That resulted in a fantastic fifth place finish in 1997/98, which saw us qualify to play in Europe's UEFA Cup in the 1998/99 season.

After such substantial progress, I was starting to believe that Graham might be able to take us to a level at which we could compete with the country's finest, namely our arch-enemies Manchester United, and our manager's former employers Arsenal.

However, disaster struck a few weeks in to my time at high school, when rumours surfaced that Graham might be set to take over at Tottenham Hotspur. Ironically, at the height of the speculation, we played out a 3-3 thriller at Spurs, a game during which the radio commentary had been dominated by talk of who he would be managing the following weekend.

Graham did indeed acrimoniously depart for Spurs, with neither our club's board nor fans wanting him to leave after the progress that we'd made. The previous twelve months had been so exciting to follow, that I was now massively concerned that we'd be heading back to mid-table mediocrity should we not find an elite-level manager to replace him.

After the Spurs game, Graham's old assistant David O'Leary took over on a caretaker basis, and presided over our first defeat of the season in his first match against Leicester City. Leicester's boss at the time, the much sought after Martin O'Neill, was reportedly our number one managerial target, and the Foxes' win at Elland Road significantly bolstered his case.

After weeks of intense press speculation, amid which O'Neill had even said goodbye to Leicester's fans, he eventually turned us down to stay where he was. I was devastated at the time, and to add insult to injury, our board appeared to take the easy option by giving O'Leary the job on a permanent basis. Not only did he have no previous managerial experience, he hadn't won any of his matches as caretaker, and I was convinced that my concerns about a return to mid-table would be realised.

One of the features of Graham's time in charge of the club had been his willingness to bring youth players in to the first team picture. Ian Harte and Harry Kewell had established themselves as mainstays in the team, while fellow academy products Paul Robinson, Stephen McPhail, and Jonathan Woodgate had been part of playing squads too.

After O'Leary's appointment, I can remember hearing a lot of talk on the radio that it had actually been he that had encouraged this fast-tracking policy, and that more youngsters were likely to get a chance under his stewardship. This was realised when eighteen-year-olds McPhail and Woodgate were given starts in our home match with Sheffield Wednesday.

To the delight of O'Leary, the two of them helped us to his first Premiership win as manager, with Woodgate scoring the decisive third goal in a 2-1 victory. As delighted as everybody associated with the club was about this, an away game at Premiership giants Liverpool didn't seem like the right environment in which to continue this youth experimentation.

One of the difficulties I'd had during my time as a Leeds fan up to that point was my frustration at how poor we were against the bigger clubs. We were particularly spineless in away matches, having failed to earn a league victory at any of the likes of Manchester United, Arsenal, Newcastle United, Chelsea and Liverpool since the start of the 1995/96 season. Winning away at a big side was essentially an unknown experience for me as a fan.

On 14th November 1998, I made the uncharacteristic decision to venture out on a Saturday afternoon. With my pal Tom having gone to a different high school, we hadn't seen each other for a couple of months, so my mum drove me over to his house at half-time of Liverpool vs Leeds. This is the same Tom that watched England vs Tunisia at primary school with me, who played for Leeds United Boys, but wasn't actually a huge fan of following football. I'd spent the car journey plotting how I could convince him to let me listen to the second half on the radio, with or without him, as a result.

With the score tied up at a very respectable 0-0 at the break, it was absolutely essential that I followed the rest of the match. I wasn't convinced that this would be possible when I walked in to his front room to find that he'd set up some indoor football nets for us, which he was rightly delighted with himself for. His parents were out, which meant that a no holds barred game of indoor 'One v One' would likely ensue, but in even better news, the TV was on, showing something that appeared to be football-related.

There was a list of scores down one side of the screen, with Liverpool 0-0 Leeds being one of them, and upon closer inspection I learned that the show was called Soccer Saturday. I soon gathered that it was a televised score-update show, a concept that I was unfamiliar with as a Ceefax and radio boy.

An incredibly enthusiastic bloke, who I discovered was called Jeff Stelling, was reading out score updates as they filtered through on a little vidiprinter beneath him on the screen, and from time to time, he would bring in one of his colleagues to provide an update on a specific Premiership match that they were watching live. I absolutely loved the concept from minute one, it was everything that I wanted a television show to be.

I'm happy to admit that as a far superior footballer, Tom would have comfortably dispatched me in a game of 'One v One' even had I not been constantly distracted by Soccer Saturday. However, with time continuing to tick away, it was soon clear that playing would be totally pointless as long as Leeds had a chance of earning a result.

Then, in a moment that didn't surprise me, but did massively disappoint me, Stelling brought in the pundit who was watching the Leeds game, who announced that Liverpool had a penalty. We'd held out for three quarters of the match, but it looked like our luck had run out.

Our goalkeeper Nigel Martyn had proved to be one of the best goalkeepers in the league in recent times, but there was an inevitability about the outcome as England striker Robbie Fowler stepped up for Liverpool. The score did indeed become Liverpool 1-0 Leeds.

At this stage, I was able to give 'One v One' my undivided attention, as I'd given up all hope of Leeds salvaging anything from the game. This might seem pessimistic with only one goal in it, but our recent inability against the bigger clubs stipulated that the view was a rational one. In spite of this, I couldn't help myself from turning and sprinting towards the TV a few minutes later, as I overheard Stelling state that there'd been another goal at Anfield.

In what I'll admit *was* a pessimistic outlook, the balance of my emotions lay at about ninety-five percent resignation to five percent hope; I had that little confidence that the goal would have gone our way. That didn't prevent me from experiencing a wonderful feeling of excited tension, as I allowed my emotion to override my rationale in anticipation of the news.

As the pundit for the Liverpool-Leeds game appeared on screen, his initial reaction was to simply say that the goal was a great finish, without specifying the scorer. The score still read Liverpool 1-0 Leeds at the side of the screen, as the man described a Leeds break, with the ball moving from Harry Kewell, to Jimmy-Floyd Hasselbaink, to David Hopkin. He then stated that the ball had bounced around the area, before falling to *Alan Smith*, who had slotted the ball in to the corner to make it 1-1.

My instinctive response was to jump around the room like a madman to celebrate us scoring a goal at Anfield, a collector's item as far as I was concerned. However, my joy was far shorter lived than my usual post-Leeds-scoring euphoria, as a bizarre feeling of doubt swept over me. I wasn't 100 percent certain that we'd actually scored the goal, and it took me a couple of moments to realise why.

Who was *Alan Smith*? Had the former Arsenal target man come out of retirement? I'd genuinely never heard of anybody in and around our football club with that name up until that point, and I honestly thought that there might have been some kind of mistake. Fortunately, my doubts about the goal's validity were soon relinquished as the vidiprinter at the bottom of the screen spelt out *Liverpool 1- 1 Leeds : Alan Smith (79)*, with Stelling simultaneously confirming that 'eighteen-year-old Smith' had come off the bench to score with his first touch in the Premiership. It was an O'Leary masterstroke, another huge impact from a budding talent.

As much as I enjoyed the fairytale moment, it would sadly mean little to me could we not secure the point that Smith had set us on course for. I had to tell Tom that I needed to stop playing football for a few minutes, as the renewed potential of us earning a draw at Liverpool was too important for me not to follow.

I knelt down within inches of the TV, which is something that I also did with the radio when listening to Leeds, somehow believing that it would increase the chances of my desired result coming to pass. I was desperate for a draw, yet within seconds, Stelling was announcing that the match at Anfield was no longer level. Once again, there were no clues as to which way the goal had gone, but that previous balance of ninety-five percent resignation, five percent hope, was now about ninety-seven percent resignation, three percent hope. It wasn't even resignation, it was despair, we'd barely equalised by the time we were almost certainly conceding again.

Liverpool 1-2 Leeds United, Jimmy-Floyd Hasselbaink. I completely lost it, as did Tom, who I had clearly infected with my extraordinarily emotional reactions. Leeds were leading at Anfield, the potential fairytale had become a potential miracle, and there were only ten minutes or so for us to hold out.

The only downside to Hasselbaink's goal was that I became a nervous wreck, as holding on to a lead is endlessly more nerve-shredding than holding on to a draw. The five minutes that followed felt like five hours. A few minutes earlier, I'd been praying for a draw. Now, encompassed by greed, a draw would be no better than a defeat.

As if the drama couldn't end, there was a fourth goal at Anfield on eighty-six minutes.

Liverpool 1-3 Leeds. Hasselbaink. Bedlam for two twelve-year-old boys in a living room in North Leeds. I'd never experienced a feeling like it as a football fan, it was unfathomable that we were 3-1 up at Liverpool having been a goal down less than twenty minutes earlier. It was total and utter ecstasy.

With the comfort of a two-goal cushion, the final few minutes passed far more quickly than the previous few had, and before I knew it, the full-time score had been confirmed. We'd done it, we'd won at Liverpool, with two goals from our main marksman Jimmy-Floyd Hasselbaink, and another from an eighteen-year-old whose name I'd already forgotten. *Alan Smith*, that was it.

In that moment, it felt as though all of the early high school concerns that I'd been feeling were forgotten, with any doubts that I'd had about David O'Leary dispelled. He'd led us to a famous victory, and in the process, provided me with the best feeling I'd ever had. As good as I'd felt at times in primary school, it didn't come close to this. This was *euphoria*.

Whelan's strike, my first ever Elland Road goal, had been a truly amazing moment, as had a number of other Leeds United strikes over the years that had followed. This was different though, there was something seminal about winning at Anfield, something defining. Maybe we didn't need Graham to reach the next level, maybe O'Leary had the potential to take us even further.

4

Sensitivity and the Ryder Cup

If there was one thing that high school exposed about me in my first year there, it was my lack of charisma. I made a lot of friends, across many different friendship groups, but I didn't even come close to becoming a social leader like I was in primary school. I hadn't fundamentally changed; I was still very capable at many different things and remained a genuinely nice person. I didn't realise that none of that mattered in high school, what mattered was personality.

I'd made the mistake of believing that I had a big personality as a result of me having been a leading figure in primary school. It's all well and good being nice, but I had few other personality traits, and the only reason that I had confidence was because of what I was doing, as opposed to who I was being.

I spent most of my early childhood in my older brother's shadow. He was the leader, and I followed him, whether that was through sport, music, computer games, or TV shows. I think I became as capable as I was because he was always pushing me to compete with him, although replicating his behaviour caused me to lack individuality. As a result, I was good at things, but I was uncertain about my identity.

The leading figures at high school were loud, funny, trendy, cool, and/or confident. I'd subconsciously believed myself to be all of these things in primary school, which made it even more difficult for me to come to terms with the fact that I was none of them. When I did, it was only natural that I became more of a background figure.

I've only recently realised that my primary school environment was so effective for me due to how much control I had over it. Every aspect lent itself to my becoming a leader, and I remained one because I could dictate terms for the most part. The interesting thing about high school was that when I realised I wasn't in control, I wanted to cede as much of it as I possibly could. I wanted either to be a leader or a follower, but nothing in between. Looking back, it's easy for me to understand why.

I'd barely experienced any conflict up to that point in my life, but I'd been extremely sensitive to it when I had done. The very few issues that I'd had with other kids at primary school had really affected me, and I'd always done everything possible to avoid altercations. As a leader, I skated above it for the most part, but as I wasn't going to be a leader at high school, the only other option was to slide beneath it.

As much as being a follower suited me, the one thing that I had to get used to was the concept of piss-taking, which hadn't been a feature of our primary school group. We'd been a very co-operative bunch, but some of these big high school characters were already adept at it.

As I was both small and quiet, I was a pretty easy target, and I took my share of grillings throughout my first year. I was neither confident nor witty, which meant that I was terrible at standing up for myself, but I was perfectly OK with simply absorbing my punishment, so long as I avoided genuine conflict.

For the most part, I got by without any issues, although not everybody was so fortunate. There were quite a few situations in which I'd see someone attempt to stand up for themselves, only to be ripped to shreds by the more charismatic characters. The funny thing was that somebody else's misfortune would yield an almost identical emotional response in me to my own.

I found myself spending quite a lot of time trying to support others in that situation, even though it was unwarranted on the abundance of occasions. Victims would often accept my attempts to aid in the immediate aftermath of an incident, but it would sometimes play on my mind until the following day. By this point, they would invariably have forgotten all about it, which would always surprise me, even if it did make me feel better. It was as though I would experience the pain of other kids more intensely, and for more prolonged periods, than they would themselves.

Early on in my second year at high school, this newly discovered trait of mine manifested itself in a bizarre manner outside of school. I was at my dad's for the weekend, and I was supposed to be heading out to go and meet some friends on the Saturday night. However, with both my sister and my brother out at respective friend's houses, I felt awful for my dad that he would be left alone. It was his weekend to have us, and none of the three of us were going to be there to spend time with him.

The reality was that if there was any man that would have been happy to be left in peace, it was my old man. It was 6.30 pm, he was sitting in his favourite reclining chair, and he had some golf on the TV; he was in his absolute element. On reflection, I think that he'd have preferred me to have gone out, but after my sensitivity got the better of me, I cancelled with the lads to spend the evening with him.

In this example, the person involved wasn't even being victimised or showing any signs of being upset or distressed. Yet, somehow, I managed to find a way to feel bad for them entirely unnecessarily. It was a nigh-on insane action to take, but one that would change my sports fandom forever.

I knew as soon as I took my seat on the couch that my sensitivity was misplaced. My dad was far too transfixed by the golf for his eyes to even leave the screen. I didn't want to disturb him, but I did want to know what the event was, so I tactfully waited for an advert break to ask the question.

He told me that he was watching something called the Ryder Cup, a three-day tournament that was contested between Europe and the USA. He said that it was being played out in the States, with the time difference explaining why it was on so late. He added that we were watching the second day's play, which was due to finish around midnight, and that he would, without doubt, be staying up to see it all.

I left it a few minutes before asking the next question, as I didn't want to irritate him when he was having the time of his life. However, when I encouraged 'we want Europe to win, right?', it was like I'd opened a can of worms.

My dad gave me a look of friendly disdain, before confirming that we, of course, wanted Europe to win. Then, just as he had with Manchester United a few years before, he explained to me that we hated the Americans, and needed to beat them at any cost. He told me that things were looking good for Europe as it stood, but that there was still a long way to go. 'Anything can happen in the Ryder Cup' is my recollection of his exact words.

He went on to tell me that the tournament was played in

the matchplay format of golf. I wasn't familiar with this, so he informed me that a player didn't win by taking the fewest shots over the course of eighteen holes, it was actually about winning individual holes.

A match started at all square, and if Europe scored a lower score than the Americans on the first hole, Europe would be 1up after one hole. Then, if the Americans won the next hole, it would be back to all square. Whoever was up by the end of eighteen holes would win a point for their team.

There were a total of twenty-eight points to play for across the three-day competition, eight on the first day, eight on the second day, and twelve on the third day.

On the first two days, each side would pick two players to represent them per match, with the morning matches contested in the playing format of foursomes, and the afternoon matches played in the format of fourballs.

Foursomes involved each team having two players playing a single ball between them, and taking alternate shots. Fourballs involved each team having two players playing a ball each, with the lowest scoring ball representing the team's score for that hole.

The third and final day was more straightforward, with the twelve players from each team playing a singles match against one of their opponents. Just as with the other formats, the individual that wins the most holes wins the match, but in this instance, it's only one ball per player. In sum, the first team to fourteen and a half points wins the Ryder Cup.

My dad was such a strong influence on me back then that his word was like gospel. His passion, particularly when it came to sport, was so infectious, that I suddenly found myself totally immersed in a competition that I'd not even heard of only fifteen minutes earlier.

I'd joined the action during the afternoon session of the second day. Europe were leading 8-4 in points overall after the morning foursomes, with the four fourballs matches being closely contested. I have two key memories of the session.

The first is of nineteen-year-old Ryder Cup rookie Sergio Garcia going wild after securing half a point for Europe. Garcia squared up his and Jesper Parnevik's match against Davis Love III and David Duval with a birdie on the 18th hole. The US pairing had been 1up after seventeen, only for Garcia's intervention to halve the match, splitting the point on offer between the two teams.

The second memory is of Paul Lawrie and Colin Montgomerie playing against an American pairing including world number one Tiger Woods. Lawrie and 'Monty', as my dad was calling him, won the match 2and1 (if a team has an unassailable 2up lead with one hole to play it means the match ends at that point), with Woods costing the USA dearly with a substandard display.

From the little golf that I'd seen up to that point in my life, Woods was the best player in the world by a country mile, and this was his first-ever poor performance as far as I knew. Still, I was elated to see Europe benefit from his apparent humanity, and my dad and I went to bed delighted that we were 10-6 ahead going into the final day. Yes, Europe were already 'we'.

The following morning, I called my mum and asked if it was OK if I stayed at my dad's that Sunday night. This was out of the ordinary, I never stayed at my dad's on a school night, even though his flat was directly opposite my school. My mum permitted it, although she probably wouldn't have had I told her that I'd be staying up until midnight to watch golf.

All Europe needed was to win four of the twelve singles points on offer on the final day to retain the Ryder Cup. If a Ryder Cup finishes in a draw, the team that won the previous edition retains the trophy. Retaining the Ryder Cup is as good as winning it, but my dad made it clear to me that winning it outright was vital. Nothing less than fourteen and a half points would suffice.

There was little doubt that the Americans had the superior golfers, with far more of them ranked inside the world's top twenty than Europeans. Still, we unquestionably had the quality to be able to win four of the twelve matches, or at least we thought we did.

On the Sky Sports coverage of the Ryder Cup, they show a scoreboard displaying all the matches that are out on the course at that time. When the Europeans are leading a match, blue envelops the score of that particular contest on the scoreboard, with red applying when the Americans are leading. I can remember my newfound hatred for the Americans increasing instinctively as a result of them being in red. They were the same as Manchester United; they were 'Scum'.

This made Europe's disastrous start even harder to take. The first six matches of the day saw Americans take leads, and the Sky Sports scoreboard displayed a sea of red. The American players were absolutely fired up, and their fans created an incredibly raucous atmosphere, roaring every time an American putt dropped and heckling the Europeans at any opportunity. I couldn't believe that golf could be so intense, it was as hostile as any football experience I'd had up to that point.

The second half of the European line-up started better, with the likes of Padraig Harrington, Jose Maria Olazabal and Colin Montgomerie getting some blue on the board. The commentators were quick to remind us that even if the first six matches went to the USA, that would still only leave them 12-10 up. It was still all to play for.

The Americans *did* win the first six matches, and the score *did* get to USA 12-10 Europe, leaving the last six matches to decide where the Ryder Cup would end up. Four of the matches were close, with the final two matches seeing comfortable leads for an American in one, and a European in another. It looked like Europe were going to require three points from the four close contests.

I can remember the score reaching USA 14-12 Europe at about midnight. Montgomerie was ahead in his match, while Olazabal and American Justin Leonard were all-square as they walked on to the 17th green. Olazabal knew that he had to win one of the two remaining holes to win his match, and thus give Montgomerie a chance to retain the Ryder Cup for Europe by making it 14-14 in his contest with Payne Stewart.

As Olazabal and Leonard reached the green, you could see that Leonard was a fair distance further away from the hole than Olazabal. It's incredible how you recall these things, but I can distinctly remember the commentator discussing Olazabal's advantage. The extra distance that Leonard's putt had to travel would make it tough for him even to get close to the hole, and his playing first would show Olazabal the line that his ball might take, with them having similarly angled putts.

As Leonard stepped up to take his putt, all that every European fan was concerned with was how far short, or past, he would leave his ball relative to the hole. It wasn't even an afterthought that it might go in.

As the ball trundled it's way up the hill, it was clear that it had enough pace. The line started to look better and better as it closed in on the cup before the camera zoomed in to confirm it's fate. I put my hands on my head in disbelief as the ball disappeared into the earth, before looking up to see that my dad had done exactly the same.

As if things couldn't get any worse, Leonard's teammates charged on to the green to mob him in celebration, completely violating the golfing code of conduct. Olazabal still had a putt to match Leonard's score and take the match on to the 18th hole, yet the Americans ran right across his line, jumping and screaming as though the Ryder Cup was already over. I was no golfing expert, of course, but I could see that this wasn't right.

A few seconds later, Leonard, who had caused the scene but was not responsible for it, was quick to recognise that his teammates had been bang out of line, and gestured for them to get off the green. When the camera returned to Olazabal, he looked visibly distressed, which caused a stirring of unexpected rage inside me. It took the human reaction of our player for me to fully comprehend how appalling the Americans' swamping of the green had been.

When Olazabal was eventually able to take his putt, I was devastated to see his ball drift past the hole. Having been four points clear before the start of the singles, we'd somehow lost the Ryder Cup.

As much as I remember of the golf itself, the abiding memory that I have of Brookline 1999 is European vice-captain Sam Torrance's interview in the aftermath. Torrance tore into our opponents for their 'disgusting' behaviour after Leonard's putt, and with it, considerably heightened the anger that had so suddenly come over me. About thirty hours earlier, I hadn't even been a golf fan. Yet, here I was, totally overcome with emotion, and desperate for us to exact revenge upon these awful American golfers and fans as quickly as we possibly could. My dad's final answer of the night was to tell me that we'd have to wait two years to be able to do that.

It took me a while to get to sleep that night, and a couple of days to get over the disappointment of my first Ryder Cup experience. However, I'd just had a wonderful weekend, and I had a brand new sporting interest to show for it. Had I not suffered a bout of irrational sensitivity that Saturday evening, watching the Ryder Cup with my dad might not have become a tradition that we've shared every couple of years since.

5

A chase to Zidane

For those of you that aren't familiar, let me explain the concept of 'getting a chase' for you. Step One: find an environment in which some kind of authority figure is enforcing any kind of law. Step Two: make it abundantly clear to that authority figure that you are not complying with the laws they are there to keep. Step Three: continue not to comply with those laws until the authority figure has no choice but to try and physically reprimand you.

As my struggles with identity continued throughout my second year of high school, I found myself moving between different social circles and sitting in the background of all of them. I'd become quite good friends with one of our school year's biggest troublemakers by way of him being in my form group. When he invited me to hang out with him outside of school, I started socialising with a crowd that exclusively contained troublemakers.

I was by no means a troublemaker myself, but spending time with these lads encouraged the boundary-pusher in me to start breaking them. I was put on report at school for truanting and answering back to teachers, I started shoplifting, and made a hobby out of 'getting a chase'.

One of my favourites chases came on the Leeds Metropolitan

University campus. One weeknight, we jumped a fence to get on to the athletics track there and started running around the track as though we were taking part in a 400-metre race. We weren't there to run, of course, we were there to 'get a chase'.

After a good while of charging around and making a considerable amount of noise, we achieved our desired result, when a security guard made his way out on to the track and started walking towards us. At this point, we posed like athletes about to start a race in separate lanes, waited for him to get to within about twenty metres, before setting off sprinting around the first bend of the track. The guy didn't run after us, but we all laughed our heads off in complete disregard of his authority.

After it became apparent that we weren't going to clear off as he'd hoped, he disappeared from whence he came, leading us to goad him further. We continued to mess around on the tracks for another five minutes or so, before I was alerted to police sirens in the distance. The lads laughed at me for anxiously bringing it to their attention, but the sirens grew closer before we saw flashing lights in the distance coming towards us.

Seconds later, a police car was speeding up to the car park adjacent to the track, which was our cue to run. We could see the officers getting out of their vehicle as we jumped back over the fence, and then sprinted hell for leather across the pitch-black fields towards one of the lads' house. Partway there, one of the lads fell, and even though the police weren't anywhere near us, stopping to help the man down back to his feet heightened the thrill. We eventually reached safety and revelled in our achievement of being responsible for a police callout. When my mum asked whether I'd had a nice time when I got home that evening, I told her honestly that I had.

The story of my second year of high school was one of becoming very sensitive to negative situations, and insensitive to positive ones. I continued to struggle with any conflict, whether it was mine or that of others, while the things that would ordinarily give me pleasure became somewhat bland.

I lost my passion for playing football, my enthusiasm for school subjects that I'd previously enjoyed, and the desire for ordinary socialising. It was as though I had a skewed emotional threshold that made me more susceptible to anxiety and more resistant to excitement.

The positive that came from this, if it was a positive, was that once I did experience excitement, I felt it more strongly than I'd ever felt it before. If something got me going, it really did get me going, although this feeling only seemed to surface in response to potentially destructive actions, like 'getting a chase'.

Nothing personally productive could yield this overwhelming feeling of excitement, which is why I owed a great deal to the rise of Leeds United.

I'm not going to say that I'd have gone down the wrong path without my football team, but I certainly feel like Leeds came very good for me at a time of need. After that famous victory at Anfield in November 1998, we went from strength to strength in the 1998/99 season to secure a brilliant fourth place finish. David O'Leary blooded yet more youngsters and transformed our playing style to deliver the most successful season since my inception as a fan.

On the eve of the 1999/00 season, I was left as concerned as I'd been when George Graham had left the club, as star striker Jimmy-Floyd Hasselbaink departed for Atletico Madrid. As brilliant as our youngsters had been, I'd seen Hasselbaink's goals as the cornerstone of O'Leary's success, and genuinely believed him to be irreplaceable. However, twenty-one-year-old Michael Bridges, signed from Sunderland that summer, scored eleven goals in a spectacular opening half of the season that saw us bring in the new millennium atop the Premiership.

Although we experienced a bit of a dip in form in January and February to fall away from a potential title challenge, I received some great news on a personal level as a fan. My mate Linley, his dad, and his sister had become season ticket holders at the start of the 99/00 season. As happy as I was for him, it'd been slightly heartbreaking to listen to his match reports on Monday mornings at school. As ever, I'd loved listening to the games on the radio or watching on Sky, but Linley's first-hand reviews undoubtedly made me feel like I was missing out.

Despite our excellence, Linley's sister somehow started to lose interest in early January, before deciding that she no longer wanted to go at all in February. With Linley's dad allowing him to take a friend in her place, I went to almost every game for the rest of the season and revelled in watching our wonderful young team play some of the best football that I'd ever seen. That wasn't just from a Leeds team either.

We went on to reach the UEFA Cup semi-final and finish third in the league, securing Champions League qualification for the 2000/01 campaign. There were multiple highlights in terms of specific results, a 2-0 win at bogey team Chelsea standing out as a particular statement of intent, but it was our style of play that really blew me away. We were so good to watch at times that I actually couldn't believe it was a Leeds United side.

In terms of personnel, Bridges finished with twenty-one goals in all competitions, while Jonathan Woodgate, Ian Harte, Lee

Bowyer and Alan Smith all came of age as our young players became the heartbeat of our team. Still, few sides reach that level without at least one truly top-class player.

Since his first-team debut in 1996, Australian Harry Kewell had been the one academy product of ours that had shown the potential to become world-class. We'd brought many quality youngsters through in that time, but Kewell was on a different level, and had been terrorising defences in the Premiership and across Europe for some time before 99/00.

Still only twenty by that August, O'Leary recognised the magnitude of Kewell's talent by giving him a free role, allowing him to roam from his starting left-wing position to wherever he wanted in the attacking third throughout matches. It proved an astute move, as Kewell was the best player on the pitch in almost every game that I watched, and produced goals and assists the likes of which I'd not seen from a Leeds player before.

In a critical game at Sheffield Wednesday towards the end of 99/00, Kewell received the ball in a central position about twenty-five yards from goal, before taking a touch to get it out of his feet. He took a glance up, before hitting a specu- lative effort with the outside of his left boot that floated over Wednesday 'keeper Kevin Pressman's head. The ball hit the underside of the crossbar and bounced into the back of the net, causing the commentators to marvel at the scope of Kewell's ability. It was a moment that solely special players are capable of, with the only downside being the questions that followed about whether we'd be able to keep hold of our prized asset.

When the domestic season finished, the crest of the Leeds United wave that I was riding carried me excitedly towards Euro 2000. After the heartbreak of World Cup 1998, I was incredibly excited to see whether England could go deep in a tournament that the quality of our players suggested that we should. Sadly, it was a disastrous campaign in which we exited at the group stage, but to my great surprise, that did not signal the end of my interest in the tournament.

I intended to watch plenty of Champions League football in the 00/01 club season for obvious reasons, although I'd seen little of Europe's premier club competition up to that point. Being largely unfamiliar with domestic Italian football too, Euro 2000 felt like a personal expose to a French magician called Zinedine Zidane.

I'd seen Zidane play before, specifically in the 1998 World Cup final in which he scored two headed goals to guide his country to victory, but I'd not paid much attention to his football prowess back then. However, watching him at the Euros that summer gave me the first experience of awe and wonder that I'd ever had.

I didn't see any of France's group games, but I tuned in for their quarter-final with Spain from the box room of my dad's flat. With something supposedly more important on the main TV in the living room, I dusted off an old, out-of-use one from a cupboard, plugged it in, and started to play around with the aerial to get a plausible signal. After a frustrating five minutes or so, I almost gave up in a fit of rage but stuck at it until I eventually had a picture. I'm so glad that I did.

For the entirety of that match, I barely acknowledged twenty-one of the twenty-two players on the pitch, merely watching one in astonishment. It wasn't just Zidane's sublime free-kick against Spain that captivated me; there was a presence about him that I couldn't quite put my finger on. He seemed to glide around the pitch with supreme elegance, yet whenever an opposing player could actually manage to get close to him, he'd shrug them off with consummate ease.

Until the free-kick, I couldn't tell whether he was right-footed or left-footed, such was his ambidexterity. His passing was inch-perfect, he moved with the ball as though it wasn't at his feet at all, and seemed to know where every single one of his team-mates was without having to look. The whole game was effortless to him.

I became so transfixed by Zidane that I turned down opportunities to play football specifically to watch him in both of France's semi-final and final matches of Euro 2000. If ninety minutes of seeing him in action wasn't enough of a privilege, both games went to extra time, with his genius defying my understanding of the game of football en route to Les Bleus lifting the trophy.

As good as Leeds had been to watch over the previous couple of seasons, the euphoria that I'd felt as a fan hadn't necessarily come from us being awe-striking to watch. It had been a combination of our performances, the results, and the magnitude of my fandom that had helped me go beyond my unusually high threshold of positive emotion. Remarkably, Zidane's outrageous footballing ability alone had got me there too, and the amazing feeling that I experienced when watching him made me want to talk about him constantly, to anybody that would listen. It was almost *obsessive*.

That was just a sign of where I was at the time in my life. I had so little enthusiasm for anything, that when I did experience a positive emotion, I felt it extraordinarily strongly. 'Getting a chase' and Zinedine Zidane might have been two very different avenues for yielding that feeling, but at least I had football as a non-destructive outlet for it.

Had I been less resistant to that level of excitement, then maybe I wouldn't have felt so strongly about Leeds United at the time. I hadn't reached the limit of my passion for my football club there though, not by a long shot.

6

A bedroom sanctuary and a European adventure

If anybody asks me what the best present that I've ever received is, only one answer springs to mind. After my mum, brother, sister and I moved house to go and live with my mum's new partner in July 2000, I asked her if I could have cable TV in my bedroom for as many birthday and Christmas presents combined as it would take.

After my dad left, we got cable in the back room at the old house to provide a permanent place for my brother and me to watch sport. It was a bit of a masterstroke from my mum, as it kept the two of us permanently occupied, and when Matt started going out with his friends more, it became a haven for me.

With my mum's partner's two daughters likely to be at our new house quite often, I recognised that my sport-watching livelihood was likely to come under threat. I was smart enough to know that compromise would be an essential part of making the new arrangement work, and with five kids around, television was something that we'd need to share. I had no problem with all the other aspects of this significant change, but sport was something I felt simply incapable of compromising on.

Although Leeds United were on a pedestal, I was now an established fan of cricket, tennis, golf, rugby league, and rugby union. There was nothing I'd enjoyed more after a day at school, aside from a chase, than switching off with a bit of sport in my back room sanctuary. I knew that it was an ambitious request to try and replicate that environment in my new bedroom.

After a long period of deliberation, my mum delivered for me, and I was the happiest that I'd been since primary school in terms of my general mood. For the first time in my life, I felt as though I had everything that I needed from the confines of my personal space, and although I was out with friends from time to time, I spent the majority of the summer alone in my new sanctuary watching sport.

A close second place to that present was my dad's gift of a Leeds season ticket for the 2000/01 season. My dad knew Linley's dad well, and they came to an arrangement by which I would take Linley's sister's ticket from her permanently. I couldn't have been more excited by the prospect, and I still feel grateful to this day for the way each of my parents provided something incredibly important to me at the time.

Their gestures prompted a bit of a change in mentality in me, and when I returned to school that September, I knuckled down and stopped playing the class clown. I got on with my work, stopped hanging around with the troublemakers, and paid less and less attention to the high school politics that I'd worked hard to navigate during my first couple of years.

Trying to make sense of where everybody else and I fitted had been an exhausting process, and I stopped caring and making effort in third year. All I needed to do was get by, safe in the knowledge that my bedroom sanctuary awaited at the end of each day. In the space of a few weeks, I replaced all of my destructive behaviours with one that yielded an equally powerful emotional response, *solitude*.

I was so happy on my own that I barely socialised at all outside of school at this stage. I'd stay out at a friend's from time to time, and attend the odd little gathering, but I found that the new craze, house parties, took more out of me than I took out of them. Being around people felt like a tremendous effort, whereas withdrawal felt blissful, which left me perfectly happy to have just one regular social interest.

After a mixed start to the 00/01 Premiership season, there was lift-off for Leeds United on the first-ever Champions League night at Elland Road. We were given the dream draw in the first group stage, pitted against European giants AC Milan and Barcelona, as well as Turkish side Besiktas. We harboured no ambitions of winning the competition of course, so just knowing that we'd be visiting the San Siro and the Nou Camp was more than which we ever could have hoped.

I loved every second of watching Barca demolish us 4-0 on ITV in our opening fixture, with the surreal feeling of seeing our players in competitive action at the Nou Camp far outweighing the football itself. Unfortunately, not every Champions League game was broadcast live back then, which meant that I had to settle for the radio for our second match when we didn't get tickets.

I was listening in from my dad's flat as we reached the 90th minute at Elland Road all square at 0-0 with AC. With the match in it's dying embers, and a remarkable draw on the cards, my dad told me to prepare to leave to head back to my mum's.

I jumped up to grab my things, but can specifically remember stopping myself in my tracks as the voice of the commentator on 96.3 Aire FM became a little animated. He described Lee

Bowyer picking the ball up on the edge of the Milan box with real promise, before instantly deflating after a tame attempt went straight at goalkeeper Dida. I resumed as I was, before receiving the biggest, and most beautiful shock of my sporting life.

In a turn of events that could only happen when listening to a match on the radio, I heard a massive cheer come from my dad's hi-fi speaker, with the commentator going berserk about a second later. With conditions wet and the ball slippery, Dida had unwittingly palmed the ball into the back of his own net when attempting to pat it safely on to the ground in front of him. The commentator must have been so sure that the 'keeper would comfortably gather it, that he'd literally taken his eye off the ball. Bowyer had scored, in the most dramatic of circumstances, to give us a last-minute lead over one of the world's footballing powerhouses.

My dad and I went wild, unable to comprehend what we were hearing; it was unbelievable. Even my little sister joined in with our celebrations, without really knowing what was happening before we all stopped dead to listen to stoppage time as it played out. The goal had knocked the stuffing out of the Italians, and we saw out the final moments to claim the most remarkable of victories.

I thought that all my Christmases had come at once when the draw had come out, never mind how I felt after we beat AC. Yet, somehow, things got even better the following week, when we annihilated Besiktas 6-0 at Elland Road, in what was by far and away the most I'd ever enjoyed listening to a game on the radio. There was an element of it not feeling real with how often I found myself celebrating.

If the ecstasy of the result wasn't enough, there was also the relief of Mark Viduka grabbing his first goal for the club. The summer signing from Celtic had come in for a bit of stick from the supporters at the start of the season for his languid approach, with the Elland Road faithful expecting nothing more and nothing less than hard work from their players.

With Viduka being 6'2" and built more like a rugby player, he didn't seem like the type that would spend ninety minutes charging around a football pitch. It was evident that he'd have to earn the fans' respect through pure ability, something that I hoped his first goal would help to unleash.

I'd spent the first few weeks of the 00/01 season riddled with concern, just as I had in 98/99 and 99/00. When George Graham left in '98, and then Jimmy-Floyd Hasselbaink in '99, I perceived us to have lost the most important individual at our football club. Although Harry Kewell didn't leave in the build-up to 00/01, it was devastating when he suffered a serious injury.

Given that manager David O'Leary had built his team around Kewell, I was concerned that we didn't have another player with which we could do the same. I'd liked what little I'd previously seen of Viduka and fellow new signing Olivier Dacourt, but couldn't imagine how we could build a team around either of them. The answer was to build it around them both.

Within just a few weeks of his debut, Dacourt had become our equivalent of Roy Keane or Patrick Vieira. Tough tackling, fantastic on the ball, brilliant at reading the game, and relentlessly driven, he formed excellent central midfield partnerships with whoever O'Leary picked to play alongside him. He wasn't just a great footballer either; he was also captain material.

While Dacourt ran the show from midfield, absolutely everything that we did going forward went through Viduka. It seemed like whichever one of our players had the ball, they were looking to get it to Viduka as quickly possible, and it didn't matter whether it went to his head, his chest, or his feet. Alongside Dennis Bergkamp, Viduka had the best touch of any player that I'd seen play at Elland Road up to that point.

Not only did the ball stick to him, but defenders would bounce off his robust frame if they ever tried to barge him off it. I was amazed by the vision he had to be able to link the play with his back to goal too; he so often found the likes of Bowyer, Alan Smith, Michael Bridges and Eirik Bakke when they ran beyond him. It was as though he had eyes in the back of his head.

Having not scored in the Premiership before the Besiktas game, Viduka hit ten goals in the six league games immediately after it. The undoubted highlight of the run came when he scored all four in an incredible 4-3 victory over Liverpool, which remains the best match that I've ever seen at Elland Road. That was the game that made the majority of our fans recognise that we might have a genius on our hands.

If things were picking up in the Premiership, the unimaginable was happening in the Champions League. After drawing 0-0 at Besiktas, we knew that a victory at Elland Road against Barcelona would be enough to send us into the second round, with the La Liga giants having lost to both Milan and Besiktas since hammering us in Spain.

Although it was disappointing that such a massive match wasn't televised, it was another matter of not being able to believe what I was hearing when Lee Bowyer gave us a fifth-minute lead. We came so close to what might have classed as the most famous Leeds United victory ever at Elland Road, only for Rivaldo to equalise in the 94th minute. It was a crushing goal to concede, and when the radio commentator described a scene in which some of our players were in tears on the pitch, I sensed that the dream was over.

The reality was that we only needed a point at the San Siro to qualify for the second group phase, which is far easier said than done of course.

As my brother, his friend and I sat down to watch the ITV build-up of AC Milan vs Leeds United at my mum's house, we naively hoped that Milan would rest a score of their stars with them already having qualified. Sadly, Paolo Maldini, Gennaro Gattuso, Demetrio Albertini, Andriy Shevchenko and Oliver Bierhoff were all in the starting line-up, which left me fearing a mauling like we'd received in our first group match at Barca. My brother's friend was quick to remind me that we'd come a long way since then.

When Shevchenko, one of the world's top strikers at the time, missed a first-half penalty, we started to believe that an omnipotent power was shining down on us. Then, in the most disbelieving moment of our adventure yet, Dominic Matteo headed past Dida from a rare corner to give us a lead on the stroke of half-time. When we reached the whistle at 0-1, we knew that if we could concede less than two goals in forty-five minutes of football, we would qualify from this group of death.

As expected, Milan came out and dominated after the break. Although we weren't thinking about anything other than qualifying, Matteo's goal had meant that we were going through as group winners as it stood, something that our Italian counterparts didn't appear willing to accept. Serginho equalised midway through the second half with a magnificent solo goal, which left us with about twenty-five minutes to survive. It felt more like twenty-five hours, and I spent the majority of it watching through the gaps in my fingers after my head involuntarily found it's way into my hands.

After our heroic defenders absorbed everything that Milan could throw at us, we clung on to secure one of the most famous results in our club's history. We had qualified for the second group phase of the Champions League, and dumped Barcelona, *Barcelona,* out of it.

Since moving house, we'd had a few run-ins with our new, well-to-do neighbours for making too much noise while playing in the street, but I think they all must have been following events in Italy. They even smiled and waved at my brother, his friend and me, as we celebrated deliriously.

Overcome with euphoria, we did two topless laps of our neighbourhood crescent, bellowing out every Leeds United chant we could think of until our throats were sore. We would stop to hug each other or fall in worship-like fashion to the ground every few steps, as the magnitude of what our football club had achieved very slowly started to sink in.

Anybody would have thought that we'd won the thing, but qualification from that group was our equivalent, relative to expectations. That's just the issue with expectations, though; they can change. They're the reason that I consider those post-Milan celebrations to be the last time that I experienced innocent, youthful joy.

7

Obsession: A flick of a switch

I can pinpoint the exact moment at which my interest in Leeds United became an obsession. It was just before midnight on Tuesday 5th December, I was sitting on my bedroom couch watching ITV's *Champions League Highlights* show, and the ball was just about to reach Alan Smith as part of a replay of the goal that he'd scored in Rome that night.

To give you some context, Leeds were playing away at Lazio in the second group phase of the 2000/01 Champions League. We'd just paid £18m to sign a twenty-two-year-old centre-half called Rio Ferdinand from West Ham United, who was being billed as a future world-beater. Our star of the previous season, Harry Kewell, had just returned from a lengthy injury lay-off to bolster our potent attacking options further. In sum, I was more excited to be a fan of my club than I ever thought I could be.

Although our match at the Stadio Olimpico wasn't to be televised, I was still immensely excited to listen to it on the radio. However, in a disastrous turn of events, my sister's Christmas Concert had been scheduled for the same night, and my mum informed me that my attendance was not optional. My brother was in the same boat, so we sulked as a pair en route to my sister's school that evening.

Matt had made arrangements for a friend of his to send us

regular text message updates throughout the evening, and I'd spent almost the entire concert furious as nothing had come through. Then, just before 9.30 pm, he discreetly pulled his Nokia 3210 out of his pocket, which confirmed that he had indeed received a text message, causing me to fall into an unwitting state of hyper-nervousness.

The message seemed to take an eternity to open, with the combination of anticipation and frustration making me feel as though my whole body might explode into smithereens. Then, on the tiny screen, appeared *1-0 ALAN SMITH.*

With the room silent and the concert playing out in front of us, I had no option but to squeeze Matt's arm as hard as I could to release a mere fraction of the adrenaline flowing through me. About fifteen minutes later, with the concert still going on, I clenched each of my fists and pushed them forcibly against each other as a second text of the night read *Full Time: Lazio 0-1 Leeds, COME ON!.*

When we finally got out of the concert hall, Matt and I embraced as though the goal had just been scored, before dancing our way back to the car as we tried to come to terms with another miracle. There was absolutely no doubt that I was staying up to watch the highlights.

Arsenal's match against Bayern Munich had understandably commanded the majority of the ITV show's allotted time, although when Leeds eventually came on, it couldn't have been more worth the wait.

There were very few highlights worth screening before the goal apparently, which meant that I was caught by surprise when Smith's strike was shown so quickly. On first viewing, I'd seen Kewell pick up the ball out on the wing before it eventually reached Mark Viduka on the edge of the area. Smith made a driving run behind Viduka, detracting my attention away from the ball, before it somehow ended up at Smith's feet inside the Lazio penalty area. When the ball hit the back of the net, and Smith ran off in celebration, I felt perplexed more than anything else as to how on earth the ball had reached him in the first place.

I watched the replay with added intensity to try and make sense of what had happened, and I can distinctly recall putting my hands on my head, and my mouth falling open in aston-ishment, as I saw what Viduka had done.

While holding off an opponent, our number nine had performed a disguised 'Cruyff' flick to send the ball in between two defenders and into the path of Smith, whose run was 180 degrees from his line of sight. It was a moment of utter magic, the best team goal that I'd ever seen from my side, and one that instantaneously made me believe that David O'Leary's Leeds United were the real deal.

When I'd watched Zinedine Zidane at Euro 2000, I'd been in absolute awe of the way that he made football look like art. He was poetry in motion, and my take was that no ordinary player would ever be capable of doing some of the things that he did. The understanding between our players during Smith's strike at Lazio told me that this Leeds side was no ordinary team, as only one of real quality could have produced some-thing so brilliant.

Amid my utter disbelief at my side's play, there was a subcon-scious shift in my expectations. Over my years of watching Premiership football, I'd only seen the brilliant Manchester United and Arsenal sides score goals such as that. The way

I saw it, if we could start producing football of that quality consistently, I didn't see why we couldn't challenge them. We had a considerable gap to bridge, but I genuinely believed that the foundations were already in place.

The issue that comes with an expectation shift is how it correlates with your mood state. As a general rule, the further you surpass your expectations, the happier you are. Conversely, the further you fall short of your expectations, the more miserable you are.

I'd seen my team surpass expectations by such a distance under O'Leary, that I'd been in a near-constant state of euphoria for over two years. Now, as I started to believe that we might have it in us to challenge among the elite, it was going to take even greater achievements to yield similar emotional responses. You don't think in that depth when riding the crest of an emotional wave as a just-turned fourteen-year-old boy though.

The good news for my mood state was that I perceived our bid to challenge to be a long-term project. I didn't expect it to happen overnight, but the starting point would be to produce performances and goals like those at Lazio consistently. That was the benchmark that Scum and Arsenal had set; it was just a matter of whether we could replicate it.

With Kewell back fit and Ferdinand having come on board, I believed that we now had a team capable of competing with anybody on our day. *On our day*, I emphasise:

Goalkeeper: Nigel Martyn
Right-back: Danny Mills
Centre-back: Rio Ferdinand
Centre-back: Jonathan Woodgate

Left-back: Ian Harte
Right-midfield: Lee Bowyer
Centre-midfield: Olivier Dacourt
Centre-midfield: David Batty/Eirik Bakke/Stephen McPhail
Left-midfield: Harry Kewell
Striker: Mark Viduka
Striker: Alan Smith

Of these players, seven were twenty-three years old or younger, while Oliver Dacourt and Viduka were coming in to their prime at twenty-six and twenty-five respectively. Nigel Martyn remained a top-quality goalkeeper even at thirty-four, although twenty-one-year-old Paul Robinson was a ready-made replacement in that department. That just left one central midfield position that I believed we could improve in, although David Batty, Eirik Bakke, and Stephen McPhail were all solid performers.

The key thing was the spine of the team, as I genuinely believed that all four of Ferdinand, Woodgate, Dacourt, and Viduka had the potential to be world-class, with Kewell also falling into that bracket. Bowyer and Smith might not have been able to match these guys for natural talent, but their work-rate, dedication, and knack for a big goal made them equally important. My expectations may have increased, but I saw no reason why this team couldn't at least win a domestic cup competition in the not too distant future.

It didn't appear that 2001 would be that year when we were knocked out of the FA Cup by Liverpool in January, having exited the League Cup to Tranmere Rovers back in October. A defeat to Newcastle United at Elland Road on 20th January left us twenty-seven points behind leaders Manchester United in the Premiership too, emphasising just how far behind them we were. That left the Champions League as our only possibility of a trophy, which was too unlikely even to contemplate.

The Lazio victory had come after a home loss to our second Spanish giants of the tournament, Real Madrid, who we'd drawn along with Belgian champions Anderlecht in the second group phase. We were second in our group after two games, but with our third match not until mid-February, we badly needed something to cheer about before then.

Results did improve in the league, as we managed three wins and two draws before Anderlecht came to Leeds, but we hadn't played well in a single one of those games. The way I saw it, signs of real progress would come through performances and style of play, and they'd been a long way off that of the Lazio game.

We did brilliantly to battle back from a goal down to beat Anderlecht 2-1, and leave ourselves in with a great chance of another miraculous qualification. However, I wasn't as full of joy as I might previously have been after listening to the game on the radio, as I could tell that we hadn't deserved to win. That was now fifteen games without a quality display since Lazio, but I remained convinced that one was just around the corner.

Our absence from the FA Cup meant that we had a weekend off before the corresponding fixture with Anderlecht. Our young, inexperienced side had played an awful lot of games up to that point in the season, and I can remember wondering whether that little break might just be the revitalisation period that we needed. With the Belgians having won nine straight European home matches, including the four that they'd played that season, we'd most likely need a lot more than a rest to have a chance of pulling off a result.

I have no shame in admitting this, but I spent the first five days of a holiday to Florida with my mum thinking of nothing other than my football team. She and her partner had utilised the half-term break at school to take their combined five kids to Disney World, a place that I'd always dreamed of going to, but never expected to visit. However, I'd also never expected Leeds United to visit Brussels with a potential Champions League quarter-final at stake.

I knew that the game was being televised, which made it even more heartbreaking to be missing it, but my mum did the best she could by arranging a 5 pm phone call to my dad on the day of the match. With us being five hours behind in Orlando, we knew the game would have finished by then.

It was Wednesday 21st February 2001, and I can remember being beside myself with nerves when we arrived back at our hotel after a fantastic day at Busch Gardens theme park. I'd just spent six hours riding some of the world's most exhilarating rollercoasters, yet my body's adrenaline levels peaked that day as I walked towards a payphone in our hotel car park.

My mum put a couple of coins into the machine before dialling my dad's phone number, leaving my brother and me to each hold an ear to the phone in anticipation of him answering. When he did, he didn't mess around; he knew exactly why we were calling and had never been one for pleasantries himself.

'Anderlecht one, Leeds United.... FOUR!!!' After an instinctive scream of 'YEEAAAHH' down the phone, I took off around the car park, sprinting, jumping, screaming, and punching the air. My mum had to tell me to shut up, which

I did, but she had no problem with me deliriously bounding about for between five and ten minutes before my brother called me over to the phone.

My dad told me that it was the best performance that he'd ever seen from a Leeds United team in over thirty years of him supporting us. He also said that he'd taped the match so that I could watch it in its entirety upon my return. As if things couldn't get any better, Lazio had failed to beat Real Madrid, which meant that we'd qualified for the quarter-finals of the Champions League. Even my new expectation levels couldn't prevent an overwhelming feeling of ecstasy from encompassing me.

There is no question that I particularly enjoyed the last two days of my holiday to Florida as a result of that phone call. I had more energy, I made more effort with everybody, and the theme parks seemed even better than they already had been; I felt at perfect harmony with the world. I was, in essence, behaving as though I'd just fallen in love, except it was a football team, not a person, that was causing me to be an all-round better individual.

We flew home overnight on the Saturday, without having had an avenue to check how Leeds had got on at Tottenham Hotspur that day. After we landed in Manchester on the Sunday morning, I darted into the first airport newsagents that I came across, picked up a paper, and rejoiced at the discovery that we'd won 2-1. I was now heading back to Leeds to go to my dad's flat, with highlights of a Premiership victory, and an entire Champions League victory to watch.

That afternoon, my dad sat with me and watched the full ninety minutes of a match that he'd already seen. He had said that it was the best performance that he'd ever seen from a Leeds side of course, and as I watched the action, I couldn't have concurred with him any more.

Smith's second goal, which made it 3-0 after only thirty-eight minutes, gave me an identical feeling to the one that I'd had after his Lazio strike. Viduka, Dacourt, and Batty toyed with Anderlecht's players in the middle of the park with a series of one-touch triangular passes, with the last of these seeing Batty release Smith in on goal. After racing clear of the defenders, Smith scooped the ball over the onrushing Anderlecht goal-keeper with his first touch, sending our travelling contingent of fans into raptures as the ball nestled in the back of the net. It was an absolute work of art, and proof that Lazio hadn't been a one-off.

Everything about that 4-1 win was unforgettable, but I was arguably happier with the way that we backed it up three days later. The comeback win at Spurs was another brilliant team performance, while we also showcased more of the wonderful football that had fundamentally changed my fandom of Leeds United on that December night in Rome.

The real question was whether we could perform at that level over a long-term period, just as all the title-winning Manchester United sides that I'd had to suffer over the years had done. Those two Alan Smith goals had me consumed in a belief that we could, and what better way to test that theory than by facing Scum at Elland Road the very next week.

8

Hope to belief in 300 days

In the year 2001, there was a 300-day period in which Leeds United were not just the *most* important thing in my life, but the *only* important thing in my life.

Don't get me wrong; I'm not saying that I stopped loving my family, or I fell out with all my friends. What I am saying is that there was this one thing that made me feel so, so strongly, that everything else in the world just stopped mattering.

I woke up on the morning of 4th March, the day after we'd drawn 1-1 with Manchester United at Elland Road, and thought, *we could win the Premiership next season*. I got into bed on the night of 29th December, with Leeds having earlier won 1-0 at Southampton, and thought, *are we going to win the Premiership?*.

Scum came into that game off the back of a 6-1 pummelling of their closest rivals Arsenal, which essentially confirmed them as champions before February was out. They were so far superior to every other team in the league that year, but I was convinced we could beat them, *on our day*.

With all that I'd been thinking about in the three months since Alan Smith's goal at Lazio, I saw this match as the real acid test of our credentials. The game didn't mean anything in terms of our respective Premiership seasons, but it would mean everything to me personally if we could give them a game. It was the perfect opportunity to see just how far behind Scum we were, and whether I was mad to have thought we could even get close to them.

It was a privilege to be at Elland Road that day. The atmosphere was out of this world, the quality of football was incredible, and the match itself seemed to have everything.

We totally outplayed them in the first half and had the chance to take a deserved lead when Fabien Barthez kicked Ian Harte inside the penalty area as part of an off-the-ball incident. Barthez should have been sent off but was only give a yellow card, a decision that was compounded by his saving of Harte's subsequent spot-kick.

We started the second half well too, but disaster struck when Nigel Martyn could only parry Ole Gunnar Solskjaer's shot during a rare foray forward from the visitors. The ball fell straight to Luke Chadwick, who slotted into an empty net to make the score 0-1, against the run of play.

A red card that wasn't, a penalty miss and a fortunate rebound were more than enough to make me think that it wouldn't be our day. However, the crowd were unbelievable from the moment we fell behind and were the inspiration for a brilliant team move that culminated in Mark Viduka heading past Barthez with just six minutes to go. It was an unbelievable moment, primarily because of how much we deserved it, and there was only one team that I thought could win it from there.

In the last minute of stoppage time, the ball fell to Lee Bowyer inside the penalty box on the right-hand side. He played the ball across in search of an unmarked Viduka, which caused Wes Brown to dive desperately towards his own goal to try and prevent the ball from reaching our goalscorer. In doing so, he turned it into his own net, sparking delirious scenes at Elland Road.

As I was about to start going bonkers myself, Linley immediately stopped me, while pointing towards the linesman. He'd flagged for offside, and with us being at the direct opposite end of the ground, we were in no position to know whether it had been or not. The final whistle went almost immediately after, and although we were left to contemplate what could have been, everybody at Elland Road knew that we'd outplayed the best team in the country.

Replays would later show that the outstretched leg of Jaap Stam, who had leapt in front of Bowyer to try and prevent the cross, was comfortably playing Viduka onside, against whom the flag had gone up. With us being so far behind the Champions League qualification places at the time, I didn't think that there was any significance in this, I was just happy with how well we'd played. I couldn't have known that we'd win our next six games and hunt third-placed Liverpool down in the process.

A few days after the Scum game, we were brilliant again, and although we lost 3-2 to Real Madrid at the Bernabeu, we fully merited a draw. The six-game league winning streak that followed included a 2-1 win at Anfield and a 2-0 home victory over an excellent Chelsea side. Amid our superb Premiership form, we also beat Deportivo La Coruna over two legs in our Champions League quarter-final.

Our season had been dead and buried at the end of January, but within three months we were Champions League semi-finalists, and bang in the race for a top-three spot in the

Premiership. The only doubt that I'd had about our credentials lay in our ability to perform consistently, but those three months had laid that to rest.

Although I feel it necessary to talk about that quarter-final in a bit of detail, as it was truly spectacular to watch and listen to, I found the knockout stage to be a very different experience to the two group phases. I can remember the first Deportivo leg perfectly; I watched from my bedroom couch with my brother as Harte, Smith, and Rio Ferdinand goals gave us a sensational 3-0 lead at the halfway point in the tie. We almost threw that away in La Coruna, when the second of two Djalminha goals made it 2-0 on the night, and 3-2 on aggregate, with about twenty minutes remaining. It was excruciating to listen to on the radio as we came under siege, but we held out to book a last-four date with Valencia.

As amazing as that felt, and as pessimistic as this seems, there still wasn't an ounce of me that believed that we could win the Champions League, even with only four teams left in it. Bayern Munich or Real Madrid awaited in the final, which partially explains my negativity, but the strangest part was that I didn't even look forward to the Valencia matches. There was so much at stake, and we'd been on such an incredible adventure. Yet, I just wasn't that bothered about it.

Upon reflection, I think that I'd already focused my mind on the next domestic campaign. Our performance against Manchester United, and subsequent league form, had turned my hope that we could soon challenge for the Premiership title into a concrete belief that we could win it the following season. Although I suspect that it was mathematically more probable that we would win that season's Champions League, I had no faith that we would.

Obviously, it's easy to say this after I was proven right, but I don't have any regrets about how I approached our season-defining month of May. We'd been so brilliant throughout February, March and April, that the future of this Leeds United team felt more important than the outcome of the enormous games we had in front of us.

Strangely, I found our 2-1 league defeat at Arsenal harder to take than our 3-0 aggregate defeat to Valencia in the Champions League. With Liverpool still to play Chelsea in the league, a game they went on to draw, we'd have piled the pressure on both the Gunners and the Reds with a win at Highbury, but playing those three games in six days was always likely to prove a step too far for our brave squad.

We hammered Bradford City 6-1, and beat Leicester City 3-1 in our final two league games of the season, but missed out on that third Champions League spot. Liverpool won 4-0 at Charlton Athletic on the last day to pip us by a single point, and it wasn't until then that I realised how critical that incorrectly disallowed Wes Brown own goal had been. It would turn out to be bigger than we could ever have imagined.

If I could have made a deal with the devil to skip the ninety days between the end of the 00/01 Premiership season and the beginning of the 01/02 Premiership season, I'd have done it in a heartbeat. There's nothing that can more clearly define how little anything other than my football team mattered to me back then, as I genuinely would have foregone time if I'd have had the choice. Although this wasn't an option, what I *did* do that summer gives a clear insight into just how obsessed I was with Leeds.

I designed my own Premiership fantasy football game, created a website for it, and nearly paid £60 to get it up and running on the internet before my dad talked me out of it. I listened to every one of Leeds' pre-season matches on the radio, apart from the Harrogate Town game, which I attended with my friend Mel. I played Championship Manager until I won the Premiership with Leeds in my first season, which I eventually managed at the fourth attempt. Last but not least, I repeatedly spray-painted my hair in the Leeds colours of white, yellow, and blue, and wore it proudly even though it looked awful.

The madness even affected the way that I watched other sports. I'd always loved Wimbledon and was heavily invested in Tim Henman by this point. Still, during his semi-final match with Goran Ivanisevic, I can remember feeling concerned that I might be using up all my 'good luck' if he were to finally win it. I didn't actively want him to lose as a result, but a little part of me felt relieved when he did, as I perceived that all my 'good luck' was still intact for Leeds United. It was a slightly warped perception of the concept of *Karma*.

On the eve of the new football season, I went to Headingley with my dad to watch day two of the fourth Ashes Test in the cricket. When he surprised me with the news that he'd got us tickets a few days earlier, I was genuinely devastated that I wouldn't be able to follow all the Premiership build-up shows instead, although I didn't express that to him of course. I ended up having a fantastic day, but the most exciting part of it was when I got home. That was when it became a reality that I was just a single sleep away from the return of the only important thing in my life.

When I got into bed that night, I was as excited as I'd ever been. I felt like a young child on Christmas Eve, desperately trying to drift off in the knowledge of what the following morning would bring. Ninety days had felt like ninety years, but the season that I truly believed could be ours was finally here.

I woke up after a perfect night's sleep and walked down to Headingley from my dad's flat to meet my pals Mel and Rodney. With the Linleys having gone on holiday, I'd ended up with three tickets for the match, and I saw nobody better to give the spares to than my two great Leeds-fan pals from primary school.

As part of the Leeds United fever we were experiencing, we bought some face-paint and emblazoned our cheeks with Leeds United crests. We bumped into Rodney's older brother just after we'd done it, and he rightly called us 'total fucking goons'. You shouldn't be painting your face at nearly fifteen years old.

As we made our way to the ground, I felt different from how I'd felt on the opening day of the previous seven seasons. Arguably the most beautiful feeling for a football fan is the opening day optimism; it doesn't matter what's been and gone, or what state your football club is in at that time, the first game is a chance for a team to make every fan dream that this could be a good season. For me, it was no longer about whether we *could* do well; I believed that we *should* do well.

The smell of the freshly cut grass, the sight of the sun-drenched pitch, and the sound of 40,000 fired up fans weren't as special as they ordinarily were that day, as for me, it was about getting the job done. We were playing at home to Southampton, and winning wasn't optional; we couldn't afford to let the big clubs get ahead of us after just one game if we meant business this season.

I was in a state of panic when the game reached the hour mark at 0-0. My mindset was that if we couldn't win this game, I'd have felt betrayed for having spent an entire summer devoted to the thought of our prospects of winning the Premiership. I didn't feel like we had to win the league for me to be satisfied, but we did have to show that we belonged among the big boys. Manchester United, Arsenal and co. would beat Southampton at home on the opening day, so we had to do it.

Fortunately, as he so often did, Lee Bowyer came up with the crucial goal on sixty-seven minutes to send Elland Road into raptures. About fifteen minutes later, his fellow fans' favourite Smith came off the bench to wrap the game up at 2-0, and the glorious day that I'd hoped for had indeed come to pass. However, on the journey home from the match, I experienced a brand new post-victory feeling, one that came with the territory of my amended expectation levels. While joy accounted for about twenty percent of my happiness, this was heavily outweighed by eighty percent of the more inhibitory emotion of relief. Winning had just become a lot more serious.

Three days later we travelled to Arsenal for the first big test of our credentials. Mel and Rodney joined me at my dad's, and there was hysteria in a North Leeds flat when an Ian Harte free-kick gave us a first-half lead. However, having stated pre-game that I'd have been happy with a point, the goal made me greedy.

When Sylvain Wiltord equalised just a couple of minutes later, I went off on such an aggressive, foul-mouthed tirade that my dad threatened to kick me out. The swearing didn't bother him, but he was embarrassed by how much I was overreacting to us conceding a goal, particularly with there still being an hour to go in the match. He mustn't have considered all of the potential ramifications when he was indoctrinating me into becoming a football fan.

To explain my anger, we'd not won at Arsenal in years, and the fantasy-like thought of it happening had become a reality after Harte's strike. Feeling that excitement getting ripped away really hurt, which was what caused my explosive response. Fortunately, my superb team ensured that I was not to be denied.

Viduka came up with a big goal early in the second half to make it 1-2, and despite red cards for both Bowyer and Danny Mills, we held out to claim a huge victory over one of our prospective rivals. It was a massive early marker for us to lay down.

The moment that I believe pinpoints when the whole footballing community started to take us seriously was when Ole Gunnar Solskjaer scored a last-minute equaliser against us at Old Trafford to rescue a point for Scum. My dad and I had gone down to watch the match at the Linleys' house with it being such a monumental occasion, and we all went ballistic when Viduka gave us a deserved lead on seventy-seven minutes. Desperately, we couldn't quite hold out for a first away victory at Manchester United in my lifetime, but the commentators made it clear that we could no longer be ignored. We were title-contenders.

We didn't suffer our first defeat until our 12th game when an impressive Sunderland side beat us 2-0 at the Stadium Of Light. If the loss was a sign that we might not have it in us to sustain a title challenge, we countered by signing goalscoring supremo Robbie Fowler from Liverpool a few days later. We really did mean business.

A few weeks later, Fowler hit his first Leeds hat-trick to give us a 3-0 win at Bolton Wanderers on Boxing Day. That left us just one point behind leaders Arsenal heading into a game at Southampton on 29th December, 300 days on from when I'd first believed that we could challenge for the 2001/02 Premiership title. It would turn out to be a pivotal day in my life, but not just for footballing reasons.

9

Alcohol, a summit, and a cliff edge

At first, I didn't get all the fuss about alcohol. On each occasion that I'd been in and around it, I'd had a couple of cans of beer, not particularly enjoyed it, and barely felt any different. Yet, on the few occasions that I'd been to house parties with my friends, or street corners if we were feeling a little more classy, I'd watched on with indifference as everybody appeared to be having the time of their lives.

It was as though whenever they had a few drinks, Leeds United had just drawn in the San Siro to qualify for the second group phase of the Champions League. They would charge around chaotically, hug and jump on each other, roll around on the ground while singing, screaming or shouting at the top of their voices. None of it made any sense to me, so when Linley asked me if I wanted to go to our mate Rich's house party while we were listening to Southampton vs Leeds on 29th December 2001, I said 'no'.

I'd gone down to Linley's specifically to listen to the game that day, as we both knew how significant it was. While we were set to face West Ham United at home on New Year's Day, Premiership leaders Arsenal didn't have a match scheduled, which meant that if we could beat both Southampton and West Ham, we could hit the Premiership's summit.

I'd been the instigator of the two of us listening to the game on the radio, and with an unentertaining affair locked at 0-0 with ten minutes remaining, Linley left me on my own in his bedroom. His dad was watching Soccer Saturday downstairs, which he reasonably assumed would be more interesting to follow.

As the game entered its 90th minute, Southampton were the ones looking more likely to snatch a winner, and when James Beattie hit a post, I started to accept that a point wouldn't be a bad result. Then, with my hands still coned over my mouth and nose in relief, the 96.3 Aire FM commentator became a lot more animated.

He described the scene as we broke away downfield, making our way deep into Southampton territory. The ball broke to Mark Viduka on the edge of the Saints' box, who held it for a moment, before finding a trademark late Lee Bowyer run with a typically ingenious reverse pass. 'It's Viduka, who finds the late run of BOWYERRRRRRR'.

As soon as I heard the Leeds fans' celebratory cheers in the background, I went insane. I screamed at the top of my voice in a house that wasn't even my own, showing total disregard for all Linley's family members. Fortunately, the sound of heavy footsteps bounding up the stairs transpired to be Linley and his dad, who hadn't learned of the goal via Soccer Saturday. They flung open the door and charged over to join me in bedlam.

It was such a huge goal, and so much emotion had just poured out of me, that I almost ended up in tears. When Beattie had hit the post, I'd instinctively realigned my expectations to be happy with a point. As a result, when that man Bowyer struck in the last minute, the improbable surpassing of these new expectations left me overcome with ecstasy.

I regathered myself to listen to the final few moments, which Linley and his dad remained with me for, before unleashing another enormous cheer when the full-time whistle went. In a direct reversal of how I felt when we beat Southampton on the opening day of the season, my joy far outweighed my relief.

Amid my euphoria, Linley intimated that I now *had* to go to Rich's house party, as I'd be doing a disservice to my football club if I didn't properly celebrate the result. It was a terrible sales pitch, but there was no doubt that I was in the right frame of mind, I felt as high on life as I had after the San Siro. There was no reason for me not to go, other than the fact that I didn't want to, which doesn't class as a valid excuse at fifteen years old.

We had a couple of beers at Linley's before his dad dropped us off at our favourite street corner en route to Rich's place. The plan was to have a drink or two there before making our way to the party, but how cold it was left us no choice but to head to Rich's early. Everybody else must have ended up in the same situation, as we arrived to find a packed house at about 8 pm.

Unlike some of the other guys that we'd met at the street corner, there wasn't a specific girl that I was hoping to talk to, so I set out to find anyone that I knew liked football, the go-to conversation for me even at fifteen. However, when I asked one of the lads whether they'd followed the match, a bloke that wasn't so keen on football overheard me.

At fourteen years old, our mate Lee already looked twenty-four and was by far the biggest bloke we knew in terms of his build. He was known for being able to drink twice as much as anybody else, and he was already well on his way by the time he overheard me talking about football. Lee needed no reason to challenge somebody to a drinking contest, but I'd just unwittingly offered him one.

'I'll 'ear no fuckin' football talk tonight, now get 'ere and do a shot'. I hadn't seen Lee when he'd shouted this at me, as he was sitting on the floor next to a table lining up whiskey shots. As usual, nobody was remotely interested in joining him, but he always seemed to find somebody who would submit. When one of the other lads opportunistically stated that mentioning football around Lee constituted having to do a shot with him, I thought 'why not'.

Lee had poured out two mammoth measures that had the people around us looking both disgusted and dismayed. I hadn't drunk spirits before, so I was unfazed by the task, how bad could it be? Lee and I picked up our glasses, toasted each other, before seeing off what must have been a triple shot.

By no means did it taste nice, but I barely grimaced after putting it away. The problem was that a couple of the lads that had seen this sensed an opportunity, as they started shouting to the room that I'd just beaten Lee in a drinking contest. After hearing the jibe, Lee was having none of it and subsequently challenged me to do another shot with him.

Lost in the moment, I went again, draining the drink before touching my glass back down on the table just before Lee did. In amazement of what they were seeing, a now considerable crowd of people started taunting my opponent, as he sat there struggling to believe that he was losing.

When partisan chants of 'ONE MORE, ONE MORE' followed, Lee poured out two more hefty shots, which we each polished off with aplomb for the third time. I don't think that I did beat him on that occasion, but I think that the lads were so impressed with my totally out of character behaviour that they awarded me a 3-0 victory.

The reason that I'd not enjoyed house parties before that night was because they were a bit too much for me. I'd always struggled with big crowds, and when I was in an environment in which a lot was going on, I found the endless stream of stimuli coming at me exhausting to try and process. I hadn't realised it at the time, but while many people were able to be in that kind of situation and easily focus on one stimulus, I didn't seem to have that filter. Everything would go in, and my brain couldn't organise it all, which I found totally overwhelming. Fifteen minutes after my shot-drinking contest with Lee, all that changed.

I can remember walking around Rich's house with a massive smile on my face, totally overcome by what I was feeling, while also being able to focus on people and things in a way that I never had before. The alcohol had suppressed my sensitivity to my surroundings, and for the first time, a mass gathering of people didn't feel intense.

I'd never been one to say too much, but I was chatting away to everyone at the party. I'd never been one of the jokers in the pack, but I was joining in with any stupid game or prank that I stumbled across. Furthermore, I found myself blessed with an ability to be interested in any conversation that I had with any person, something that I'd spent so much of my time at high school feigning.

This newfound clarity lasted for about an hour before everything became a bit blurry. I involuntarily fell over a couple of times, and all of a sudden, I was the centre of attention, but in a very positive way. Fortunately, I was now part of a friendship group that was full of genuinely nice kids, and they all ensured that I was OK amid their endless piss-taking.

Disastrously, Rich's mum unexpectedly came home early and told us in no uncertain terms that we had to leave. I can remember stumbling upstairs at this point in a bid to inform anybody that hadn't received the message, which I did so by whispering. I don't know why I thought that whispering would help matters, but at least I meant well.

They say that alcohol can uncover what you truly feel when you have too much of it, and my reaction upon leaving Rich's certainly suggested that to be true. There was no angst, no sadness, and no drama with a drunk me; I just charged around this unfamiliar suburban neighbourhood shouting 'BOWYEERRRRRRR', before diving on to the concrete in 'Klinsmann'-esque fashion. All of my innermost feelings were Leeds United-related, which perfectly reflected where my priorities had lain over the previous 300 days. Maybe I'd have been crying on somebody's shoulder had Beattie, not Bowyer, found the back of the net.

I somehow managed to navigate my way back to my mum's house, and after stumbling through the door, I ran into the downstairs bathroom and vomited in the sink. There was a perfectly good toilet right next to it, but the sink seemed like a more logical choice at the time.

Fortunately, only Matt had heard me hurling, and he looked after me in true big brother style by telling me to 'fuck off to bed' while he cleaned up my mess. I tiptoe-swayed upstairs, walked into my room, and jumped straight into bed fully-clothed. Even with my head spinning and my stomach churning, I can still vividly recall my last thought before passing out; *are Leeds*

United going to win the Premiership?.

Remarkably, I slept for about twelve hours straight that night, but the first few minutes of Sunday morning were appalling. My head was now pounding, my stomach was still churning, I couldn't believe how awful the taste in my mouth was, and I noticed blood all over the clothes that I was still wearing.

My body was battered and bruised, and I would later learn that the cuts on my hands had occurred when one of my Lee Bowyer dives had been straight on to some broken glass in the street. After about half an hour of writhing around in bed, I eventually pulled myself together and jumped in the shower.

I'd heard of total absences of memory after a heavy night's drinking, but I could recall almost every detail of the previous night perfectly, even my inability to stand up. However, one of the few things that I'd forgotten as I made my way downstairs to get some breakfast was the sink, of which my brother dutifully reminded me. He was fine about it, and he even joined me in my bedroom to watch the previous day's Premiership highlights. Seeing Bowyer's goal was the perfect hangover cure, and as bad as I'd initially felt upon waking up, I already couldn't wait for my next night out on the booze.

Two days later, on the night of the 1st January 2002, came the pinnacle of my Leeds United-supporting tenure. It might have been sub-zero degrees, but there was a metaphorical warmth around the stadium that I'd not experienced at Elland Road before. Never had I known every facet of my football club, from the fans, to the players, to the coaching staff, to the board, to so poignantly embody the name, *United*.

We were 2-0 up within seven minutes courtesy of a Viduka brace, and from that moment on it was party football. Every move that we put together was reminiscent of those Smith goals at Lazio and Anderlecht; I couldn't put a number on how many times our play yielded 'ooh's' and 'aah's' of marvel from the crowd in the first half alone.

An outrageous dink from Robbie Fowler to make it three at the start of the second half just about summed up our overall performance, but when the final whistle confirmed our place at the top of the league, I can distinctly recall a very different kind of celebration.

As the players walked over towards the Kop to show their appreciation to the fans, the crowd didn't only applaud back; they roared with encouragement. I'd never heard this kind of response post-match, the game was over, but it was clear to me what was happening.

Just like me, the expectations of every Leeds United fan had changed, and winning a game in such style wasn't enough. We had to look to the next match immediately, and the players on the pitch seemed to recognise that they faced a new challenge too. We'd reached the peak of English football, but it was as though the mentality of everybody at the club instantaneously changed now that we had something to lose.

The unity that I experienced at Elland Road that night suggested to me that we had it in us to sit on that summit until the season's end. However, with so many outstanding sides scrambling up the mountain behind us, I also knew how easy it would be to slip back down. The real problem was that nobody had considered the cliff edge on the other side.

10

Wildest dreams to wildest nightmares

There's something poignant about the cross-section of me taking up drinking and the collapse of Leeds United. Alcohol firmly established itself in my life just three days before we hit the Premiership's summit, yet within twenty months, we were bottom of the league, and favourites for relegation. Obviously, the two were unrelated, but there was a direct correlation between the increased frequency with which I drank and the decline in performances of my football team. At least my social life experienced the opposite effect.

Alcohol fundamentally changed what socialising was to me. My idea of a good time had been to meet up with just one or two friends in a quiet location, usually with a specific activity in which to partake. The concept of the bigger, more grandiose occasions just hadn't appealed to me, as I fundamentally hadn't known how to enjoy them. That's where alcohol came in, and my relationship with it just seemed to get better and better from the start of 2002. I wish more than anything that I could say the same about Leeds.

On 3rd January 2002, just six days after my first time of being drunk, and only two after Leeds went top of the Premiership, our seemingly flawless young manager David O'Leary announced the release of a book that he'd been writing.

It was called *Leeds United On Trial* and was a chronicling of his experiences with us over the prior couple of years. It might sound like a harmless endeavour, but it wasn't merely a recounting of our recent footballing adventures.

The reason that it was called *Leeds United On Trial*, and the reason that O'Leary felt compelled to write the book, was because of an extremely serious off-the-field issue that had been hanging over the club since January 2000.

Two of our best and most promising players, Lee Bowyer and Jonathan Woodgate, were on a night out in Leeds city centre when they got into an altercation with a young Asian man called Sarfraz Najeib. Najeib was seriously injured in the incident, and Bowyer and Woodgate were charged with causing grievous bodily harm to him, with intent.

A case was then built against Bowyer and Woodgate over the next year, with a full trial beginning in January 2001. The trial lasted for over two months, before being dramatically thrown out because of a newspaper article that suggested that the attack was racially motivated. With the jury potentially compromised, on the very day that the verdict was expected, the judge had no choice but to delay the trial for six months, at which point a new jury could be appointed.

The second part of the trial started in October, and on this occasion, it did manage to conclude. The verdicts were delivered in December, with Woodgate only found guilty of affray and Bowyer acquitted entirely. It was considered an excellent outcome for the two of them overall, and the hope was that after almost two years, the club could put the whole ordeal behind them, and focus solely on trying to win the Premiership.

I don't think there could have been a good time for O'Leary

to have released that book. However, I can imagine few worse occasions than just two days after we'd gone top, at the beginning of a fresh start of a new year, with the club seemingly as united as it had ever been.

O'Leary had mostly positive things to say about Bowyer and Woodgate in the book. Still, the very fact that the incident was thrown straight back into the public eye, just as the two of them were starting to try and put it behind them, can't have been good for relations. I don't know if the book truly did impact that dressing room after 3rd January 2001, but events on the field suggest that something did.

Three days after it's release, we travelled to Cardiff City in the FA Cup third round, in a match that was being shown live on Sky Sports. Things had looked good after Mark Viduka had given us an early lead, but Cardiff equalised before a red card for Alan Smith. We'd looked comfortable with ten men, but Scott Young pounced with just three minutes to go to send the fans of a team two leagues below us into absolute raptures. If O'Leary's book wasn't the problem, then maybe the humiliating nature of this defeat was.

The Cardiff loss was the first game in a run of ten without a victory. Imagine that happening in the present day, the Premier League leaders going *ten* games without winning. In our defence, it wasn't the easiest of runs, with the four league matches after West Ham being against Newcastle United, Arsenal, Chelsea and Liverpool. A point against Arsenal was all we managed from a possible twelve.

We then failed to beat Middlesbrough, Charlton Athletic, and Everton, while also being dumped out of the UEFA Cup by PSV Eindhoven. By the time we beat Ipswich Town at Elland

Road on 6th March, we were out of all cup competitions, and Champions League qualification looked out of reach, never mind the title itself.

We won six and lost three of our final nine games of the 2001/02 Premiership season, but the damage had been done. We finished fifth, five points adrift of the top four, which was now the threshold for qualifying to play among Europe's elite. Had fourth place earned Champions League football in 2000/01, we'd have made the cut.

Not too long after the season had finished, O'Leary was sacked by chairman Peter Ridsdale. It was true that we'd had a disastrous second half of the season, but I thought it seemed both harsh and hasty to dismiss a man that had achieved so much during his time in charge. I was genuinely devastated, as O'Leary had been responsible for almost all of my most cherished moments as a fan. However, life had to go on, and I was excited by the appointment of Terry Venables as his replacement.

Soon after that, we sold Rio Ferdinand to Manchester United for £30m. I actually thought that such a vast sum of money was good business at the time, but rumours surfaced about us needing it to support the club financially. Apparently, our substantial player investment over the previous couple of years had happened on the premise that we'd be in the Champions League, which was a far bigger source of revenue than any of us fans realised. We'd just failed to qualify in 01/02, and having missed out by a single point in 00/01, that incorrectly disallowed Wes Brown own goal suddenly seemed far more significant than we'd realised at the time.

However, we still had an excellent squad on paper, and

things looked up after our sixth game of the 02/03 season against Scum at Elland Road. Upon his return, Ferdinand was slaughtered by our fans for committing the ultimate betrayal of joining our biggest enemies, just as Eric Cantona had been in the early 90's. In a poetic turn of events, a Harry Kewell header secured a 1-0 victory and sent us top of the Premiership, which Ferdinand had left us to try and win. Sadly, it was the most false of dawns.

We won only one of our next eleven, and despite a mini-resurgence in December, January shed light on the fact that our club was in a mess of cataclysmic proportions. Chairman Ridsdale had to publicly admit that we'd massively overspent in a bid to fulfil the fans' dreams over the previous couple of years. He was the one that had taken those decisions, yet he laid the blame more squarely at our failure to qualify for the Champions League, which he confessed had been nothing short of a monetary disaster.

Robbie Fowler, Bowyer and Woodgate were all sold, while Olivier Dacourt left on loan. I can remember Venables and Ridsdale doing a press conference together after the sale of Woodgate, and the manager looked in total disbelief about what was happening. It suggested that he hadn't been aware of the full picture at Elland Road when he'd decided to join the club.

After another awful run of one win in eight between January and March, Venables departed. Ridsdale soon followed him out of the club, after the fans made it abundantly clear where they believed the blame to lie for our demise. Most of our players wanted out too, which begs the question as to why Peter Reid took the job with us fighting a genuine relegation battle in 15th place. It took a stunning 3-2 win at Arsenal in the penultimate game of the season to confirm our safety, and the 3-1 final day victory over Aston Villa spelt the end of an era for me personally.

Now sixteen years old, I'd secured a job working in a supermarket, with the only shift that they'd had available for me being a 12-8 on a Saturday. I was devastated to have to give up my season ticket, but I can't deny that I felt a little relieved at the same time.

It had been so painful to witness such a dramatic decline, so soon after our incredible rise, that I knew that it might not be the worst thing for my self-esteem to be away from Elland Road for a little while. However, I felt conflicted in terms of loyalty, as I knew deep down that I'd have turned the job down a couple of years earlier amid our ascent. I couldn't bring myself to admit that to anyone at the time, and writing this is the first occasion on which I have.

That summer, a friend of mine's dad managed to arrange a week's work experience for me at the Yorkshire Evening Post newspaper. My fascination with sport, combined with my relentless reading of post-match articles, had inspired me to want to become a sports journalist, and it was an ideal opportunity to start building both a contact base and a portfolio. On my first day there, one of the chief writers asked me if I was a gambling man, to which I said that I enjoyed the odd £1 football bet if I wasn't ID'ed in the bookies. There was so much shock-value in his response that I can recall it word-for-word. 'If you fancy making yourself some money this season put every penny that you own on Leeds to get relegated'.

I knew that we were coming off the back of a difficult season, but I fancied us to bounce back from our disappointing 02/03 campaign by re-establishing ourselves in the top half of the table. I voiced this in riposte to his bold claim, which made him almost fall off his chair with laughter. I was quite offended by this at the time, but on reflection, I have no idea why I didn't agree with him.

In the nineteen months since that wonderful night against West Ham, we'd sold Nigel Martyn, Rio Ferdinand, Jonathan Woodgate, Lee Bowyer, Olivier Dacourt, Harry Kewell, Robbie Fowler and Robbie Keane, while loaning out Danny Mills, Stephen McPhail, and recently emerged seventeen-year-old prospect James Milner. We'd paid money for one player in that time, Nick Barmby back in July 2002 for little more than a couple of million. He also left on loan.

Our new squad consisted of the few players that had either wanted to stay to help fight for the cause, or who hadn't been good enough to warrant bids from other clubs, as well as a crop of unknown loan signings. We were an absolute mess, a total shambles, although it remained a surprise to the footballing world that we were bottom of the Premiership as we travelled to newly-promoted Portsmouth on 8th November 2003.

That was the day that I knew my football fandom, and the course of my life was about to change forever. Less than a week after my 17th birthday, I started to prepare my goodbyes to Leeds United as I'd always known them. Portsmouth 6-1 Leeds United. Thank fuck I had alcohol.

11

The Rugby World Cup and sporting glory?

It was probably a good thing that Leeds United's decline saw them step back down from being the *only* important thing in my life, to the *most* important thing in my life. It might not seem like a huge difference, but I can see upon reflection that my obsession with my football club had detracted from my development as a person.

I'd been struggling with high school before we embarked on our remarkable rise to the top of the English game. I lacked confidence, I was overly sensitive, there wasn't anything about me as an individual that defined me, and I was losing interest in anything that had previously mattered. Ultimately, I lacked self-esteem, and our brilliance as a team had subconsciously provided me with an external, but very real form of it.

Although going out drinking became a key hobby as Leeds declined, by no means was it like a passing of the proverbial baton. My newfound social life had filled part of the void that the elite level version of my team had left, but it's quite clear as I look back that I needed something more. Inadvertently, this produced many positives.

I'd tentatively started to learn both the guitar and the piano in 2001, and I invested far more time into them through-out 2002 and 2003. I rejoined the school football team, and was even fortunate enough to play against a kid called Aaron Lennon, just a few months before he was to make his Leeds debut. I put a lot of work into my final high school exams and came out with some excellent grades. I also rekindled my interest in watching other sporting events, having allowed these to disintegrate during Leeds' rise.

Despite exiting at the quarter-final stage to eventual winners Brazil, I loved every minute of a solid World Cup performance from England's football team in 2002. I watched all of our games at my friend Laurence's house and quickly realised that drinking and watching football with my mates was an ideal social environment for me. My superior knowledge of the game was a form of comfort, confidence and self-esteem, and I felt an undoubted sense of identity when I was in the act of being a football fan.

I really enjoyed uncompromisingly supporting Tim Henman that same summer, although it was hard to come to terms with the fact that his semi-final defeat to Lleyton Hewitt had probably been his last chance of Wimbledon glory. I'd been cheering Henman on for six years by that point, but with the standard of tennis improving by the year, I didn't know where we were going to find the next British contender.

A particular highlight was Europe's regaining of the Ryder Cup from the USA in the golf, with 2002 captain Sam Torrance poetically lifting the trophy after his infamous rant in 1999. Celebrating Paul McGinley holing the winning putt with my dad made me feel like we'd personally exacted revenge upon the Americans, and how much satisfaction I took from it surprised even me. Still, nothing could fill the void of a competitive Leeds United, as I found out to my peril at the 2003 Rugby World Cup.

I'd watched bits and pieces of rugby union over the years, but it was similar to golf in that it was my dad's interest that made me properly invest in it. I'd never seen any of the domestic game, with the annual Five/Six Nations Championship in February and March being my sole outlet for watching the sport up to that point. It took the remarkable finale of the 2003 Six Nations for it finally to capture my imagination.

I hadn't seen any of England's victories over France, Wales, Italy or Scotland that year before I sat down with the old man on a Sunday afternoon to watch us play Ireland. He was particularly excited for the match as the victors would complete the Grand Slam, which a team wins when they beat all five of their Six Nations opponents. Ireland had also won all four of their games up to that point and had home advantage, historically a massive difference-maker in the Championship.

I watched in awe as we demolished them 42-6 in their own back yard, but was even more taken aback by the post-match analysis. I assumed that there was a fair amount of bias involved when the pundits claimed that England had every chance of winning the World Cup later that year, but my dad reassured me that we were the real deal.

I'd heard nothing but cynicism in the past about England's chances at World Cups, but that was usually related to football. Newspapers and other media outlets had always been so quick to dismiss us for whatever reason and had seemed to take a degree of pleasure in criticising us after defeats. Something felt different before this Rugby World Cup though; it wasn't a pessimistic approach tinged with hope; it was an optimistic approach filled with belief. On top of this, there are two other reasons that I invested heavily in that World Cup.

The first was the influence of my dad, as his passion was massively contagious when I watched our group games with Georgia and Samoa with him at his flat. With Australia hosting the tournament, the time difference meant that the matches were on in the morning in the UK, and with these games being at weekends, I would often wake up still a bit drunk from a booze-up the night before. That gave me an extra bit of fire in the belly and added to the enjoyment of celebrating tries with my old man.

The second related to that emotional void left by the plight of my football club. I didn't know this at the time, but with my football team having stumbled off that cliff-edge in their pursuit of glory, I think a part of me was hoping that England's rugby team could provide the sporting fulfilment that I so badly craved.

Despite this, there could be no doubting that my support of England through the knockout stages was substantial. I watched the comeback victory over Wales in the quarter-finals at my dad's, and remember celebrating Will Greenwood's try as raucously as I would a Leeds United or England goal.

I then watched the semi-final dismissal of France alone on my bedroom couch at my mum's, having set my Sunday morning alarm to get up and watch it after a Saturday night knees-up. I was definitely still drunk on that occasion, and I can remember being stunned by the commentator's words 'England are in a World Cup final' at the end of the match. Even at seventeen years old, I'd already thought that I might never see the day as a fan of any sport.

I spent the week that followed looking forward to the final, without feeling massively excited about it. I found with Australia

'03 that the rugby engrossed me once it was on, but I thought little about it between matches. During a football World Cup, or throughout a whole season of being a Leeds season-ticket holder, I'd always be engaged in something related, whether that was a conversation with other fans, reading articles, or watching highlights. As much as I'd have liked it to have been, it just wasn't quite the same with it being rugby, which almost entirely explains my behaviour on the morning of Saturday 22nd November 2003.

I watched England's World Cup final victory over Australia with hazy eyes from my mate Chur's bedroom floor on a tiny television screen, feeling like total shit. My entire group of friends had been on a massive night out on the eve of the match, and for some reason, I ended up staying at Chur's instead of heading back to my dad's. If I'd have stayed at my old man's, I'd most likely have got up and had one of the most memorable experiences of my life up to that point. As it was, I missed the first twenty minutes after falling back to sleep in my hungover state, before barely mustering a moment's enthusiasm for the remainder of the match.

My first memory of the game is of Ben Kay dropping the ball with the try-line at his mercy. I honestly think that I was too all over the place to have even focused on what the score was at that point, but when Jason Robinson crossed just before half-time, I do recall a massive smile coming to my face as I saw Australia 5-14 England.

I then went back to sleep at half-time, before waking up with only ten minutes of the game remaining. The first thing that I recall after that is Mel, who was also staying at Chur's, commenting that he had no idea how we'd thrown the match away after Elton Flatley drew Australia level at 14-14. Fortunately, I was now wide awake and *did* manage to see those incredible extra-time scenes.

I can't imagine what it would have been like to have watched it with my dad. The drama of us going back ahead at 17-14, only for the Wallabies to draw level once more at 17-17, would have been an emotional rollercoaster that I wouldn't rather have ridden with anybody else. As it was, I let out a tame, pathetic cheer as Jonny Wilkinson slotted over that famous drop-goal, and barely felt a thing after the full-time whistle sounded. I instantly knew how badly I'd fucked it, and that wasn't even the worst of it.

I received a message from Rich, whose house party had got me into drinking in the first place, and it turned out that a considerable crowd of people had gone back to his house after the night out. He wasn't a huge rugby fan but had very much got into the spirit of the occasion, and the crowd had stayed up all night drinking, right through until Wilkinson's drop-goal. Knowing that I'd been following England closely throughout the tournament, he messaged to tell me what they'd all done, and how amazing it was that we'd won a World Cup. I think his exact comment was, *if I'm this happy, I can't imagine how you must be feeling.*

I was so distraught that I'd watched it at neither Rich's nor my dad's, that I literally couldn't face up to the reality of it. When I messaged Rich back, I stated that I was feeling euphoric, that Wilkinson was my absolute hero, and that I'd thought the worst when Kay had dropped the ball back in the first half. I hadn't thought the worst; I hadn't been able to think at all in the state that I was.

Then, when my dad came to pick me up from Chur's, I ran up to the car, jumping around wildly in celebration, before getting in and hugging him with feigned delight. We talked about England's brilliance on the way back to his flat, and he was keen to stress how our dominance of the game should have seen us out of sight long before extra-time. I wholeheartedly agreed with him, without having a clue whether that was the case or not.

The one shred of comfort that I took was that if I was capable of sleeping through that match, then I must not have cared about it that deeply. I'd thoroughly enjoyed the World Cup, but had England's potential glory truly meant that much to me, no hangover would have kept me from watching the final. There's no way that the same would have happened had it been England's football team or a critical Leeds United game.

The most interesting part, of course, was my inability to admit my *actual* World Cup final experience. My reaction to my dad was a very real one, as I was genuinely too heartbroken to face up to the fact that I hadn't watched it with him. My relationship with my old man had always been brilliant, with sport a binding interest for us throughout my childhood. We should have shared that moment, and even if England winning a Rugby World Cup wasn't as important to me as I might have thought, I knew it was important to him.

I see my message to Rich as being far more significant, for the very reason that I was seventeen when I sent it. My behaviour mirrored how I'd acted in primary school when I'd perceived that I was somehow important for being the biggest sports fan. I honestly think that I couldn't tell him because I was trying to protect a reputation. The reality was that neither Rich, nor anybody else, could have cared less about how big a sports fan I was, but clearly, I still wanted to be defined this way. At seventeen years old, I had little more identity than I'd had at nine years old.

Later that day, as I had a rare Saturday off work, Linley and I went down to Elland Road for the first time in Leeds United's torrid 2003/04 Premiership campaign. We watched our managerless side fall to a 2-0 home defeat to Bolton Wanderers, leaving us rooted to the foot of the table. How many sports fans can say that a day on which their country won a World Cup final was one of the worst days of their lives?

12

The footballing extremes

I feel grateful for the 2003/04 football season having coincided with my first year in further education. I'd opted to stay at my high school to go to its sixth-form college after I finished my exams in June 2003, although I had thought about going elsewhere after my mixed high school experience. The fact that all my friends were staying on made that decision for me in the end, and things couldn't have worked out any better.

I spent plenty of time with the lads that summer, but mostly in big-group situations, and usually with a lot of alcohol involved. Don't get me wrong, it was a tremendous amount of fun, but I preferred the year in education that followed.

In my first year in sixth-form, I felt like I was actually getting to know my friends as individuals for the first time. The number of people in our year dropped from 270 to about seventy, with pretty much all of the less cooperative characters having left, and our common area became a calm, open environment in which people felt free to express themselves. It was so refreshing after all the high school politics and was a gateway to uncovering personality traits.

I was still struggling for confidence and identity to some degree, as my post-Rugby World Cup final behaviours attest to, although I found that the more time that I spent listening to and learning from my mates, the more confident I became. Furthermore, the sensitivity that I'd elicited in high school started to become a positive thing, as instead of absorbing the pain and negativity of others, I began to form a persona based on the different strengths that my friends brought to the table. It wasn't necessarily an identity, but it was a start.

My slightly weaker character meant that I was rarely a leader, but I did find that I had a quality of being able to bring people together. Aided by the strong individual friendships that I was forging, I took a lot of pleasure in encouraging the lads to play off each other's strengths, which I think helped a great group of individuals to become stronger collectively. The most important thing for me was that my friends were now having a massively beneficial effect on my self-esteem at a time when my football team was doing the direct opposite.

I can remember my last Premiership game at Elland Road like it was yesterday. It was a Tuesday night in April 2004, we faced Everton, I went with my dad for the first time in years, and the atmosphere was electric. I didn't realise this at the time, but it was almost ten years to the day since my first meaningful matchday experience against Manchester United in April 1994; the start of my Leeds United journey. I'd been through so much as a fan since then.

The Everton match was a must-win. Pre-game, we sat in the final relegation spot, three points behind Blackburn Rovers and Portsmouth, but had just won consecutive league games for the first time all season. I can remember cherishing that isolated feeling of hope, but with an unbeatable Arsenal side to come a few days later at Highbury, there was no margin for error.

The match was a story of three footballers, two of whom

I perceived would play prominent roles in my future as a football fan, and one of whom had been highly significant in my past. Frustratingly for us, thirty-seven-year-old ex-Leeds 'keeper Nigel Martyn rolled back the years in the Everton goal, making a string of saves in each half, although he hadn't been able to keep out our outstanding eighteen-year-old James Milner on fifty minutes. Unfortunately, Milner's strike was only enough to earn us a 1-1 draw, which spelt big trouble heading to Highbury.

As incredible as Arsenal's 'Invincibles' side were to watch, their 5-0 demolition of us was not what I needed to get me fired up for the Friday night out that I was about to go on. With our goal difference already in dire straits, we now effectively needed defeats for Blackburn and Portsmouth on the Saturday to have a realistic chance of escaping. Both sides won, and when Pompey outplayed us for three points at Elland Road a week later, the end was nigh.

We were so far into the mire going into the Portsmouth game, and then performed so badly that day, that I was already quite far along with my grieving process when we travelled to Bolton Wanderers on Sunday 2nd May 2004. With me still working Saturdays at this point, I was grateful for the game's selection for Sunday TV coverage at the time. Sadly, I'd probably have been better off stacking shelves.

There was brief hope for my dad, Rodney and me at my dad's flat when Mark Viduka gave us a first-half lead with a penalty. However, Viduka was then sent off for two bookable offences just five minutes later, and we were not just a man, but our best player down. We managed to hold out until half-time but imploded soon after the restart.

The team battled hard, in particular Leeds through-and-through striker Alan Smith, but we collapsed to a demoralising 4-1 defeat. When the final whistle sounded, and the camera focused in on a distraught Smith, the reality that we were all but relegated hit home. We could still mathematically stay up at six points from safety with two games remaining, but with our goal difference thirty-six worse off than 17th-placed Manchester City, the jig was up.

At seeing the heroic Smith's tears, my dad had to leave the room to ensure that he didn't cry himself. Rodney left soon after in a similar emotional state, whereas I sat there, feeling numb, but also quite philosophical as a result of the psychological preparation that I'd done. The hardest thing to come to terms with was the thought of us not being on Match Of The Day, or ITV's The Premiership as it was at the time, but I was confident that we'd bounce back soon. We were too big not to, I'd mused.

It was far more painful for me to see Smith, a lifelong Leeds fan, move to Manchester United a few weeks later. In his final home game against Charlton Athletic, when it had become clear that he was going to have to leave to help the club bring in some money, the fans poured on to the pitch and showered him with worship. Almost everything about the team had been awful that season, but Smith remained a hero by way of his apparent willingness to die for the cause.

I didn't personally resent him for moving to Scum, he'd fought harder for the white shirt than any other player that I'd seen in my ten years as a fan, and he deserved the chance to play on the biggest stage. However, the incredible memories that I had of his goals at Lazio and Anderlecht, his oh-so authentic kissing of the badge, his deep connection with everyone at Elland Road, and his entire Leeds United legacy soured when he made that move. Somehow, another Old Trafford-bound player would have a more significant impact upon my summer in 2004.

I'd seen Wayne Rooney play at Elland Road before my final time watching Leeds in the Premiership. It was November 2002, just a week after he'd turned seventeen, and only two weeks since he'd announced himself on the national stage with that spectacular strike against Arsenal, when he came off Everton's bench with only a quarter of an hour remaining. Within five minutes, Rooney had dribbled past four of our defenders like he was in a school playground and tucked the ball into the bottom corner. He was still a child but looked like a king among men as he won the match for his team 1-0.

By the time of our April 2004 match-up, an eighteen-year-old Rooney was already better than any player that I'd seen play for Leeds at Elland Road. He was lightning quick, strong as an Ox, could pass and cross the ball brilliantly, flew into a tackle, worked harder than anyone else on the pitch, and had an absolute rocket of a shot on him, as his early goal that night displayed. He was the complete player, and although I could only wish that he played for Leeds, I felt eternally grateful that he was English.

The fact that the happiest time of my childhood came just before I turned eighteen says it all about how much I enjoyed Euro 2004. I didn't stop to think about it at the time, but I'd so quickly developed this incredible group of friends, I was watching the best England team that I'd seen during my time as a fan, and I felt as free as I'd ever felt in my life.

We only played four matches, but every one of them was special beyond measure. I went to my mate Mel's for our opening group match against France, and about eight of us drank beers in his bedroom for a couple of hours before kick-off, even though we had exams the next day. The French went into the game as clear favourites, as they still had the likes of Zinedine Zidane, Lilian Thuram, Patrick Vieira, and Thierry Henry in their side. We didn't look too bad either with David Beckham, Steven Gerrard, Paul Scholes, and Michael Owen in our eleven, but it was a player that had never appeared on the big stage that completely stole the show.

Rooney pulverised France from the first minute, showing far more desire, energy, and most importantly, ability than all of the supposed world-beaters he was facing. All on his own, in one half of football, Rooney had me believing that England's thirty-eight-year wait for glory could be about to end.

Frank Lampard's header gave us a half-time lead that we more than deserved, and we really should have wrapped up all three points when Beckham had a penalty saved with fifteen minutes remaining. Rooney's driving run to win the penalty epitomised his superiority and had Head Coach Sven-Goran Eriksson not taken him off a couple of minutes later, we might not have gone on to lose the game.

With us still leading in the 90th minute, Zidane reminded the world of his brilliance by scoring a free-kick and a penalty in stoppage time. France may have stolen victory, but their celebrations on the pitch afterwards conveyed how lucky they knew they'd been.

I was devastated, but pragmatic after the match. Yes, we'd been beaten, but it was the best performance I'd seen from an

England team at a major tournament, and we should have won the game comfortably, never mind not even getting a point. I spent an hour afterwards feeling crushed, but as soon as I got over the injustice of the result, I started counting down the hours until I got to see Rooney and co. play again.

I reckon there were twelve of us packed into my mate Andy's living room for the Switzerland game four days later, as Rooney hit two as part of a 3-0 cruise. By no means were the Swiss a bad side, but we dominated every aspect of the game, and I don't think anybody would have begrudged us a fourth. It was a challenge not to get carried away with the quality of football that we were producing.

Having been so good in our first two games, it didn't feel right that we couldn't afford to lose our final group game against Croatia. We deserved to be through already, which is why my mate Laurence's living room was a very quiet place when Niko Kovac put the Croatians ahead after just five minutes. However, that goal is the only time that England have conceded at a major tournament and I haven't gone into meltdown. With Rooney on the pitch, and the rest of the team playing as well as they were, I just knew that we'd be OK.

Lo and behold, Scholes equalised later in the first half, before the boy wonder got in on the act on the stroke of half-time. We went on to win the match 4-2 and had completely outplayed our opponents for the third consecutive game at a European Championships. I can remember the lads taking the piss out of me when I over-excitedly stated, 'WE'RE THE BEST TEAM EVER, WE'VE GOT THE BEST PLAYER IN THE WORLD, WE'RE GONNA WIN THE EUROS'. It felt special to be so proud of an England team.

I think that we had twenty lads at Laurence's for the quarter-final against hosts Portugal, and when Owen gave us the lead after just three minutes, I felt that it was going to be another night to remember. We'd all had a few beers before the match and went wild after the goal, with talk already starting about how big an occasion a major tournament semi-final would be. However, the room soon fell quiet, as disaster struck.

Portugal didn't equalise, and we didn't have a man sent off; it was much worse than either of those things. Rooney had gone down with what looked like quite a serious injury, and moments later, he was limping off down the tunnel. Here we were, 1-0 up in the quarter-final of Euro 2004, and an injury to an eighteen-year-old made me feel like we had just been knocked out.

The 300 minutes of glorious tournament football that England had just produced suddenly felt like a long-forgotten dream. It was like Leeds United's journey to the top of English football, a temporary building of disbelieving euphoria that vanished in the blink of an eye. Even as we reached half-time with our lead still intact, there wasn't an ounce of me that felt anything that I should have been feeling.

Although Portugal were barely any better than us in the second half, they just about deserved their equaliser when it came with little over five minutes remaining. Despite the loss of Rooney, getting that close and conceding was extremely hard to take, but I soon found myself bouncing off the lads' energy as they found a way to fire each other up for extra-time.

When Rui Costa gave Portugal the lead on 110 minutes, we all assumed that it was all over. The living room was a sorry sight, with a group of crestfallen seventeen-year-old lads staring at the floor in defeated acceptance, while also preparing to pour all of their emotion into the one tiny shred of hope that would exist until the referee blew the final whistle.

Then, in a moment similar to Lee Bowyer's strike at Southampton, Lampard pounced after a goalmouth scramble to make it 2-2, sparking a different kind of celebration among our twenty-strong crowd. It was shock, it was relief, it was euphoria, it was passion; it was every positive emotion imaginable. We all went mad, and I can remember locking eyes with my mate Chur amid the pandemonium, before punching his back repeatedly during the most masculine of embraces. By the time the bedlam had subsided, there was a full-time whistle and an imminent penalty shootout.

So little had happened for such a long period of the match, but the half an hour that we'd just been through together was as dramatic as tournament football gets. In an act of overwhelmed and confused unity, we all decided to take off our tops, before forming an arm-in-arm arc around the perimeter of Laurence's living room.

As a replica of the two sets of players that were standing on the halfway line in Portugal, we anxiously awaited the fate of our emotions. With a beer in one hand and the other nervously hitting the top of a pal's shoulder, I felt eternally grateful for my friends and football in that moment. I may have been beside myself with nerves, but everything that I loved about life at that time was right there in that tiny, enclosed space.

Captain Beckham stepped up first for England, and ballooned his penalty over the bar, a second crucial penalty miss of the tournament. Portugal then scored their first two, with Owen and Lampard converting for England before Rui

Costa missed his penalty to bring us back level. Once again, we were seemingly back from the dead.

Hope and excitement enveloped me three times as a Portugal player stepped up after we'd gone ahead in the shootout. A miss from either of the last two would have sent us through, but the three Portugal players beat David James with their penalties. Then, as Darius Vassell set out on the long, lonely walk from the halfway line, the words 'there's no way *he's* scoring' cut through me like a knife.

It was a simple, meaningless prediction from one of the lads, and someone in the room had probably said it before every one of our previous penalties. However, I couldn't have agreed with the comment more; I just couldn't envisage Vassell beating Portugal 'keeper Ricardo.

Despite the foresight, I couldn't prevent a crushing sinking feeling from piercing the pit of my stomach as Ricardo palmed Vassell's penalty away. To somehow make matters worse, Ricardo then stepped up himself with a place in the semi-finals at stake and smashed the ball into James' bottom corner. It was absolutely heartbreaking.

As brilliant as we'd been in the group stage, it wasn't until Owen's goal in that quarter-final that I'd truly believed that England were going to win Euro 2004. I'd not thought like that before at a major tournament, and I've not done so since, but I take a lot of pride in being able to look back on having a bona fide belief in my national team. We were a genuinely good side that was made a lot better by a fearless teenager with the world at his feet. I wish that I could say that I took solace in the prospect of England's future with Rooney at the time, but the pain of the moment was too overwhelming.

Leeds United's relegation from the Premiership, and England missing out in a tournament that they definitely could have won paints a pretty bleak picture of the summer of 2004. However, as I reflect on the year leading up to and including the Euros, it was undoubtedly the best of my childhood.

13

Ashes 2005

Personally, I don't believe that any child owes their parents anything. Invariably, if two people decide to bring someone into the world, it is out of *their* desire to do so. I'd challenge anybody to find a couple in the world of whom neither had any desire to have a baby, but did so anyway for reasons that are free of societal pressure.

Maybe I'm wrong, maybe some folk do have children for a mysterious altruistic reason that I'm not aware of, but even if they did, I still don't think that their kids would *owe* them anything. However, I do believe that any child that is brought up by two caring, attentive parents should be more thankful for it than anything else.

There's very little that I'd change about my upbringing. Yes, my parents separated, but I'd say that it only served to bring me closer to each of them as individuals. I'd venture that the different lessons that I learned from spending time with them separately actually benefited the shaping of my morals, ethics and abilities. I'm sure most people with split parents wouldn't say this, but I'm genuinely glad that it happened.

My dad was incredibly involved me with me from a very young age to teach me how to do things, in particular play sports. He took me to and watched me play in every match that I partook in throughout my childhood, whether it was his weekend to have us or not. He also took me to watch more football, rugby and cricket matches than any friend of mine's parents combined. And, as I got older, he helped to instil a working discipline in me, and even drove me around my paper-round route, while also taking me up to and picking me up from every supermarket shift that I did whilst staying with him.

My mum is the most naturally intuitive person that I've ever met. Her ability to detect when something wasn't right for me growing up, and find a way to help put it right, was nothing short of remarkable. She had a bit of a temper from time to time, but if I got it in the ear, it was likely because she was aware that I'd knowingly not done something to the best of my ability. She always made me feel loved, and as though I was good enough, regardless of the trouble that I brought upon myself. And, partly because she was a teacher herself, she always knew when I wasn't quite working hard enough at school and was excellent at picking the right moment to have a word.

The most important thing that my parents did was to allow me to do *whatever* I wanted and be *whoever* I wanted, within reason. They gave me a tremendous amount of freedom, encouraging ambitions and placing few restrictions upon the various things that I pursued. For better or for worse, I always liked to push boundaries as a kid, and they were happy to let me learn from the mistakes that I would inevitably make. Before I did though, there would always be some gentle guidance or advice offered, with it being left to me to decide whether to take it.

The only time that I didn't heed my mum's educational advice was in and around Euro 2004. It took place just before, and during, my AS-level exams, and she expressed concern that

I wasn't quite doing enough. Deep down, she *knew* that I wasn't doing enough, but didn't tell me what I should or shouldn't be doing, instead encouraging me to consider my efforts.

That open and compromising approach made it all the more difficult to deal with when I received my very disappointing results that August, but it also inspired me to sort myself out as I headed into my final year of schooling. The reality was that although I'd had the best year of my childhood in my first year of sixth-form college, I'd only burned the candle at one end.

I found a far better work-life balance in my A-level year, working hard at college, continuing my Saturday shifts at the supermarket, while going out with the lads just a couple of times a week, as opposed to the three or four that it had been the previous year. The excitement of turning eighteen brought a few extra booze-ups around November time, but it was timed well after I re-sat my two failed modules from the previous year on my birthday itself. I was always busy but had a clear direction and purpose of securing good enough grades to earn a place at university.

As the months passed by, it became clear to me that it was going to take a lot more than my intelligence alone to get the grades that I needed. I was studying English Literature, Maths, and Psychology, and while the content of the work was challenging enough, the sheer amount that I had to do was the more overwhelming part. Fortunately, I had a place in which I could spend every day after college, Saturdays after work, and all day on Sunday to get it done.

From the confines of my bedroom, I watched more sport between late 2004 and the summer of 2005 than I had throughout my entire childhood. I got into a lovely routine of completing every essay, project, and mock exam paper on my couch with Sky Sports on in the background. It didn't matter whether it was football, rugby, cricket, tennis, golf, darts, athletics, boxing, or even pool's Mosconi Cup just before Christmas, sport accompanied and supported me through the only truly challenging year of my education.

I watched England record an incredible Test series victory in South Africa, our first there for over forty years. I found there to be no better sport to write essays to than cricket, with its slow pace providing only the occasional distraction, while also bringing an intensity that keeps you wanting to watch more. With my brother as mad about cricket as I was about football, I'd watched many a Test series over the years, and this was undoubtedly the best England team that I'd seen. It made the prospect of facing the Australians in the Ashes six months later particularly enticing.

In golf, I watched almost all of the 2005 Masters, including the entirety of Sunday's dramatic final round. Tiger Woods and Chris DiMarco were neck and neck for pretty much the entire eighteen holes, only for Woods to pinch the Green Jacket on the first play-off hole. I can remember the exact project that I spent the day doing while I watched it, Psychology Statistics coursework, although when Woods holed his now-legendary chip on the 16th, I put my pen down for the night.

Wimbledon was on during my final exams and provided daily background entertainment as I was off college on study leave by this point. Tennis was a sport that I found engrossing, particularly when Tim Henman had been playing, although his second-round defeat meant that the majority of the tournament was conducive to revision. To my surprise, there was another Brit that piqued my interest, with eighteen-year-old wildcard Andy Murray beating 14th seed Radek Stepanek, and taking two sets from 18th seed David Nalbandian before falling to a courageous defeat. There was a steel and a belief about Murray that excited me though, and I certainly hoped to see him in action again.

It wasn't necessarily a bad thing for my studies that it was a modest first season in the Coca Cola Championship for Leeds United, with new manager Kevin Blackwell leading us to a 14th-placed finish. Typically, I listened to or watched every non-Saturday game of the season, even when it became clear that our campaign was fading into meaninglessness from as early as January. Not for the first time in recent years, though, the most important events were occurring off the field.

The very future of our football club had come under significant threat after our relegation from the Premiership, with the ownership changing hands twice during that period. Considerable investment was required to clear the massive debts that remained from our overzealous Ridsdale-era spending, and to balance a wage-bill that still included many players that had long since left. Apparently, after failing to qualify for the Champions League in 2001/02, we'd been so desperate to get rid of our highest-paid players that we offered to subsidise their salaries to encourage bids from other clubs.

Towards the end of 2004, the word 'liquidation' was bandied about alarmingly frequently, and there was genuine concern for our club's future. There had been weeks of talk about us going out of business if we couldn't find a buyer that would inject some cash, and at the 11th hour, an infamous, colourful character stepped forward.

With Leeds and Chelsea having history, former Blues chairman Ken Bates' takeover was not well received, but every sound of mind fan knew that the days of us being choosers were long behind us. When a minority let Bates know what they thought of him, he was quick to remind them that they wouldn't even have a football club without him. His presence at Elland Road made us all a little nervous, but we merely had to hope that he and Blackwell between them could plot a route back to the Premiership in 2005/06.

One of the greatest feelings of freedom that I've ever had in my life came after I finished my final A-level exams. Having worked hard all year, I felt utterly euphoric as I walked out of the school hall after that English Literature exam, knowing that I could do absolutely anything that I wanted henceforth.

After a couple of days of total relaxation, a group of thirty-four of us took off to Kavos in Greece for a two-week lads' holiday. It was a pretty chaotic experience, and one that overwhelmed me in the first few days, but I soon got into the swing of getting drunk out of my mind with all my best mates every night. Ultimately, it wasn't an environment that suited me at all, but a combination of the lads' energy and alcohol eventually proved the perfect tonic.

Soon after we got back, I got my exam results and found out that I'd got into Northumbria University in Newcastle to study Psychology. I'd spent my last couple of years at high school planning to become a sports journalist, but I'd enjoyed Psychology so much at A-level that I changed my degree plans late on.

I also made a late decision to defer my university entry for a year to go travelling with my mates Chur and Neil. I had no idea what travelling constituted, but I'd turned in to a perennial 'yes man' during sixth-form, and it sounded like an incredibly exciting prospect. The plan was to get full-time jobs, work until March, and then take off on an adventure around the world. The thought of it alone excited me beyond belief.

While Chur and Neil quite quickly found jobs post-Kavos, I decided to take the entire summer off. The notion of being free to do whatever I pleased, whenever I pleased, was an opportunity that I knew might not come along again, as I recognised that in that exact moment I was lying on the cusp between childhood and adulthood. There was also a titanic sporting series lying ahead that I did not want to miss.

The 2005 Ashes doesn't just represent an amazing series of cricket as I look back on it, but a period of time in which I was living my dream lifestyle. I had a near-constant stream of dramatic sport, I wasn't working, I was out with my mates a couple of nights a week, and every day that I woke up to was my own. I was totally and utterly free, and the cricket was supreme.

There were only two days between my return from Kavos and day one of the first Test at Lord's. I'd read a lot about the series in the newspapers and online, and spent the evening before day one watching Channel Four's preview, in which many of the pundits were tipping England to run Australia close at the very least. After that magnificent win in South Africa and a more recent home demolition of Bangladesh, I was more hopeful than I'd ever been heading into an Ashes series, although that wasn't saying a great deal.

The top three batsmen of Marcus Trescothick, Andrew Strauss and Michael Vaughan, alongside the four frontline seam bowlers of Steve Harmison, Matthew Hoggard, Simon Jones and Andrew Flintoff, had formed a formidable fulcrum to the team. There was a bit of concern over our middle order, with the inexperienced Ian Bell batting at four, and the supremely talented but unproven one-day specialist Kevin Pietersen selected to make his Test debut at number five. Flintoff was to bat at six as the all-rounder, with wicketkeeper Geraint Jones at seven, and the solid but unspectacular spin bowler Ashley Giles in at eight.

The way I saw it, we had a chance of nicking a match or two, but the flawless Australian team was far too good for us to be able to win the five-match series.

Matthew Hayden and Justin Langer had long been the best opening partnership in the world, I'd been in awe of numbers three and four Ricky Ponting and Damien Martyn when they'd made brilliant hundreds four years prior at Headingley, Michael Clarke was extremely highly-rated at number five, and Simon Katich was a specialist top-order batsman, not a number six. Throw in one of the greatest wicketkeeper-batsmen of all time in Adam Gilchrist at seven, the ingenious Shane Warne at eight, and the lightning-quick Brett Lee at nine, and you have a team that bats very deep. With Jason Gillespie at ten and the best seam bowler I've ever seen in Glenn McGrath completing the line-up, you have arguably the greatest Test team ever assembled.

I didn't leave my bedroom for the entirety of that first day, and hope sprang eternal from the opening session. We skittled Australia for just 190, and the ferocity of our bowling attack was reminiscent of West Indians Curtley Ambrose and Courtney Walsh in their pomp. The Aussies' supposedly impenetrable batting line-up couldn't cope with Harmison's raw pace and bounce, while the variety of Flintoff, Hoggard and Jones posed all kinds of other problems. It was like watching Leeds United at Anderlecht or Wayne Rooney's England in Portugal all over again; I thought I was in some kind of wonderful dream.

I woke up very soon after, when the unplayable McGrath made a mockery of our top-order, removing Trescothick, Strauss, Vaughan, Bell and Flintoff to leave us 21-5. Pietersen showed some grit to make a half-century, but 155 all-out represented a disappointing return after the brilliance of that first morning.

The Australian batsmen redeemed themselves for their substandard first-innings performance, making 384 to set us a target of 420 to win, an almost impossible task with McGrath and Warne around. The geniuses took four wickets apiece, removing us for just 180, and all of a sudden there was an ominously familiar pessimism in the air.

I can remember exactly what I was doing when the news filtered through that McGrath had suffered a freak injury in the warm-up to the second Test. My mum must have been out, as I was eating Weetabix in the living room while watching the build-up to the start of play. In scenes like I'd never witnessed during TV analysis, the body language and the tone of voice of the pundits completely changed; everybody knew how significant this was.

Australia won the toss and elected to field, only for our batsmen to take advantage of McGrath's absence by making 407 on a superb first day. I only saw snippets of day two, as twenty-one of my friends and I had arranged a game of cricket of our own at a local cricket club. However, I nipped over to the pub while my team were batting, and I can remember seeing Ashley Giles snare Michael Clarke while I was sinking a quick pint. We eventually dismissed the Aussies for 308 to leave ourselves in a commanding position.

The Football League season started the following day, which left me flicking between Soccer Saturday and events at Edgbaston at my dad's flat. Australia fought back brilliantly, with Warne taking six wickets to remove us for 182, which left them with an achievable target of 282 to take a 2-0 series lead. It could have been far worse for us had Flintoff and Simon Jones not put on fifty-one for the final wicket.

The irrepressible Flintoff then bowled the over of his life to remove Langer and Ponting, en route to our attack reducing Australia to 175-8 at the close. With 107 runs still required to win, and only two wickets remaining, we were now overwhelming favourites to win the match. I don't think anybody anticipated that it would end up being so, so close.

The wicket of Michael Kasprowicz to give England a two-run victory over Australia in the second Test of the 2005 Ashes is a moment that I hope I never forget. I was at Elland Road, having a pre-match pint before Leeds' first game of the 2005/06 season, and about 100 blokes had gathered around a tiny screen about ten minutes before kick-off. Kasprowicz and Brett Lee had somehow taken their side from 220-9 to 279-9, and our bowlers looked like they'd run out of both steam and ideas.

With only one boundary required to win, Harmison ran into bowl at Kasprowicz with the Australian readying himself to become a national hero. I'd been so happy when he'd been thrust into their bowling attack as a result of McGrath's injury, but here he was, on the brink of pulling off the most unlikely of victories for his team with the bat.

Then, as the ball clipped his glove, and wicketkeeper Geraint Jones flung himself low to his left to take the catch, there was absolute bedlam among Leeds United fans. We hadn't even kicked off, yet a section of Elland Road was celebrating as though we'd just scored a goal to win the Premiership title. It was incredible sport, and Leeds went on to win to complete the best day of the summer thus far.

The drama that followed in the third Test was scarcely believable, particularly bearing in mind everything that had happened at Edgbaston. After thirty-five pulsating hours of Test cricket, Australia clung on for a draw at the end of day five at Old Trafford, with England requiring just one wicket to win. I'm sure any non-cricket fans reading this will believe that the phrases 'pulsating' and 'Test cricket' should never be used in the same sentence, but I dare you to watch that Test match back and not find it entertaining, it was astonishing to behold.

Then, with a few Australian cracks starting to appear, England moved ahead in an Ashes series for the first time in eight years at Trent Bridge, after another absolute thriller. Having won the toss and elected to bat, we registered an imposing 477 over the first couple of days. We then ripped through Australia's top order to reduce them to 99-5 at the close of day two, which they could only turn in to 218 by the time they were all out. In another historic moment, this allowed captain Vaughan to enforce Australia to follow-on against us for the first time since 1986, when I was just two-weeks-old. I back myself to have been watching that match if my dad or two-year-old brother will have had anything to do with it.

In typically resolute fashion on a difficult wicket, Australia made an outstanding 387 to give themselves a chance of an against-all-odds victory. Still, bearing in mind how well we'd batted throughout the series, 129 looked like a straightforward task, and everything was going to plan when Trescothick and Strauss guided us to 32/0. Enter Shane Warne.

Flanked brilliantly by three wickets from Lee in the absence of McGrath, Warne took four as we crumbled to 116/7, thirteen runs short with only our bowlers remaining to try and bat us to victory. Fortunately, Giles and Hoggard were coolness personified and steered us home to secure our second victory of the series in another utterly dramatic Test match. 2-1 England with just one Test to go.

The strangest thing about the fifth Test is that I can only remember day five. There are so many specific details that I can recall about the whole series, yet that pivotal match escapes me almost entirely. I can only assume that I spent the entire five days locked inside my bedroom, as that's where I was when Kevin Pietersen announced himself as a batsman like no other with an incredible 158 on the final day.

I'd never seen batting like it, as I watched Pietersen take the game away from Australia. He was marching down the wicket to 90mph deliveries, hitting Warne and Lee all over the park, and making the returning McGrath seem like a novice. Pietersen had regularly been the centre of attention throughout the series for a variety of reasons, and it seemed appropriate that he should take centre stage to decide The Ashes.

With Australia having a target of over 300 to win the match, with less than an hour in which to do it, everybody knew it was over. Despite this, there was something very unsettling about the Australian openers coming out to bat for only a few balls, before being called off due to bad light.

After a series of pure drama, involving some of the best cricket ever witnessed, The 2005 Ashes ended farcically. I can remember spending about half an hour watching both sets of players stew restlessly on their respective balconies before the umpires finally walked out to the middle and knocked the bails off, signalling the end of the match. We'd done it, we'd won the Ashes for the first time in eighteen years, although in absolutely bizarre style.

Within a couple of minutes of the end, my mate Rout called to tell me to watch the news that evening, as the BBC had filmed him celebrating in the pub. I can remember finding the footage hilarious, as they had no idea how to respond to such a contradictory moment while being oh-so aware that they were on camera.

Not for the first time, I felt conflicted after witnessing what should have been one of the greatest sporting moments of my life. I tried to embrace the fact that England had just beaten arguably the best cricket team of all time, but the anticlimactic nature of it made celebrating feel somewhat unnatural. However, the moment itself wasn't the most important thing.

The aftermath of the fifth Test signalled my last few days of freedom, as I started full-time work the following Monday. That utterly astonishing series had been right at the centre of an unforgettable couple of months, and I wouldn't change those experiences for the world, which was exactly what I was about to go and see.

14

One night in Sydney

Before Chur and Neil asked me to go travelling with them back in my first year of sixth-form college, I'd had a clear plan in my head; school, college, university, get a job, see where life takes me. I'd not stopped to think that there might be other options available during my childhood; I'd just assumed that everybody followed the same basic societal model. Before the two of them mentioned it, I hadn't even known what travelling was, and if I'm honest, I still didn't as I boarded a flight to Bangkok in February 2006.

I worked in a warehouse for six months to save up for my trip, and my colleagues had often asked me what I was doing there. With most of them being working-class lads from Wakefield, they hadn't been used to having a 'posh cunt' around, and whenever I explained that I was saving money to go travelling, the standard response was 'what the fuck are you doing that for?'. Not once could I give them an explanation, but just as I had throughout sixth-form, I'd been happy to follow the lead of my mates.

Of all the people travelling the world between February and June of 2006, I must have been the least cultured. I did no prior research into the places that we intended on visiting, I hadn't listened to the expert during our travel agency consultation, and I genuinely didn't know what people spent their time doing when they were in other countries. Sure, I'd had a few holidays in southern Europe in my time, but that wasn't South-East Asia, Australia and New Zealand. For the entire four months that we were due to spend away, there was only one thing that I'd expressed a desire to do; watch a rugby league match in Australia.

Something that I'd become very good at throughout high school and sixth-form was adapting to situations. In the earlier years, I'd found it to be the best method for navigating complex social scenarios, particularly those that involved aggressive or uncooperative characters. Conversely, it became a pleasure in the later years to adapt to the lads that I grew closest to, as they all had so much confidence in their identities, and passion for their interests. Those adaptation skills meant that I took to the travelling lifestyle like a duck to water, even if Chur and Neil were the ones coming up with the plans.

The first interesting thing that I learned in South-East Asia was that the travelling itself was what I enjoyed most. When I stuck my headphones in and looked out of a window on a long bus journey, I found myself experiencing these unexpected waves of euphoria. It all seemed to stem from my thought processes, as the simple consideration of the fact that I was in Thailand or Cambodia or Laos was astonishing to comprehend. I was just your average nineteen-year-old lad from Leeds, but here I was cruising through the scenic South-East Asian countryside; none of it quite seemed real.

Conversely, I found most of the activities on offer pretty dull. Whether it was a cultural thing like visiting temples or staying with a local family, or something more active like hiking or kayaking, it all made me feel like I was going through the motions to some extent. The reality was that drinking with the lads was my favourite social activity, which was made even better on a Saturday or Sunday evening.

I was hugely surprised to discover that Premiership football was everywhere in South-East Asia. People were walking around in English club shirts wherever we went, and there were more matches televised than there were back in England. One thing I had heard before I'd left the UK was that many South-East Asian countries were impoverished, but there seemed to be more folk out there with satellite TV than back home.

With Chur a Birmingham City fan and Neil a Liverpool fan, we'd often get to watch their teams play very late at night due to the eight-hour time difference, but that played perfectly into the hands of watching football while out drinking. I can remember sloping off alone from a beach party one night to watch Tottenham Hotspur vs Blackburn Rovers in the 4 pm Sunday kick-off, which was midnight my time. I didn't care about the game, but the very concept of being able to watch English football on a beach in Thailand was enough to have me heavily invested. It turned out to be a 3-2 thriller.

Unfortunately, there wasn't any Championship football shown over there. Still, I followed the Leeds United scores every week without fail by sitting in internet cafes between the hours of 11 pm and 1 am. Sometimes, I'd even have to ask the locals to keep their places open just for me, and it was both heartwarming and relieving that they were happy to do so. I may have followed Chur and Neil throughout the week, but I was uncompromising in my demands to follow football at weekends.

Up until we departed the UK, I attended every Leeds United home game of the 2005/06 season and travelled to my share of away games too. Having missed out throughout the 2003/04 and 2004/05 seasons because of my Saturday job, it was wonderful to be able to go and watch my team again, and with my Leeds-fan mates Andy, Bill, Rodney and Wardy all saving for trips of their own, we always had a cracking crowd on matchday.

Kevin Blackwell had managed to assemble a solid Championship squad for his second season in charge, and by the time that I left the UK, we were closing the gap on the automatic promotions places. However, after briefly threatening to chase down Reading and Sheffield United in March, we faded badly in April and had settled for the play-offs by the time the lads and I arrived in Cairns in Northern Australia.

Having spent my first twelve years as a fan with my team in the Premiership, I'd not watched much of the Football League play-offs before. The one game that I could remember had been a stunner though, with Charlton Athletic beating Sunderland on penalties with their play-off final having finished 4-4 after extra-time. Although I had no interest in either side, the drama of the occasion consumed me, particularly with there being so much at stake after such a long season.

When the 05/06 play-offs came around, it seemed like an eternity since I'd watched the Ashes at Elland Road before we beat Millwall on the opening day. Here we were though, nine months later, with me on the other side of the world, and Preston North End standing between us and the so-called richest game in football.

Soon after arriving in Cairns, Chur and I had met up with

our pals from home Luke and Rodney, who had also just flown in from South-East Asia. Neil had decided that he wanted to spend some time on his own and flew to Melbourne in the south with a plan to travel north up the coast, whilst we planned to do the opposite.

After spending a few days contemplating what our best travel style might be for the east coast, the four of us eventually hired a campervan. Only Rodney and I could drive, but I was more than happy to do the majority of the work as I loved being behind the wheel. I was both delighted and surprised to learn that the Australians drove on the same side of the road as us, and although it felt a little different being in such a large vehicle, I was into the swing of it in no time.

The freedom that I felt as we first hit the open road of the Bruce Highway was indescribable. I hadn't had a clue what this lifestyle had constituted before I'd departed of course, but I think that resting my arm on the driver door's open window, with music blaring out, while the lads drank beer in the back was my idea of travelling. Only sport had given me moments that had paralleled or surpassed that feeling, and as though it sensed a potential rivalry forming for my affections, football soon delivered a timely reminder of who was boss.

After drawing the first leg of our play-off semi-final with Preston 1-1 at Elland Road, we headed to Deepdale as slight underdogs. The lads and I had just reached Sydney, and we'd arranged to meet our pal Andy, who was also travelling in Australia.

Rodney and I had followed the first leg through an online vidiprinter from a Byron Bay internet cafe, but now being in Australia's biggest city, we held slender hopes of finding somewhere that would be screening the match. We embarked on a mission to find a 24-hour place that might somehow show English Championship football and eventually stumbled across a sports bar in the somewhat seedy area of King's Cross. The barman informed us that they'd be open all night, but couldn't guarantee that the game would be on.

The 8 pm kick-off back home represented a 5 am kick-off for us. There was talk among Andy, Rodney and me to stay up all night, but coming off the back of a colossal booze-up with Chur and Luke, we took the more sensible approach of staying in a hostel and setting our alarm for 4.30 am.

I'd had two hours sleep in our campervan in an inner-city car park the night before, which helped me to drift off in an instant at 8 pm that evening. I slept solidly for six hours, but when I stirred at 2 am, there was no way that I was getting back to sleep.

I can remember lying there for that two and a half hours, listening to my MP3 player, thinking of nothing other than Leeds United. If we could win that match, we'd be one game away from a return to the Premiership, and who knows what could follow from there. I didn't suspect that it would be an instant return to the glory days of our Champions League run, but merely winning a Championship play-off final would be glorious enough in itself. It was the first stepping stone towards producing a team that my home city could genuinely be proud of again.

I shot up the instant that my alarm went off, excitedly shook Andy and Rodney awake, before we threw our clothes on and headed out into the night. It took us about twenty minutes to walk to the bar, and we found nothing but a short, balding, middle-aged man with a familiar accent when we arrived, who was arguing the case for the channel to be changed. Of course there was another Leeds United fan on the other side of the world remonstrating with a barman to search for a football match in the middle of the night.

There were major concerns among the three of us, and our new friend, as the clock struck 5 am, and we'd not managed to find the match on TV. Our comrade did our dirty work for us by imploring the barman to flick back through the channels again, and after accepting that it might be time to find another internet cafe, something truly glorious happened.

I shouted for the barman to go back one channel, as a green screen appeared, complete with some moving figures in either white or dark blue shirts. As the green screen re-appeared, a caption in the top corner of the screen read *PNE 0-0 LEE*. The match was on.

I'd been away from home for about three months at this stage, and it was a thing of beauty to be able to see the players that I'd watched so often that season before going travelling. Something hadn't felt right as we'd walked away from Elland Road after our February clash with Luton Town, it was so unnatural to know that we weren't going to see out a season that we'd invested so much in to. Still, we were managing to watch from 10,000 miles away, so the three of us pulled up chairs, grabbed ourselves a beer, and revelled in how fortunate we were to be watching Leeds United.

The first half was turgid. Both sides were awful, and could barely string two passes together, but that came as no surprise to any of us. Since we'd dropped down to the second tier, the standard of football had disintegrated with it, and I genuinely hadn't seen a single team play good football in two seasons. However, this league wasn't about playing good football; it was about finding a way out of it at all costs. We just had to find a way to win this game, if it could be completed that was.

Just after the game reached half-time at 0-0, the analysts reported to us that the floodlights had failed at Deepdale. Here we were, in a Championship play-off semi-final, and unless the technicians could sort out the problem, the game would have to be abandoned and replayed. It was a total and utter shambles, but one that the commentators believed might work in our favour.

With Blackwell having picked a team full of experienced old pro's, one of the pundits claimed that Preston's young guns would be more likely to be psychologically disrupted by the distraction. It seemed like a slightly long-winded viewpoint, but with so much at stake, I was happy to cling on to anything that might benefit Leeds. The delay had lasted more than twenty-five minutes by the time the lights came back on, and as the second half started, we looked like the more composed side.

On fifty-five minutes, we earned a corner, which veteran right-back Gary Kelly jogged over to take in front of the travelling Leeds fans. I perched on the edge of my seat hoping for a good delivery, and as Kelly swung the ball over, a huge space appeared in the middle of the penalty box. Preston' keeper Carlo Nash stayed on his line, before our striker Rob Hulse met the cross with his head. I couldn't believe my eyes when the ball nestled in the back of the net.

I can remember catching the barman's eye amid my delirium. There was no doubt that he'd never seen a celebration like it; he looked almost frightened by the pandemonium that had ensued in his bar. There was such an overwhelming outpouring of emotion from Andy, Rodney and me in that moment. All the elements of the occasion felt accentuated as Hulse ran off celebrating; where we were, the fact that we were managing to watch it, the significance of the goal, it all exploded in one moment of delirious ecstasy.

After thirty seconds or so of our riotous behaviour, we re-took our seats and desperately attempted to regain our composure. I tried to maintain my state of hope, battling to reject the tsunami of belief that was drowning my every feeling and thought. Then, just a few minutes later, it was bedlam once more.

Goalscorer Hulse received a pass just within the left-hand side of the penalty box, before shrugging off his man and attempting what appeared to be a strike at goal. However, the shot turned in to the perfect pass, the ball falling square to Frazer Richardson on the edge of the six-yard box, who hit a scuffed shot just inside the right-hand post.

The goalkeeper did well to reach it but spilt the ball into the corner of his net while trying to keep it out. Richardson ran off towards the travelling fans at Deepdale, while three lads in a desolate Australian bar jumped around in jubilation, grabbing and hitting each other hysterically. 2-0, 3-1 on aggregate, in a Championship play-off semi-final. We were on the brink of the most important occasion of my time supporting this football club.

One positive thing about the lack of quality that we'd seen in this division was that you felt very confident once you were two goals ahead. We had an organised team at this stage too, with experienced centre-halves, and solid central midfielders, and we managed the rest of the match brilliantly. Preston couldn't break us down, and the referee blew up to seal our fate. We'd done it; we were in the final.

With the sun now up and the day upon us, we found the nearest internet cafe and logged in to MSN Messenger to see if any of our family and friends were online. All three of my dad, my brother, and Mel were on there, and I thrilled them with our story of finding an Australian bar that showed the match.

Having revelled in joy until about 8 am, I wrapped the internet session up by e-mailing the travel agency that we'd booked our trip with to ask if it was possible to change my flight home. The way I saw it, I could nip over to New Zealand briefly, before taking the long journey back to watch one of the biggest games in my club's history. I never received a reply and didn't even have the £1500 that an agent in Auckland quoted me for a one-way flight back to London. If it would have been £500, I'd almost certainly have done it.

15

One priority

The closer I grew to my mates in my late teens, the harder I worked to be the best friend that I could to them. I valued them so highly that I poured a tremendous amount of effort into getting to know them on a very personal level, and would always be happy to reach beyond halfway to ensure that they were getting as much out of the friendship as I was. I don't know this for sure, but I like to think that Chur and Neil recognised these efforts with the sacrifice that they made for me in New Zealand back in May 2006.

After the hugely successful road trip that Chur and I had enjoyed in Australia, the three of us bought a dirt-cheap campervan in Auckland. Chur had expressed an interest in visiting a nature area a few hundred miles north, so we ventured up there and stayed for a couple of days as a starting point for our latest journey. Once again, I had no idea what New Zealand had to offer, and was just delighted with the adventurous quality of being behind the wheel of a camper on the opposite side of the world.

On one of our rare visits to an internet cafe, I discovered that I'd received an e-mail from Rodney. He told me that he and Luke, as well as the other travelling Leeds contingent of Andy, Dan and Danny, were in a place on the south island called Queenstown. Rodney described it as being the best place that he'd ever been and issued a personal plea for me to get myself down there for the Championship play-off final. It was a Wednesday night at the time, the game was on the Sunday, and Queenstown was almost the full length of the country away. However, with that glorious night in Sydney emotionally compromising me, I asked Chur and Neil if we could take the plunge.

At this point, I think Neil felt similarly to me in that he was just happy to be on an adventure. I don't think he was too bothered as to how we approached our time in New Zealand, he just wanted to have fun, and getting down to all the lads in Queenstown was undoubtedly the route to that. As the more cultured one, Chur had plans for the north island and was not keen to spend four straight days driving so that I could attempt to watch Leeds United with my fellow fans. Still, having experienced the intensity of my relationship with my football club first-hand over the prior thirteen weeks, he gave me the thumbs up.

If there were any doubts as to how much more important football was to me than anything travel-related, I even managed to locate a pub that was showing Arsenal's Champions League final with Barcelona early on the Thursday morning. We were in a town called Whangarei on the north island, and the landlord agreed to open at 6.30 am for us so we could watch Europe's Wednesday night final over breakfast.

It was a hugely entertaining match, with Barcelona coming back to win 2-1 against a resolute ten-man Arsenal, and with the game having finished by 8.30 am, we were on the road in great time.

We drove about 250 miles to a place called Rotorua, spending a few hours there before pressing on further south to spend the night in Taupo, a picturesque lakeside town. The plan had been to move straight on early the next morning, but I was in no state to drive after the three of us embarked on a massive Thursday night out. We ended up spending the Friday strolling around the lake and enjoying the fresh mountain air, before staying for another night in the knowledge that we still had two days to get to Queenstown.

We left for Wellington, the capital city on the southern tip of the north island, early on the Saturday morning. We'd intended to arrive around midday to catch an afternoon ferry over to Picton on the northern tip of the south island. It was typically naive teenage behaviour to assume that there would be ferries departing whenever we required, and the plan to reach the lads was under real threat when we were told there no spaces available for campervans until the following morning; matchday. There was a brief moment at which we considered giving up before we booked the 8 am ferry.

We didn't arrive into Picton until about 11.30 am on the Sunday morning, with the match starting at 2 am that night. We had a 500-mile drive ahead, in a clapped-out banger of a campervan, with about fourteen hours in which to do it.

As we sped down NZ highway one along the south island's east coast, Chur made a point of informing us of the activities on offer in each town as we passed through them. He was understandably annoyed to be missing out on these things but made light of it by joking that he'd much rather be sitting in a van than going out to sea to whale-watch in Kaikoura. It's both hilarious and excruciating to reflect upon at the same time.

Having passed the city of Christchurch at nightfall, and feeling exhausted as the sole driver, I'd lost all sense of responsibility in my desperation to reach Queenstown in time. An hour or so later, with over 150 miles still to travel, the petrol light flashed on.

I asked Neil to study the road map that we'd acquired to find out how far it was to the next town, which he did with the aid of a head torch. Much to my relief, he informed us that we only had another twenty miles or so to go. It was about 7 pm, still seven hours before kick-off, and after we'd topped up at a petrol station, I'd only have a couple of hours of driving remaining.

The town came upon us unexpectedly, with only a few establishments dotted along either side of the highway making it up. We came across a couple of motels, a late-night shop, and a single pub, but there was no sign of a petrol station. Then, to my horror, I saw a large, flat roof in the distance, only for the building that was attached to it to be lightless. There was a petrol station, but it was closed.

I can't remember what went through my head at that point, but I didn't stop the van, and I didn't ask how far it was to the next town. We were still in the upper echelons of the low petrol part of the meter, and the only option in my one-track mind was to make it to Queenstown.

As we steadily progressed, I put the van into neutral every time we reached a downhill slope, letting it roll where possible, and only stepping on the gas when necessary. The further we travelled, the lower the needle on the petrol gauge slipped, causing the anxiety coursing through me to grow ever more overbearing.

Chur and Neil didn't say a great deal, and I said absolutely nothing, acutely aware that I would be entirely responsible if the van were to shut down and leave us stranded. They started to suspect that we were in trouble as I allowed the van to roll on almost flat terrain, knowing that we must have had only had five or six miles left in us. For this reason, it felt like a miracle when we saw some lights in the distance.

At nearly 10 pm, we chugged up to a tiny town called Cromwell, only thirty miles short of Queenstown. If I'm honest, the idea of making it to our final destination had lost all importance by this stage; I just felt relieved for having dragged my friends to civilisation by the skin of my teeth.

Cromwell seemed so small that I accepted that there might not even be a petrol station at all, never mind an open one. I came up with a contingency plan to find an expensive hotel or motel, that might have satellite TV, that might have sports channels, that might show the game. However, as we crawled through the desolate settlement, we saw what looked like some petrol pumps with lights above them on the side of the road.

I pulled the camper in alongside one of the pumps and confirmed that they contained petrol. There was a machine attached to them that stated that it accepted card, which led me to dig deep into my backpack to find the two debit cards that I'd brought travelling with me.

The first card didn't even seem to activate the petrol pump at all, as though it wasn't even a real debit card. The second one did activate the pump, before a message on the small screen stated that only Kiwi cards were accepted.

At that point, I fully came to terms with the fact that the final shred of hope of reaching Queenstown had disappeared. Then, like an angel sent from heaven during a time of desperation, a police officer pulled up next to the van to ask if we needed any help.

It transpired that the man was from Sheffield, and he'd recently emigrated to New Zealand. I told him that I was from Leeds, and he instantly chimed in with a reference to the match. What on earth was a police officer from Sheffield doing out at this time on a Sunday night in a tiny town in the middle of nowhere talking about English Championship football? Whatever the reason, I felt as though I owed him my life.

After our pleasant exchange, the man told me that he would use his credit card to help us fill up our van in exchange for cash. He told us that there wasn't a functioning cash machine in the town, but fortunately, I had fifty dollars in my wallet.

My incredibly helpful fellow Yorkshireman then did my pump work for me, before I turned on the ignition, forgetting what it was like not to see the low petrol light. The sight of the gauge's needle clearing the low zone sent a multitude of emotions rushing through my body, and I pulled back on to the highway unable to believe that we were going to make it.

Having set off from Whangarei in the north of the north island at 9 am on the Thursday morning, we arrived into Queenstown in the south of the south island on the Sunday night at 11 pm. There was so much of New Zealand that we'd missed en route, but it had been a truly spectacular achievement to have made it in such a short space of time. Now, it was just a matter of finding the rest of the lads.

We popped into a late-night internet cafe to see if they'd e-mailed. They hadn't, so I sent one to both Andy and Rodney in the hope that they'd have the presence of mind to consider the possibility of us having made it. Half an hour passed with no response, which led me to give up on trying to contact them and prioritise finding a place that was showing the match.

I spent a further half an hour popping into bars in search of the friends that we'd driven all that way to meet. Eventually, I looked at the two friends that I'd dragged along with me on the ridiculous journey and recognised that it was time for us to go for a beer, something that we all massively needed.

We made our way back to the most lively bar that we'd come across, and I can still recall how magnificent that first sip of lager tasted as it touched my lips. It had been a chaotic day, and as much as I knew that the chaos hadn't even started yet, I allowed myself to relax for the time that it would take to consume one pint.

I wasn't even halfway through it before I heard someone call out my name from the other side of the room. As I looked in the direction of where it was coming from, I saw two lads that I'd played Sunday League football with during high school bounding towards me. Although I wasn't close with either of them, I couldn't quite believe that I'd bumped into somebody that I knew on the opposite side of the world, having had no idea that they were even travelling. On the one hand, I was disappointed that it wasn't the people I was looking for, but on the other, it was amazing to have come across yet more men from Leeds.

I asked the two of them if they planned to watch the game, which was now only two hours away, and they said that although there weren't going to be any bars open for it, they knew that their hostel had the channel that was screening it. They invited me to go back to watch it with them, and after the most intense day of my entire life, I could finally fully relax.

I introduced the two sets of lads that I was now with to each other, and we spent the next couple of hours playing pool and crushing beers. It was a magical little spell, one of the best of my entire trip, as the alcohol exacerbated my excitement, relief and anticipation. It had been such an insane day that I'd not even had the chance to contemplate the fact that Leeds United might be back in the Premiership by the end of it.

We made our way back to the hostel at 1.45 am, and the place was utterly silent. Our two new companions told us not to speak as we made our way through to the hostel's TV room, bearing in mind that they'd snuck us in after-hours when we weren't staying there. One of them switched the screen on, and after some flicking around, I saw the two teams in the tunnel at the Millennium Stadium. In that instant, the magnitude of the game registered with me. It made me feel uneasy.

The overriding feeling that I had as the players walked out was that I wasn't psychologically prepared for the match. For every enormous Leeds United occasion I'd experienced before that, I'd been through a process both with myself, and with at least one other fan, by which I'd consider how the game might go, whether we'd put out the right team, and what the most likely outcome was. I'd done no such thing in the immediate build-up to this match, although I can't assign any blame to that for the ninety minutes that followed.

I felt as though I deserved so much better than a horrendous 3-0 defeat at the hands of a modest Watford side. After the drama of the journey that I'd just had, one I'd made entirely for my football team, I knew that we'd lost from the minute that Jay DeMerit headed Watford into a first-half lead. It got worse and worse as the match progressed.

Watford's second just after half-time summed up our entire ninety minutes, a combination of shambolic defending and awful luck. The Hornets played with little flair or enterprise but were well worth their 3-0 victory by the time Darius Henderson wrapped the game up for them late on.

I'd only seen us in one cup final up to that point in my life, another 3-0 humbling, at the hands of Aston Villa in the League Cup final ten years earlier. I may have only been nine-years-old back then, but here I was at nineteen experiencing the most horrible feeling of deja vu. Not a single player on the pitch had turned up, and it was impossible to understand why we'd saved our worst performance of the season for the grandest occasion. The only consolation I drew from it was that I'd not managed to find the lads; I was feeling bad enough myself without having to absorb the despair of both Andy and Rodney at the same time.

I had a bit of a routine back then as to how I dealt with a significant Leeds United defeat. I needed about an hour alone, during which I could come to terms with the always over-whelming feeling of disappointment by allowing my racing mind to wear itself out. It was about 4 am by this point, but I knew that if I was to climb into the campervan, which we'd left in a car park by a lake a short walk from town, there was no way that I was going to be able to sleep.

As the lads got into the van, I sat down on a rock by the lake about fifty metres from the car park. All I wanted to do was sit there alone and think, but with us being nearly as far south in the southern hemisphere as you can get, in late May, it was far too cold for me to be able to relax. I couldn't think of many worse positions to be in after such a devastating defeat;

all revved up with only a freezing campervan with two snoring blokes in which to go.

After reluctantly climbing in next to the lads, I reckon it took me until about 5.30 am to drift off to sleep. At 6.30 am, a man from the local council woke me up by banging on the side of our van, telling us that we were illegally parked. As the sole driver, I had to switch the lights on and drive us about twenty minutes uphill and out of town in the dark to a spot that would be suitable to be able to sleep undisturbed.

To round off a perfect few hours, I woke up later that morning to discover that I'd left the headlights on. The battery was flat, the van wouldn't move, we were a long way out of town, and I had the crippling sinking feeling of Leeds United's miserable failure encompassing me. It was entirely my fault, but I still allowed myself to wallow in self-pity.

As brutal as that experience was, I couldn't have been in a better place in which to get over it. The view from halfway up the hill that I'd driven up really was something to behold. It was an incredibly quaint little town, flanked by two enormous turquoise lakes and surrounded by spectacular mountains. Rodney hadn't been exaggerating, Queenstown did look incredible.

We found the other lads later that day and proceeded to spend a week with them having an absolute blast. I was with a load of my best mates, in this unreal town, getting pissed by night and having an incredible time by day. We did a bungee jump and a skydive, both of which exhilarated me, while I also took immense pleasure from taking a couple of solo strolls by the lake.

I found that having a bit of solitude among the incredible

scenery gave me the same euphoric buzz that I'd experienced while on long bus journeys in Asia, or while behind the wheel in our Australian campervan. It was as though I needed to either partake in the most extreme activities or do the direct opposite. I'd not cared for anything in between throughout the entirety of the trip.

Little did I know that this polarised way of being would dictate the next few years of my life.

The Second Half

16

A personal cliff-edge

The best way that I can summarise my childhood experience is through four pillars of self-esteem. The first pillar was positive reinforcement, which I received based on the things that I could do, and defined my time at primary school. The second pillar was an indirect sense of achievement, stemming from the joy I received from Leeds United's performances, which defined the happiest period of my time at high school. The third was vicarious confidence, which I experienced when spending a glorious couple of years with my charismatic friends throughout sixth-form college. The fourth was entirely artificial, and I'll come to it later.

Within just a few weeks of me setting out on what I considered to be real adult life, I suffered the consequences of this childhood. As good as it had been in so many ways, and as grateful as I remain for it to this day, the path that I went down as I arrived at university exposed the fact that it had been somewhat fraudulent.

I call it fraudulent because none of the self-esteem that I experienced stemmed from my personality. I'd been extremely fortunate that my primary school environment was one in which I was designed to succeed, with the high ranking that came with my sportiness and intelligence serving as the self-esteem source. Leeds United's spell of being one of the best teams in the country was the only time that I was truly happy in high school, a displaced form of self-esteem. My sixth-form college happiness was borne out of me feeding off the characteristics and strengths of my friends, with the same happening while I was travelling, bar the odd moment of solitary euphoria that I'd not been able to understand. From the minute that I arrived in Newcastle, I was starved of all of these things, and in turn starved of psychological stimulation.

Even during the periods in which I'd found things difficult as a child, I'd still been stimulated in some way. With my first couple of years of high school having been so chaotic, I'd effectively been on red alert at all times, in a permanent state of survival mode. Later on, my sensitivity to my surroundings had made me feel quite vulnerable in big groups, and albeit a negative experience, I was still stimulated. When university provided neither positive nor negative stimulation, my self-esteem went with it.

My childhood had essentially provided me with a multitude of distractions from myself. Yes, I'd spent my share of time alone, but I'd always had either sport, schoolwork, or some other kind of activity to keep me occupied. At each stage, there'd been some kind of direction, some kind of purpose, and when I found myself with almost unlimited time to think about this, and no direction or purpose, my mental health declined.

All the people that I met at university were genuinely nice. They meant well, were pleasant to me, and had no ulterior motive or agenda in anything that they were doing. However, I'd spent the last three years of my life with highly intelligent, funny, witty, intellectual, and substantial folk. Pretty much every student I came across during my first few weeks was so limited in comparison, and although it was only a bit trying initially, it became a real problem for me after a couple of weeks.

I couldn't grasp how so many of these people became a part of what they all saw to be one big happy family in such a short space of time. I can remember hearing some folk expressing that they were already best friends for life, and others saying that their new acquaintances were the best people they'd ever met. Some folk would say it to me from time to time, and when they did, I'd smile awkwardly, nod my head, and usually respond by saying something like 'you're alright too I guess'. I didn't even think they were alright; I thought they were superficial, idiotic morons.

The reality was that the quality of the friends that I'd made back in Leeds had made me entitled. There was nothing wrong with these people, but I very arrogantly believed that I deserved better. The lads back home had always been good for an interesting conversation, for making me laugh relentlessly, or for partaking in an enjoyable activity of some sort. What I found at university was that these students could only *chat* about nothing, as opposed to *converse* about something, the loudmouth, apparent jokers among them couldn't have been less funny, and none of them seemed to have any interests or hobbies. I was fortunate to find the odd football fan, although this was a time at which I didn't much feel like talking about my team.

During a time of need in high school, when I'd been a bit lost and lacking focus, Leeds United embarked on that unforgettable rise to the top of English football. My football fandom provided me with stability, it was a form of meaning at a time when I had none, and with that one key interest, I was able to become productive in every other area of life. It was one thing that had truly stimulated me, which was all I needed to find overall balance. Unfortunately, they were unable to do the same for me early in my first year at uni.

Four days after I arrived in Newcastle, our manager Kevin Blackwell was sacked, just four months on from our Championship play-off final defeat to Watford. I'd been to the first couple of games of the season that summer, and we'd started well enough with a win and a draw. At that stage, there was no reason to think that we wouldn't go one better than the previous season by securing automatic promotion over the play-offs, but then we lost five of our next six league games. A play-off final at the end of one season, to the relegation zone after eight games of the next; it felt like we'd fallen off a second cliff-edge in just four years.

Having acted swiftly to remove Blackwell, chairman Ken Bates brought in a figure that intimated that he was trying to anger our fans. The Elland Road die-hards had struggled with Bates' Chelsea links when *he'd* arrived, so when former Blues captain Dennis Wise was appointed as our new manager, I intuitively felt that there could be trouble moving forward. I couldn't possibly have known how much trouble.

With me being indifferent about the people that I'd met, and Leeds having an awful time of it, I can remember making a big point of wanting to go to the pub for England's Euro 2008 qualifiers against Macedonia and Croatia. I'd never been one to get hugely into qualifiers, as England were very much expected to win them, but with me getting so little out of my club at the time, I felt a desperate need for something to cheer on and about.

In the most embarrassing few days that England had endured in my lifetime, we drew 0-0 at home to Macedonia on the Saturday, and lost 2-0 in Croatia on the Wednesday. We were catastrophically bad in each game, and the fact that we couldn't even muster a goal meant that I'd not even had the chance to cheer across those 180 minutes of football.

With no indirect sense of achievement coming through football, and no vicarious confidence coming from the people that I was around, that just left positive reinforcement. I'd barely received any ego-boosting positive reinforcement since primary school when I'd got it for standing out for my abilities. The reality of being among thousands of other people in their first year of university, while not having any standout qualities to gain attention and adulation for, is that you're going to have to do something remarkable to receive a high level of positive reinforcement.

Starting out at university felt a bit like starting out at high school. You're thrown into a sea of people, knowing absolutely nobody, and everybody is rightly looking out for themselves in an attempt to establish a safe environment, as quickly as they can. By way of both that and my lack of standout skills, I didn't receive the kind of feedback that I needed to feel good in the absence of an indirect sense of achievement and vicarious confidence. I didn't have any of the three pillars of self-esteem that had made me happy during my childhood, which just left the final pillar, the artificial one.

17

Alcohol and football

It was only very recently that I learned that a person doesn't have to be an alcoholic to be *dependent* on alcohol.

I believe that the definition of a healthy relationship with alcohol is when someone drinks solely to enhance the happiness that they're already feeling. In my opinion, drinking to make something that you're already enjoying even better is the only reason that anybody should do it. Still, people have many other motivators for seeking out alcohol.

I started drinking heavily at fifteen years old when I realised that it enabled me to manage a situation that I didn't enjoy. It was back in high school after that Lee Bowyer goal at Southampton when I discovered its capacity to numb me from the stressors of a frantic group environment. Although I was drinking to counteract a negative, it did end up leading to something very positive.

The more occasions on which I entered big group situations, the more time that I spent getting to know my friends. Over time, I learned to enjoy those situations because although they remained quite chaotic, the presence of all these interesting folk kept me positively stimulated. When I then went on to drink alcohol, the positive experience of being with my friends was enhanced.

At university, I drank to help myself deal with the negative effects of chaotic environments but didn't have the positive of spending time with people that interested me. I found the social situations so under-stimulating, that I started to drink to excess, as a way of trying to escape the environment that I found myself in, and the lack of enjoyment that I was experiencing.

You'd think that the obvious thing to do in a situation like that is to avoid socialising altogether, but that wasn't always possible. I did start to spend a lot of time on my own in my room during my first year of university, as it was a therapeutic way of recovering from the mundane chat that would happen in and around daytime lectures and seminars. I'd have been perfectly happy to stay in on my own at night too, but there was an internal driving force that I couldn't ignore as a twenty-year-old man.

I did OK when it came to girls during my first year, but I wasn't in the right frame of mind to impress them like I'd wanted to. I wasn't looking for a girlfriend, it's something that I'd never had an interest in for whatever reason, but I was hoping to hook up with a few along the way. Ultimately, I found most of the girls that I met to be sinfully dull, just as I did the blokes, which I believe was because I couldn't get to know any of them due to this big group mentality that they all had. Everybody blended into one, and nobody had any identity, which made me resent both the group situations and the individuals themselves.

It's only recently that I've delved into the psychology behind this to make sense of the intense dislike that I felt for these people. It's so often the case that if you're feeling resentment towards others, it's as a result of a fundamental problem that you have with yourself. As I reflect, it's clear to me that I was projecting a degree of self-dislike on to these perfectly nice people, as I blamed their lack of individuality for the lack of individuality that I had myself. I disliked them all for not being interesting, funny or charismatic, even though I wasn't any of those things myself. That's where my issues with alcohol started.

I felt a need to go into group situations because I wanted to get with girls, but I found group situations so unenjoyable and under-stimulating that I drank excessive amounts to feel like I was escaping them. The subconscious element to my drinking was that I was also trying to escape my own personality, which I will have known deep down was inadequate to have impressed girls. The booze did help to numb the mundanity, and also helped with girls due to the artificial confidence it gave me, but it was hiding the serious underlying problem that I had with my lack of identity.

During identity crises in the past, I'd always been able to turn to sport. It was the one thing that I truly did identify with, and it had been there to provide me with that indirect self-esteem hit during every period in which I'd struggled. I was only a couple of months into my time at uni when I realised how much I needed it, and wasted no time at all in throwing myself entirely into my sports fandom.

Between November and January, I regularly stayed up all night to follow England's 2006/07 Ashes tour of Australia. After our outstanding performance in that hugely dramatic 2005 series, I'd been incredibly excited to see if we could get a result down under for the first time since 1986/87. We were mauled 5-0.

With 2007 being a World Cup year, I invested a lot of time

in the Six Nations in February and March, only to see England lose twice and play some of the dullest rugby I'd ever seen. When Ireland crushed us 43-13, I virtually gave up on our hopes of being able to defend the Webb Ellis Cup, even if there were still six months until the tournament started.

One good decision that I did make for sport was to stay in my university halls over the Easter holiday period. Aware that all my flatmates were going home for three weeks, and with my flat having Sky Sports, I was incredibly excited by the idea of having a place to myself while the Cricket World Cup was on. I stayed for two weeks before heading back home to see my folks, and it was the only period that I actually enjoyed during first year. I found the solitude incredibly relaxing and peaceful, and there was a liberating freedom about knowing that nobody was going to disturb me at any point. England were awful though and deserved to be dumped out at the Super Eight stage.

If those events were bad, then Leeds United's 2006/07 campaign occurring as they were all playing out was beyond awful. Although new boss Dennis Wise had a bit of an impact after his appointment, earning nine points from his first six league games, things went catastrophically downhill from there. We picked up just twelve points from the next fifty-one on offer, which left us bottom of the Championship table at the start of March.

I'd headed back to Leeds to go and see a couple of matches during that period, and also made the effort to get to a couple of away games too. It was impossible to conceive that we'd been atop the Premiership only five years earlier, as we genuinely looked like a Sunday league team.

Our players were horrendous, the quality of football was even worse, they all looked terrified to be on the pitch, and the fans sensed that their football club was falling apart in front of their eyes. I had very little money at the time as a student, but even had I been rich, I'd have felt a bit sick to have paid to watch us play; we were an utter disgrace.

I can remember feeling so desperate for something to cheer at one stage that I celebrated a 90th-minute Michael Coulson equaliser for Barnsley at Southend United in the FA Cup. With the two sides being Championship relegation rivals of ours, the draw meant that they'd have to play out a replay, which could potentially lead to fixture congestion, which would, in turn, heighten the chances of tiredness and injuries setting in for them. It's quite funny to look back on with it being so, so pathetic, but it paints a very damning picture of the psychological place that I was in at the time.

During our most recent dramatic decline, rumours surfaced that a second relegation in three years would be financially disastrous for us. We'd all thought that our off-the-field difficulties were behind us after Ken Bates had bought the club in 2005, but apparently, we still had significant debts that would be almost impossible to clear with League One revenues. Something needed to happen quickly on the pitch, and Wise finally managed to get something out of the players in March.

We beat Luton Town in a relegation six-pointer, before picking up draws at Leicester City and fellow strugglers Southend. We then managed back-to-back last-gasp victories over Preston North-End and Plymouth Argyle to lift ourselves into 21st place, and out of the relegation places for the first time since long before Christmas. With only five games remaining until the end of the season, it seemed that we'd timed our revival well.

Unfortunately, we then lost two of our next three matches, while our rivals picked up crucial points, to fall back into 22nd place, the final relegation spot. That left us one point from safety with two games left to play, and with Ipswich Town to come at Elland Road in our penultimate match, it wasn't a game that I thought I could miss.

As abysmal a team as we were, I felt as invested in us as I ever had at that point. Both university life and sport in general had sucked so much life out of me over the prior eight months, that it felt good to feel so strongly about something again. With so much potentially at stake for everyone associated with Leeds United, the drama of our battle against relegation was curiously irresistible, and I couldn't have been more fired up on the train down to Leeds on the morning of Saturday 28th April 2007.

I can remember heading to the ground with Bill and Rodney that day, feeling a sense of considerable optimism. With Luton already down and Southend as good as, Hull City were our rivals for the final survival spot, and they had a tough match away at Cardiff City. Hull were one point ahead of us, and with it unlikely that they'd get anything more than a draw in Wales, we knew that two wins would probably see us safe.

There was a nervous, but excited tension as we took our seats in the west stand at Elland Road. Over 30,000 people had made the effort for this titanic clash, and with all the nightmarish times that they'd experienced over the prior five years, I was in awe of their loyalty. We had eleven players out on the pitch that had given us so little to cheer about throughout the season, but I could have burst with pride as the raucous cheers of encouragement greeted the players as they walked on to the pitch.

The support proved to be inspirational, as Richard Cresswell struck to give us an early lead. It was just what we needed to settle everybody down, and we looked comfortable throughout the rest of the half, reaching the break with our lead intact. Hull were drawing 0-0 at Cardiff, which meant that we were out of the relegation zone as things stood.

The three of us nipped out for a half-time pint, and I can remember feeling as though it was more like full-time, as we started to discuss how difficult it might be to win at high-flying Derby County a week later. Hull had a far easier fixture at home to Plymouth, but our take was that if victory were all that we needed to survive, we would find a way to win. We'd have to.

About five minutes into the second half, we received some desperate news. Dean Windass had scored for Hull at Cardiff, and although we were still cruising in our match, we now faced the prospect of needing Hull to drop points on the final day to have any chance of survival. It made things tough, but there was nothing more that we could do than give ourselves a chance.

There must have been so little action in that second half at Elland Road, as I can't remember a thing about it up until the 89th minute. As Ipswich won a corner, Rodney and I were far more interested in checking Bill's phone, as he was receiving regular Cardiff-Hull updates from a friend of his.

Sometimes in life, however possible something might seem, you can't comprehend that it could happen until it does. The notion of Leeds United being relegated to the third tier of English football had been a distinct possibility for the vast majority of the 2006/07 Championship season. Still, I'd never really contemplated it actually coming to pass.

As Ipswich swung the corner into the near post, a few players jumped for the ball, but Alan Lee got his head to it for the visitors. They'd done so little in the match, that I couldn't believe my eyes as the ball flew past our goalkeeper Casper Ankergren, and nestled in the far corner of the net.

I didn't realise until that moment that I'd ignored the reality of relegation all season. It was as though the trapdoor to League One had opened beneath my feet, with my body staying exactly where it was, but every ounce of feeling sinking through it beneath me. We were going down.

After a few seconds of stunned silence, I turned to my right to see Rodney in floods of tears, and I put a consolatory arm around him. It felt as though things couldn't possibly get any worse, but then I turned back towards the action to see streams of our fans storming on to the pitch from the Kop End.

There were still two minutes of normal time remaining, yet hundreds of desperate supporters burst past the powerless stewards to invade Elland Road's playing field, leaving the Ipswich players with no choice but to vacate. Our players bravely tried to reason with them, but swiftly gave up as the wave of fans charged towards the corner where the few hundred travelling Ipswich fans were sitting. I immediately feared for their safety.

I watched in horror as most of the Ipswich fans hurtled over seats towards the back of the south-east stand. Those individuals could count themselves lucky to be able to do so, as the few disabled supporters at the front sat helplessly in their wheelchairs, their carers valiantly trying to protect them. Fortunately, an army of stewards formed a barrier-like wall between the two sets of fans, and the majority of the pitch invaders repressed their animalistic instincts and showed some mercy by holding back.

Our fans stood in the corner of the pitch, shouting towards the Ipswich fans, before breaking out in song between themselves. You could see a host of middle-aged men crying their eyes out despairingly, others lying on the turf dejectedly, while some marched around looking for fights with their fellow Leeds fans. If my celebrating a Barnsley-Southend replay had been desperate, then this was a whole different level.

Eventually, after about fifteen minutes of tannoy instruction and police intervention, the fans were cleared from the pitch. Remarkably, it was announced that the game would resume, with every person in the stadium expecting it to be abandoned.

We won a couple of corners in the final moments, but the full-time whistle followed not long after. The Ipswich players immediately charged from the field, and every Leeds United fan in the stadium stood motionlessly.

A few moments later, a typically obstinate chorus of our club anthem *Marching On Together* rang out from the Kop, prompting supporters from each stand to join them in unison. One of my friends was crying, the other was sitting down for the first time that afternoon with his head in his hands, but still, they sang. It was an incredible show of defiance, but merely demonstrative that the reality hadn't sunk in.

We stayed for half an hour after the whistle, mustered the strength to applaud our players as they returned to the field to show their appreciation before I walked into the city centre to catch the bus back to Newcastle. There'd been an air of pure hostility around town, and I was glad to be out of there.

On the journey north, the reality did start to sink in. All of the things that I'd not even contemplated before Alan Lee's header registered. We'd be playing in the Johnstone's Paint Trophy; we'd be playing in the league on international weekends; we'd be playing in the FA Cup first round. I couldn't have felt lower.

Yet, as I contemplated Leeds United's relegation to League One, coming off the back of an awful experience during my first year at university, I somehow found myself enjoying my anguish. It was as though so much had gone wrong over the past eight months, that I actually started to embrace the negativity.

At the time, I perceived that although there was nothing wrong with me as an individual, I had the right to behave as I pleased as so much was going against me. With all the positivity vanquished from my life, I decided that there was only one thing to do to make a bad situation not so bad; drink.

18

Beyond the bottom

Sometimes, you only realise that things could yet get even worse, once they've become worse than you ever thought that they could get. That was the case for both Leeds United and my self-esteem after we were effectively relegated to League One.

After I got back into Newcastle after Leeds' draw with Ipswich Town, I went out and got as drunk as I could possibly get. I'd been made aware that some people were out at the students' union, so I headed there to meet them, before telling them upon arrival that I didn't want to talk. Instead, I sat in a corner and drank to excess on my own.

Let's unpack that behaviour a little. If I'd wanted nothing other than to drink alone, I'd have picked up some beers or a bottle of gin and gone and sat in my room at my halls where nobody would have talked to me. However, I decided to go to a place that I knew that people would talk to me, with a clear plan in my head to tell them that I didn't want them to talk to me. Although I was oblivious to this at the time, it was quite clearly a desperate cry for attention.

The following morning, I woke up still drunk at about 10 am, walked to a local pub, and drank eight pints; actually alone. I can remember sitting at a little table in the corner of this place and thinking about how downhill things had gone over my first year of university. It's tough to put this into words even now, but strangely, I loved feeling miserable about it all.

When I woke up on the Monday morning, I wasn't enjoying the misery so much. It was arguably the worst that I'd ever felt, everything considered, and the fact that I had an essay deadline the following day compounded it.

My Psychology degree had been another contributor to my extremely disappointing university experience, with a lot of the material feeling like a backwards step from A-level. There were many students on the course that weren't at all bright, and I wondered whether they'd dumbed down the content a little bit to make it more accessible. For me, it was just another aspect of life that left me under-stimulated.

With my personal life at a new low, Leeds United hit what I thought was rock bottom soon after, as we entered administration. The rumours about our precarious financial position were realised, and chairman Ken Bates announced that we'd failed to recover from the gross monetary mismanagement of the Peter Ridsdale era. Apparently, we were £35m in debt and had no way of clearing it with such a drop in revenues expected from playing in the third tier of English football. The club had planned for promotion to the Premiership from the 2006/07 season, not relegation to League One.

We suffered the automatically imposed ten-point deduction that happened to any team that entered administration at the time, dropping us to the bottom of the Championship, and officially confirming our relegation.

Interestingly, this was actually an astute move by Bates, as we still hadn't technically been relegated at the time of entering administration. With one game remaining, we were three points behind Hull City, although their goal difference was considerably superior to ours. That meant that we could still mathematically survive if were to win at Derby County, and Hull were to lose at home to Plymouth Argyle, with a nine-goal swing going in our favour. Recognising how unlikely this was, Bates took us into administration to ensure that we suffered the ten-point deduction during 2006/07, as opposed to at the start of the 2007/08 campaign.

Had we lost to Ipswich the previous weekend, we'd have been four points behind Hull with one game to go, which would have made it mathematically impossible for us to have survived. That would have meant that the ten-point deduction would have had to apply at the start of the following season, by way of the laws of The Football League. It certainly seemed like a fortunate technicality from which to benefit.

Essentially, Bates' idea was to clear the club of all it's debts, and start afresh in League One without having a points deficit to overcome. Yes, it was calculated, but if there was anything that Leeds United needed, it was a fresh start. I'd thought that I was now fortunate enough to be able to put football behind me for the summer, but that was by no means the case.

As a result of the questionable ethics surrounding the manner of our entering administration, a summer-long argument between The Football League, Leeds United's creditors (those that we were indebted to), and Leeds United's board of directors ensued. The job of the administrators had been to strike a deal between Bates and our creditors, to ensure that the creditors received a reasonable percentage of the amount owed, although they were all aware that they would be losing most of it.

A balancing act was required on both sides as if the creditors refused to accept whatever Bates and our board offered them, Leeds United might go into liquidation (cease to exist), which would mean they would receive nothing back at all. Conversely, nobody associated with Leeds United wanted to see us go into liquidation, and even if we didn't, we'd have our place in The Football League revoked until we could exit administration.

That was only achievable once an agreement between the club and a certain percentage of our creditors was agreed, with The Football League only willing to return our membership to us once they'd received that agreement in writing, which is known as a Company Voluntary Arrangement. What followed made me embarrassed to be a Leeds United fan.

As a club, we offered only 1p in every pound that we owed to each creditor, meaning that they would only receive one percent in return for what they had invested. There's no doubt that our board members had a lot more money available, but they chose to offer the smallest amount possible. With the offer being so derisory, the expectation was that the majority of creditors would reject it.

Somehow, the required percentage of creditors approved the 1p in the pound deal, and ownership of the club was returned to Bates and our board members. This was totally unexpected and seemed like the best possible outcome for us. We now had a blank slate, and hopefully, there would even be some money available for player investment to ensure that we had the best squad in League One for the 2007/08 season. A club of our size really should have of course.

However, the Inland Revenue (the taxman) made a legal

challenge over the deal, as they believed it to be suspect. As a creditor that was understandably unhappy with the 1p in the pound deal, they were entitled to do this, and it meant that Bates and co. would have to wait to assume ownership of the club, with it being temporarily returned to the administrators until the situation was resolved. With this being the case, multiple rival bidders came forward and offered the administrators, and the creditors, a better deal for the club than Bates was offering. This should have given them the upper hand, but it didn't.

Dramatically, rumours surfaced that the reason that Bates' offer had been accepted was that he was directly linked to certain, specific creditors, who just so happened to be owed the most money. There was no concrete evidence for this, but these creditors then offered to wipe out almost all of the debt that they were owed, on the sole premise that Bates' offer was accepted. They were essentially saying that they were unwilling to do business with any rival bidder, making it impossible for anybody else to gain ownership of the club. The drama didn't end there.

After the Inland Revenue's challenge, Bates eventually returned to the creditors with a considerably better offer than 1p in the pound, which included extra payments if Leeds were to get back into the Premier League within a particular time period. The Inland Revenue never accepted the new offer, but the administrators accepted Bates' bid because the required majority of creditors did accept the deal. This meant that we'd exited administration, and just needed to apply for our place back in the Football League with the start of the 2007/08 season now looming.

Just when we thought that the drama was over, The Football

League refused us our place in League One for the start of the new season. They said that although we were now out of administration, we hadn't submitted our proof by way of the Company Voluntary Arrangement, which was essential for reclaiming our membership. With time running out, and it seeming likely that I wasn't even going to have a team to support, it all felt totally and utterly desperate.

With August already upon us, we finally received the news that we craved. The Football League had agreed to return us our membership, and our place in League One for 07/08 was secured. At a heavy cost.

We were deducted fifteen points for failing to comply with The Football League's administration laws. Before a ball had even been kicked, we would be five wins worse off than every other club in the league, and thoughts of immediate promotion back to the Championship were vanquished. From being first in the English football ladder on 1st January 2002, we were now 68th on 3rd August 2007, and fifteen points behind 67th.

It was only as I saw my football club fall lower than I'd ever thought that they possibly could, that I recognised that we could yet fall further. Relegation was now more likely than promotion, and with all the off-the-field drama that we'd just been through, I genuinely believed that liquidation remained a possibility. At 1-0 down at half-time on the first day of the season away at Tranmere Rovers, it certainly didn't look good.

Even though we equalised early in the second half, I still feared what the atmosphere was going to be like at Elland Road the following week, as our opening game entered it's dying embers at 1-1. I was watching Soccer Saturday at my auntie's house at the time, and with plans in place with the lads to see us play Southend United the following week, I could imagine nothing other than toxicity.

I genuinely believe that things could have been very different for Leeds United had Tresor Kandol not popped up with a 90th-minute winner that day at Tranmere. Had we not nicked those three points, I certainly don't think that Bates and manager Dennis Wise would have been able to fan the flames as they did in the aftermath of the victory. Maybe if I'd have been in a better place psychologically, I wouldn't have bought into their propaganda as I did.

Both Bates and Wise had spent the week talking about how every faction of English football was against us, and that we could do nothing other than pull together in riposte. I didn't have much time for either of them, but I couldn't help but admire what they managed to do, as the club somehow became as united as I'd known us to be since the very beginning of our fall from grace. I was one of the 24,000 or so fans singing 'FUCK OFF, TO THE FOOTBALL LEAGUE', to the tune of 'Go West', as we sunk Southend 4-1. Things only got better from there.

We wiped out our fifteen-point deduction in the quickest possible fashion, with five wins from our first five games. My last game at Elland Road before heading back up to Newcastle for my second year of university was a 2-0 home victory over Swansea City, which made it seven wins from seven and saw us climb out of the League One relegation zone. It was truly remarkable and particularly special for me on a personal level.

After a trying first year at uni, and a summer spent feeling embarrassed to support my football club, the defiant unity at Leeds United was precisely what I'd needed. I felt some direction, some purpose, for the first time in over a year, and couldn't wait to see if my club could move clear of the relegation places. Who knew, maybe we could move towards the promotion picture, despite our fifteen-point disadvantage.

It had taken for us to go lower than I'd ever considered that we could for me to realise that things could yet get worse. The irony was that once I'd accepted that things could get worse, they took a big turn for the better.

Not for the first time in my life, it looked as though my football fandom might make everything OK again, or so I hoped.

19

Against the world

Here's a good question. How many twenty-one-year-old white males from a middle-class background, in the history of humanity, do you think have perceived the entire world to be against them while studying at university in a first-world country?

The answer is probably unquantifiable, as so many people that have believed that the world is against them at some point in their life still do, and would not have the courage to verbalise it. I know that I didn't have the courage to verbalise it back then, but it's how I felt.

Within a week of being back at university for the second of my projected three years, I realised that I didn't want to be there. Everything about the lifestyle was converse to what I wanted to be doing, but I didn't feel as though I could escape it.

To highlight how privileged I was, my dad was paying for my accommodation, while my mum was paying for my course fees. The extent of my appreciation for them meant that I didn't feel as though I could drop out, while I was also aware that having a completed degree would undoubtedly be beneficial for my future. Every ounce of me wanted to leave university, but I knew that I couldn't bring myself to do it.

My dislike for the lifestyle came down to me not being able

to escape people. It didn't matter whether I was going to a lecture or a seminar, heading on a night out, playing football, or going to work at the part-time bar job that I'd taken on, there were people everywhere, all the time. Even when I was at my uni house, where I was living with three of my best mates from Leeds, Mel, Rout, and Sam, I still felt like I was trapped, and they were all excellent at giving me space.

My total disdain for the lifestyle there, combined with my knowledge that I was never going to quit, left me feeling a horrendous internal conflict. I'd just spent one year partaking in something that was fundamentally not for me, and I was aware that I was about to spend two further years doing the same. There are probably billions of people worldwide that would have given anything to have been in my position, but it was my idea of hell.

The conflict manifested itself through an intense, burning anger that bubbled inside of me whenever I was around people. However, the cooperative personality that I'd carried right through my childhood remained, which meant that I didn't feel like I wanted to let that anger out in the direction of people specifically. Morally, I knew that it wasn't the fault of anybody else, even if I resented those that I perceived to have nothing about them. They didn't deserve the wrath, and it wasn't in my nature to project it.

Every now and then I'd blow off some steam to Mel, Rout or Sam at the house, or friends or family members over the phone. I'd never reach out to them specifically, but if they came to me and the conversation moved in a certain direction, I'd sometimes end up on a bit of a tirade about how much I hated everyone and everything.

It was as though there was a vortex of negativity swirling around inside of me, and if anybody came too close, I'd temporarily suck them in. In small crowds, I had the strength to suppress it quickly enough to prevent ruining the atmosphere of the entire room, but alcohol was the only route to managing in bigger crowds.

There was only one previous period of my life during which I'd endured internal conflict up to that point, which was early on in high school. I'd also found myself unhealthily under-stimulated while almost permanently surrounded by people back then, when my behaviour had manifested itself through deliberately misbehaving at school, shoplifting, and 'getting a chase'. I came out of that phase when Leeds United provided the external stimulation that I required, and it was clear that I needed sport as an outlet for my emotions during my second year at university.

As I reflect, I don't think that I *wanted* to enjoy Saturday afternoons for being able to follow football; I think that I *needed* them. It was a time at which I knew that I could let out at least some of the anger that I spent all week suppressing, and my reactions to goals scored by or against Leeds United reflected that.

Even though we were playing against clubs that were about a tenth of the size of us, any goal that we scored would yield a roar of furious delight. The reality for me was that a goal celebration was the only appropriate situation in which I could scream, which was incredibly cathartic, bearing in mind that I permanently felt like doing so. The funny thing was that even conceding had its advantages.

The level that we were playing at meant that any game that

Leeds didn't win at this stage was a huge disappointment. When I was in a healthy frame of mind, an underwhelming result for my team would make me angry, and I'd have to take myself off for some alone time to recover. However, I'd use a negative result at this time to fuel the negative emotions that were burning inside me, with the two negatives miraculously making a positive. I didn't recognise this at the time, but I was in a perpetual state of self-pity, and anything that went against me only served to vindicate and exacerbate that belief.

There could be no more evident sign of how much I was struggling than the positive outcome of my team scoring yielding anger, and the negative outcome of conceding yielding an inverted form of joy. At a time during which I felt as though I was losing in most areas of my life, I recognised that I could only win when it came to sport, in an emotional sense at least. The natural thing for me to do was launch myself into every sporting event that I possibly could.

England were awful to watch in the group stages of the 2007 Rugby World Cup, but I was still delighted when we managed to scrape through to the quarter-finals in second place. I couldn't have cared less about how badly we were playing as I sat down to watch us face Australia, as any kind of victory would represent a huge achievement after four years of unsuccessful rebuilding. As if the Australians hadn't seen enough of Jonny Wilkinson in 2003, his four penalties were enough to dump them out of France 2007, as we edged them out 12-10. The day didn't end there.

I effectively became a France supporter for the evening as they faced New Zealand for the chance to take us on in the semis. Everybody knew that we'd have had no chance against the Kiwis, which is why I was dancing around our living room as the French nicked an incredible match 20-18 against all the odds. It was one of the most dramatic days of sport I'd ever watched, with Leeds nicking a 90th-minute win over Yeovil Town at Elland Road for good measure. I couldn't have asked for a better sequence of events through which to express copious amounts of positive aggression.

The following Saturday night, an early Josh Lewsey try gave us the best possible start against France, before the hosts scored three unanswered penalties to lead 9-5 early in the second half. However, that man Wilkinson found his range once more to knock over two penalties and a drop goal to book us the most unlikely of places in a World Cup final. It was another terrible spectacle for the neutral, but our tactics had been to ruin the game to neutralise France's far superior free-flowing brand of rugby. Knowing that rugby purists around the world wouldn't have enjoyed watching it only served to accentuate my celebrations.

England had entered France 2007 with a similar narrative to that of Leeds United and the 2007/08 League One season. Everybody was on our backs, the media were slandering us, we'd been written off from day one, but everyone in the camp had used that as fuel to unite defiantly. By the day of the final against South Africa, I sensed a parallel between my personal life and our triumphant march towards glory. I was desperately hoping for a happy ending.

I sincerely hope that 20th October 2007 is the only time that I see England lose in a World Cup final and feel a degree of pleasure. We only spent ten minutes of our match with the Springboks level and were never really in it as we fell to a 15-6 defeat. I'd been hoping for some wildly euphoric celebrations that night, but at least I was the rare kind of fan that could settle for the warm rush of self-pity.

The bigger picture was that finishing second represented a fantastic performance from our squad, but I was in no mood to appreciate our over-achievement. Ultimately, it's unnatural to celebrate being a runner-up, but it was totally natural for me to relish feeling despair. I had an all-or-nothing mindset, which was, in fact, an all-or-all mindset, as I was in a position to feel intensely emotional whatever the outcome. I went out that night and drowned my sorrows in alcohol, which became a common theme that winter.

I'd say that the England football team's failure to qualify for Euro 2008 is one of the lowest moments that I've ever had as a football fan. Bearing in mind what I'd been through with Leeds over the previous few years, I was no stranger to footballing pain, but this was an embarrassment beyond which even I could understand.

We only needed a draw against Croatia at Wembley to reach the following summer's showpiece. The Croats had already qualified, and Israel had done us an almighty favour the weekend before by beating our main rivals Russia, presenting a significant opportunity to avoid the most humiliating of eliminations. Ultimately, if you can't avoid defeat at home to quite an average team that has nothing to play for, then there is absolutely no point in you being at a European Championships. We lost 3-2, while Russia got the three points that they needed in Andorra, and I drank whiskey alone in my bedroom past midnight to make myself feel both worse and better simultaneously.

I'd been following the tennis career of young Andy Murray

closely since his emergence at Wimbledon in 2005, and had been amazed by his performance against the game's new superstar Rafael Nadal at the 2007 Australian Open. Murray made it to the fourth round, before showing incredible ability in falling to Nadal in five sets, and I was full of excitement to see if he could go even further a year on. However, he was knocked out in the first round, and I took pleasure in blaming my incomprehensible misfortune as a sports fan for the defeat.

I think the funniest behaviour of all for me to reflect on from that time, particularly bearing in mind what I now know about Floyd Mayweather Jr., is Ricky Hatton's first professional boxing defeat. I'd barely watched a fight in my life by this point, but with all the media attention, and my boxing fan pal Rich insisting that I tune in, I made the effort to stay up all night for it. As little as I knew about the sport, I was genuinely excited to be watching a British man with an undefeated record fighting in Las Vegas against a supposed superstar.

After I'd watched Hatton suffer his first ever loss, I went to bed at about 5.30 am with a wry smile on my face. Forty-three professional victories and zero defeats without me as a fan. Zero victories and one defeat with me as a fan. Even had I known just how good Mayweather Jr. was, I wouldn't have cared. When you're looking to feel sorry for yourself, you find whatever it is that paints the bleakest possible picture for you, and that's exactly what the stats did.

For all of the misery that I was experiencing, the most important aspect of my sports fandom looked like it might be on the brink of performing an absolute miracle. After starting the season with minus fifteen points, Leeds United went top of League One on Boxing Day after we secured a late draw in our early kick-off at Hartlepool United. I was back in Leeds at the time and can remember celebrating the goal raucously from my bedroom at my mum's as I listened on the radio. It was a truly incredible achievement, beyond anything that we could ever have imagined after receiving that points deduction back in August. Now it was a matter of seeing the job through.

We'd lost our assistant manager Gustavo Poyet to Tottenham Hotspur a couple of months earlier, but Dennis Wise had done brilliantly to cope without his right-hand man. With the transfer window just around the corner, I hoped to see us bring a couple of fresh faces in to help bolster our promotion bid, while also keeping my fingers crossed that one player, in particular, wouldn't leave.

Our hotshot striker Jermaine Beckford was heavily linked with a Premier League move to Derby County. Still, after weeks of speculation as we moved through January, it was eventually confirmed that he would be staying. Despite our success, there was nobody at the club other than Beckford that I'd feared we would lose, but to fear losing somebody, it has to enter your mind that they might leave. There can't have been a Leeds fan in the world who predicted what happened next.

In the endless drama that was Leeds United Football Club, manager Dennis Wise resigned at the end of January after producing the best start to a season from a Leeds team in my lifetime. With there having been so much doubt and debate around Wise after he took the job, and considerable uproar surrounding him staying on after overseeing our relegation from the Championship, the fans had finally accepted him. Even without Poyet, he'd been nothing short of brilliant in 2007/08, which of course can work against you when you're in the lower leagues.

Had we not been doing so well, I highly doubt that Spurs would have pinched Poyet from us when they did. The fact that it happened was incredibly frustrating, but at least it was understandable from a footballing perspective. Had Wise been pinched by another club to become their manager, or even an assistant manager if it were a big club, I think I'd have just about been able to accept it. He wasn't though.

When else in football history has a manager left a club at which they were working miracles to become an executive director? Wise was at the peak of his managerial powers, and at just forty-one years old, it certainly seemed that he was far too young to be joining Newcastle United to move upstairs. This was Leeds United though, of course the most important person at our club was departing in unprecedented circumstances, just as we finally seemed to be moving forward after six years of moving backwards.

Soon after, former Leeds midfielder Gary McAllister was appointed our new manager. In our first five League One matches since his arrival, we faced Southend United, Tranmere Rovers, Northampton Town, Nottingham Forest, and Crewe Alexandra. We failed to win any of them; maybe the world really was against me.

20

The self-destruct button

There is no doubt that my personality lends itself to self-destruction. I'm particularly bad at dealing with imbalance and a lack of control in the absence of fulfilling external stimulation. When I find myself in that kind of position, self-destructive behaviours follow.

During that short spell in high school when I displayed signs of this, I started to thrill-seek as a result of the decreased excitement that I was experiencing on a functional level. The people didn't enthuse me, my football team weren't quite good enough to be all-consuming, and there were no specific interests that I was partaking in that would either excite me or lend themselves to ego-boosting praise.

The reality is that when you're twelve or thirteen years old, there is only so much harm that you are likely to do to yourself bearing in mind the boundaries and constraints placed upon you at that age. Excepting extreme anti-social cases, dependent children only elicit self-destructive behaviours that get them into temporary trouble, and they almost always have a parent or guardian to help guide them away from that. That's why there was no real issue with me fighting with teachers, shoplifting on a small scale, and 'getting a chase' back then. Things change when you're an independent young adult.

After Leeds United's automatic promotion push all but ended in the aftermath of Dennis Wise's exit, my self-destructive side resurfaced. In the absence of any other prominent, meaningful sporting events in the first few months of 2008, I'd pinned my incessant need for purpose and direction on our battle for a top-two spot. Those hopes vanished with that run of zero wins in five games, and the decline caused me two key emotional issues.

The first was that we only scored three goals in that period, which decreased the opportunity to express my anger through my aggressive goal celebrations. The second was that we'd done so well up to that point in the season that I couldn't find a way to wallow in self-pity authentically. That's where the self-destruction started.

I'd been drinking a lot as it was, but the scale of how drunk I got became anti-social. It was commonplace for me to get kicked out of nightclubs and bars, or even be denied entry altogether. I wasn't necessarily doing anything overtly aggressive or disruptive; I was just so unable to control myself that bouncers and security would have no choice but to ensure that I wasn't on their premises.

I'd always enjoyed gambling on football, but both the stakes and the frequency of my betting increased considerably during this period. What had previously been £5-£10 per week on an accumulator turned in to £20-£25 on every round of fixtures. That might not seem much, but it is when the financial struggles of being a student leave you having to take on a part-time minimum wage job. Due to my extensive football knowledge, I managed to snare a few victories, and by no means was I in financial trouble because of it. Had I been, my behaviour at work might have been a little easier to explain.

I quite liked working as a barman in Newcastle city centre. I found brief interactions with charismatic locals to be far more entertaining than sustained conversation with characterless students. As I was earning money, I at least felt like there was some point to what I was doing, which I didn't feel about my degree. There was always sport on while I was at work too, which I loved, although the late-night shifts that often finished at 5 am were a little less enjoyable.

With there being about fifteen bar staff in total, we needed two managers to run the place. On the one hand, I saw these managers as being quite good to me, as they gave me any overtime shift that was going as a result of my willingness to do them. On the other hand, there was a strong argument to say that they took advantage of me, as if I tried to turn an overtime shift down, they would then threaten to stop giving me extra shifts at all.

I didn't have the insight to recognise that I was a dream member of staff for them, as I would almost always cover when required, and I never called in sick or missed a shift. There were quite a few staff that were the direct opposite of that, which only increased my value, but my total lack of self-esteem at the time meant that I didn't perceive myself to have any worth at all.

I saw my relationship with the managers as being about 50:50 in terms of give-and-take, even though I was, in theory, giving more. It took one of them to display a flagrant disregard for me as a person to realise that this was by no means the case.

On my December payday, I realised that there'd been an issue with my tax code since I'd started there in September. As a student, I shouldn't have been paying tax at all, just national insurance, and I asked my manager why this was happening when I returned to work in January. He said that I'd been emergency taxed, and I'd need to call the taxman to get it sorted, which I immediately did before sending off all the required forms. The one thing out of my control was that I needed the managers to do a small amount of administration on their side to ensure that I both received an income tax rebate, and was not emergency taxed again.

When my January pay came around, not only had I not received a rebate, but I'd been emergency taxed on that month's work too. I called the taxman again at this point, who told me that they'd received all my information, but not the required documents from my employer. In short, my managers hadn't done what I'd needed them to do.

I went back to them and politely asked if they would ensure that the relevant information was sent off as soon as possible, just to ensure that I wasn't out of pocket again in February. I told them that I was now about £700 down, which was a lot of money to me at the time, and they unequivocally assured me that they would sort it.

I wasn't working on my February payday, but I decided that I was going to go in and have a friendly but frank discussion with whichever manager was on shift. I'd been emergency taxed for a third straight month, and estimated that I was now around £850 short of what I should have had. Although I knew that I would get it back eventually, I was sick of how long the situation had dragged on and felt as though this would be a perfectly reasonable thing to ask as I knocked on the bar's office door.

The shift manager for that day pulled the door open far

enough to be able to see me, but narrowly enough to make it clear that he didn't want me coming in. It was one of those situations in which somebody is implying that you need to make it quick, which is why I asked if I could 'have a very quick word'.

After he asked what it was about, and I explained that my tax code still hadn't been sorted and that I wanted to go through it with him there and then, I honestly believed that he was going to sympathise with me. At the very worst, I thought that he would say that it wasn't a good time, with the more likely outcome being that he would ask if we could arrange another time to sort it out. When he said 'not my problem', and slammed the door in my face, I literally couldn't believe it.

I'd been so angry for such a considerable period leading up to that day, that I'm surprised that I didn't kick the door in and try and kill him. However, I simply laughed, and walked out of the bar, and made the decision that I was never going to work there again, which made me feel a hell of a lot better in the moment.

The following day, I received a phone call from the other manager, who pleaded with me to work the Saturday day shift as another member of staff had spontaneously quit. Recognising that the previous day's incident hadn't been his fault, I told him that I would do it on the premise that I could have the Saturday night off, which he said would be OK. I'd had the time to process my emotions, and I didn't want to quit working there but did want to try and develop a more mutual arrangement.

When I got in that Saturday morning, the manager that had asked me to work the shift told me that the other two members of staff that were supposed to be in had called in sick. That left the two of us to work on the bar for the first three hours, and with Newcastle United playing at home that day, we both knew that it would be chaotic from minute one.

Upon opening, the manager disappeared to his office and left me to fend for myself as tens of thirsty, fired up Geordies rolled in to start their big Saturday out. It became clear after half an hour that he wasn't going to be putting in a shift behind the bar in the absence of the other staff, and I felt total despair at the thought of him sitting in his office as I ran myself into the ground. At that moment, I felt like I'd accepted that these two people had no regard for me whatsoever, and the self-destruct streak came to the fore.

The previous summer, when I'd been back in Leeds, a friend of mine had been working in a local pub and would turn up to meet us for a few beers after his shift with a wallet stacked full of cash. He wasn't known for his generosity but developed a habit of getting a round in upon his arrival. On certain occasions, he'd even offer to pay for a night out for us when we explained that we couldn't go to town with him as we were too skint. As nice as it was, it didn't stack up.

We eventually asked him how he was able to afford his extravagance, after we'd sunk a few pints of course, and he explained that he'd been stealing from the till at work.

We asked him how he was getting away with it, at which point he gave us a detailed account of how he would serve multiple drinks, while only putting one of them through the till. He'd then return the appropriate amount of change to the customer, and calculate how far up the till would be in cash compared to the number of drinks that he'd registered to it. He'd then pocket the surplus cash, with the only deficit being the amount of alcohol dispensed in comparison to the amount that had gone through the till. He said that there wasn't a bar manager in the world that checked such a deficit.

That day in my Newcastle sports bar, craving dangerous behaviour, I decided to see how far up I could leave the till by correctly charging punters while putting fewer drinks through. Within two hours, and with my manager not once having been up to support me, I'd calculated that it was £80 up. Fortunately, I'd always been good at maths.

When I'd decided to undertake this little experiment, I'd not considered what I would do once the till was up. I didn't know whether I had it in me to pocket the money deep down, but I now had two choices. I either had to rebalance the till by applying the reverse process of entering more drinks than I was taking money for, as there would be serious questions from my manager if he discovered that the till was £80 out. Alternatively, I pocketed the cash, resulting in no drama for anybody.

I must have made the decision subconsciously, as, without any thought process, I started looking up at the ceiling to see where the CCTV cameras were when I was pulling a pint. I could see two directly ahead of me at the far end of the room, and as I looked behind me over the top of the bar, there was one above each till. The one above the till meant I couldn't physically take the money out of there, while I also couldn't simply take it out of a customer's hand and slide it straight into my pocket in front of their eyes. I had to be discreet.

As I gave the guy I was serving his two pints, he passed me over a twenty-pound note. I turned to my left to walk over towards the till, took a couple of steps, and then slipped the note into my right pocket. As I was pulling the pint, I'd recognised that the bar itself would obstruct the view of both the two far cameras and any customers, while my body would prevent the cameras above the tills from seeing.

I walked over to the till, actually entered which drinks had been purchased on this occasion to bring it down by £6, before taking out £14 change to give to the customer. With £6 of drinks having been processed, £14 having been removed, and nothing having gone in, the till was now just £60 up.

I got fortunate in that the next round I served was for three pitchers. They cost £11 each, which meant that the guy would have to pass over two twenty-pound notes to foot the £33 bill, which he duly did. I followed the same process, slipping both notes into my pocket this time, and putting no cash into the till.

With both my mind and my heart racing, I realised that there was a flawed logic to my process. If anybody was to look at the CCTV footage of those two payments in close enough detail, the camera above the till would show me entering no cash, while still taking some out. The thought made me flustered beyond belief, as I realised that there was now a chance I'd be caught, but I also didn't know how I could get another £20 into my pocket to complete the job.

I ruminated on this while I served a few customers, desperately trying to think of what I could do. Then, when I received a drinks order for two pitchers of beer, I realised that I was going to receive two notes once again. Realistically, if I could slip at least one note into the till there was no way that the CCTV could know how much the round was. Provided the camera could see at least one note entering the till I would be in the clear.

As the guy handed over two twenties for his twenty-two pound round, I felt like the weight of the world had been lifted from my shoulders. I turned left, took a couple of steps, slipped one twenty-pound note into my pocket, before entering the other into the till for the cameras. I then took £18 out, handed the bloke his change, and revelled in the fact that the till was now straight. That left me with just one final task to complete my little project.

With £80 burning a hole in my pocket, I told the customers that I had to run for a quick toilet break. I charged upstairs to the changing rooms, opened the locker in which I'd put my bag, pulled out my wallet, and stashed the four twenties in as tightly as I could. As I made my way back down to the bar, I experienced both a vile, hot sensation of guilt and a filthy but exhilarating thrill at the same time.

I didn't take any more money that day. I worked incredibly hard and told myself that I'd earned the extra money having worked for three, and left work in a fantastic mood after Leeds picked up their first win under Gary McAllister at Swindon Town. I went out that night and bought multiple rounds for the people that I was with, which felt like the purest method for relieving the guilt.

With each shift that I worked that month, I grew more confident. At first, I would only steal when I was on my own on the bar. However, as time passed, I recognised that nobody ever paid attention to the intricate behaviours of their fellow bar staff, and I was soon slipping notes into my pockets at free will. I never even came close to getting caught.

Applying logic to try and justify my behaviour, I started working towards a target of £1000 in total. That was how much money I perceived those managers were going to have cost me through the emergency tax situation by the time I quit at the end of my uni year. I made a hefty dent into that before I headed back to Leeds for a short Easter break, and as my March payday rolled around without any rebate or tax break, I fully intended on completing the job upon my return to Newcastle. However, before I could, two things happened.

Although McAllister managed to back up his first win as manager with a 2-0 home victory over Bournemouth, we then suffered an embarrassing home defeat to Cheltenham Town, before conceding a stoppage-time equaliser to draw 3-3 at League One basement club Port Vale. We'd been first on Boxing Day but were now 10th, and our hopes of reaching the play-offs looked like a stretch.

However, we embarked on a run of four wins and a draw in five games to put ourselves right back in the top-six picture with just four games to go. Our form provided the sense of purpose and direction that I was so badly craving, and as I headed back to Newcastle off the back of it, there was somebody there waiting to help me.

When I went back to work for a Wednesday daytime shift in mid-April, there was a new manager in place. I'd barely got through the front door when a very butch-looking blonde-haired lady confidently bounded over to me and introduced herself. She'd just moved to Newcastle from down south and had come in to replace the guy who had slammed the door in my face. Apparently, he'd had a couple of run-ins with other members of staff, which was part of the reason why he'd left, and she wanted to let me know that she'd look after me if I ever needed anything from her.

It felt so unusual to hear somebody say that to me, that it didn't register for a good couple of hours. When it did, I reached out and told her about my emergency tax situation, and when I detailed that it had been going on since September, she went straight into the back office, printed out the form that needed sending to the taxman, and stuck it in the post that same day. When I was walking out of the door at the end of my shift, she told me that my rebate should be with me by May or June and that I shouldn't be emergency taxed for April.

I can remember listening to *Hurt* by Johnny Cash as I walked home that evening. I was exclusively listening to dark, emotive music at the time as I found that it helped to exaggerate what I was feeling, which was usually self-pity. However, one of the most vivid memories that I have of university is of feeling overcome by shock as a smile broke out across my face, even as one of the most heart-rending songs ever written played back to me.

It was the first time that I'd experienced a warm rush of dopamine in the absence of alcohol, gambling, or stealing in almost two years. It was so far removed from what I was used to experiencing that it prayed on my mind for days. I may not have been able to comprehend positive emotion, but one kind gesture certainly did have a positive effect.

I never stole another penny from that, or any other bar again. I'm still not 100 percent certain that I'd have stopped had Leeds not managed to turn their season around, but I genuinely believe that a solitary helping hand was all I needed to kick that truly awful habit. Two wrongs hadn't made a right, but one right had dispelled two wrongs.

I wasn't emergency taxed in my April pay, and I received an £880 tax rebate cheque in early May. I was considerably up from the whole debacle, but the thought of what I did still makes my skin crawl to the point at which I don't want to consider how much. I wanted to focus on the positives with things potentially looking up, and when Leeds managed to secure a League One play-off spot, I sensed the light at the end of the tunnel.

21

All roads lead

The 2007/08 League One season epitomised everything that it is to be a Leeds United fan; unprecedented drama.

It was our first ever season in the third tier of English football. We'd had to start the campaign fifteen points behind everybody else, after suffering the largest points deduction in English football history. We won our first seven games to move out of the League One relegation zone. We had our assistant manager pinched by a Premier League club. We managed to top the table on Boxing Day despite our fifteen-point deficit. Our forty-one-year-old manager left to become an executive director of another football club off the back of one of the best starts to a season a team has ever made. We temporarily collapsed under our new manager, before finding good enough form to move back into the play-off places. We staged a legal challenge to have the fifteen points reinstated, which would have guaranteed us automatic promotion when the verdict was given with two games to spare. After the challenge failed, we secured a place in the most compelling competition in English football, the play-offs. All that, and the drama was only just getting started.

After I bagged three tickets for the first leg of our play-off semi-final against Carlisle United at Elland Road for Rob, Bill and me, Bill offered to drive us back to Leeds from Newcastle for the occasion, saving us the hassle and expense of the train or the coach.

Throughout the drive home, we reminisced about our experiences as fans over the years that had passed. We discussed everything, from the first time we'd attended Elland Road, to the Champions League season, to the near-miss of the Championship play-off final, to the previous year's relegation to League One against Ipswich Town, a game that we'd also attended as a trio, to the insane nature of 07/08.

The key message that we took from the conversation was that we were all waiting to see Leeds United achieve something for the first time as fans. The two of them were adamant that we were about to watch the start of a play-off campaign that would end in promotion; I could only hope and pray that they were right.

Over the two league games during the regular season, the aggregate score was 5-4 to Carlisle. They'd outplayed us at their place, and had probably deserved something at Elland Road too. I was wary of them as a side, although we'd amassed eleven more points during the regular season. We were favourites, and rightly so, but I was so nervous that I could only immerse myself in reasons that we should be concerned.

We got to the ground and took our seats in the East Stand Upper, an area in which I'd never sat. We were pretty much bang in line with the halfway line, and I felt as though it was the best view that I'd ever had of a football match from within a stadium. The pitch was drenched in the late-evening sun, there were over 36,000 fans packed in, and as the players made their way out, the scene was set for something special.

After a lively start, both Jermaine Beckford and our experienced loanee Dougie Freedman drew magnificent saves from Carlisle goalkeeper Kieran Westwood. The visitors had a couple of half-chances of their own, but we were on top; things were going to plan.

Then, after a rare foray forward, a Carlisle corner was headed clear to the edge of the box, and Simon Hackney volleyed the ball back into the crowd of players. It hit the Cumbrians' striker Danny Graham on the back and bounced past our 'keeper Casper Ankergren into the corner of the net. Cue the sinking feeling.

The crowd tried to inspire the team with their unified cries of 'COME ON', but as I'd experienced many times at Elland Road, it was hard to feel the encouragement through the expectation, aggression and hostility. The fans were genuinely trying to get behind the players, but it seemed to have the opposite effect.

We were awful from then on, and Carlisle fully deserved their second when it arrived through Marc Bridge-Wilkinson at the start of the second half. If the first sinking feeling had been bad, this was a crushing blow.

At this point, I'd all but accepted that the promotion dream was over. I felt more deflated than I'd been after either of our recent relegations or our Championship play-off final defeat to Watford. Resting my elbows on my knees, and my chin on my palms, I watched with despair as our players huffed and puffed. Try as we might, we failed to produce a moment's quality, right through until the 96th minute.

Then, with the referee on the brink of blowing the full-time whistle, a speculative ball was launched into the penalty area.

Westwood thought about coming for it, but then held back, and a multitude of players rose to try and meet it. I couldn't see who'd won the header, but the ball landed in a pocket of space on the edge of the six-yard box. Incredibly, there was Freedman to bundle the ball past Westwood, sending those that had remained in the stadium ballistic. It was a wretched goal, one befitting of our performance, but that didn't matter a jot.

It turned out that Freedman's intervention was the last kick of the game, and although the game finished Leeds United 1-2 Carlisle United on the night, the whole complexity of the tie had changed. We'd been atrocious, and had no right whatsoever to think that we could go to Carlisle and win, but we had something that we were no strangers to clinging to at Elland Road; hope.

When I'd dropped into work to ensure that I wasn't rostered in for either of the play-off legs, the new manager had asked me what I was doing for the matches. I'd told her that I was going down to Leeds for the first leg, but that I had no plans for the second leg. In another heartwarming gesture, she told me that she would get the function room at the bar set up for me for free, and would even throw in a couple of on-the-house pitchers for the occasion. Other than going to Brunton Park, it was the best possible setup to watch my team in an enormous game of football.

Bill, Mel, Rodney and me, as well as a few other select football fans that I'd invited, headed down to my work three days after the home leg to find that the room was ready and waiting for us. The projector was on, the correct channel and the sound were sorted, and about twenty-five seats had been laid out. One of the barmaids on shift had even been assigned solely to our group.

Beers were brought through to us on cue, many more than just the two pitchers without charge, as we watched the entirety of the match's build-up. As the game was about to kick off, she even dimmed the lights for us, and as the noise picked up within such a small space among my enthused friends and me, the atmosphere was perfect.

After a frenetic start to the match, there was chaos among the group of us in no time at all, as nineteen-year-old, Leeds-born midfielder Jonny Howson fired us into the lead on the night. We'd been down and out of the tie with ninety-five minutes and thirty-five seconds on the first leg clock, but ten minutes of football later and we had parity.

The lads and I tried to settle ourselves down in the aftermath but severely struggled to regain our composure. Without conscious thought, my beer-drinking speed picked up considerably, although it did nothing to rebalance my emotions.

As we reached half-time with little else to report, I could tell that the lads wanted to venture the thought of us going to Wembley. I could see the excitement in their eyes, they were daring to dream, and although I was doing absolutely nothing of the sort, I did acknowledge that the momentum was with us.

As the second half played out, the knife-edge nature of the tie became abundantly clear to us, as both sides had opportunities to take the lead on aggregate. Carlisle had the better of the early stages, but we came back into it well, creating some decent half-chances of our own. However, as the game reached seventy minutes, both sets of players seemed to run out of steam, and almost nothing happened for the following twenty minutes.

With extra time looming, and the players seeming more

determined not to lose the tie as opposed to trying to win it, conversation picked up about how on earth we'd be able to stomach watching Leeds United in a penalty shoot-out with so, so much at stake. I couldn't even comprehend the thought.

In the time since football had introduced the policy of displaying how many minutes of stoppage time there would be, I'd never seen only one additional minute indicated. From my experience, there was almost always either three or four minutes added, with two or five declared only after particularly uneventful or eventful games. One never happened.

Within an instant of the fourth official holding up an electric board that read *1*, Neil Kilkenny picked up the ball in the centre circle, before playing an incisive pass towards Freedman about twenty-five yards from goal. He flicked the ball around the corner and into the path of Howson on the edge of the Carlisle box, leaving him with a bit of space to move forward in to. After a couple of touches, Howson got the ball out of his feet, and struck the ball with his weaker left-foot.

The ball seemed to move at the rate of a twenty-yard pass, bobbling towards it's intended target, which was the bottom right corner of the Carlisle goal. Suddenly on my feet, I stared at the screen as 'keeper Westwood hurled himself to his left. The ball beat his outstretched glove, but was it on target? I get goosebumps even now as I think about what happened next.

All the anger, hate, resentment, pain, and misery that I'd been feeling for the previous couple of years poured out of me in one utterly delirious goal celebration. I screamed louder than I ever had in my life, jumped all over Bill and Rodney, hit the walls repeatedly, before falling to my knees in utter disbelief.

I kept my face buried in the floor as the amount of adrenaline pumping around my body only seemed to increase. After everything that had happened to us as a club in the last year, it was such a huge goal, and I felt every ounce of it from that function room in Newcastle city centre. Seconds after the restart, it was all over. We were going to Wembley.

With everything that I was going through, the net rippling after a scuffed Jonny Howson strike in a League One play-off semi-final surpassed any feeling that I'd ever had as a Leeds United fan. It beat all of the Champions League goals, Lee Bowyer's last-gasp strike at Southampton, Rob Hulse's header in the 2006 Championship play-off semi-final that I'd watched in Sydney, everything.

Just as I had in Sydney through MSN Messenger, I got in touch with all the big Leeds fans that I knew. I had three of them with me of course, but I had to take the time to call my brother, my dad, and Andy, so I could take the time to soak up their emotions. Pretty much all that any of us could say was that we were going to Wembley. *We were going to Wembley.*

I woke up the following morning with an incredibly sore head and got straight into action. The game was scheduled for nine days later on the second May bank holiday Sunday, which immediately cleared any university commitments that I might have had. As a club member, I was guaranteed four tickets, which I duly confirmed for Andy, Bill, Rodney and me, although my dad called soon after to say that he'd got me, my brother and himself hospitality tickets. I couldn't bring myself to turn the old man down, even if I'd spent the last three years going to games with the lads. I decided to compensate for that by turning our big day out into a full weekend city break in London.

One of Rodney's best mates from uni, a bloke called Mat who was one of the very few folk in Newcastle that I liked, had come along to the pub for the Carlisle match as a show of support, even though he wasn't a big football fan. On hearing that we'd got tickets for Wembley, he decided that he'd head back down to London that same weekend, as he was born and raised in Putney. I'd assumed that we might meet him down there for a few pints but thought little more of it than that.

Not only did he offer to drive us down there, but he also arranged for us to stay at a penthouse flat that his parents owned in the centre of the city. As Rodney informed me of the plans, I felt like the balance of the universe was being a whole lot more than restored after the incredibly challenging time I'd had over the previous couple of years.

I had a few exams to negotiate between that glorious semi-final second leg and the bank holiday weekend, but when the Friday morning finally came, I felt like an over-excited child.

We had a few cans on the journey down, before heading over to Mat's parents' place upon arrival in London. As if they weren't already doing the nicest thing I could imagine by gifting us a penthouse flat for the weekend, they greeted us with food and drinks, before almost immediately insisting that we got on our way to go and enjoy ourselves. It was perfection.

I couldn't believe what was happening to me when we arrived at the flat. It was a huge open-plan space, with three bedrooms and a state-of-the-art modern kitchen and living room. There were two double beds and one set of twin beds between the four of Mat, Andy, Rodney and me, as Bill had only planned to come down and meet us on the Sunday. For one weekend only, I was royalty, and all roads led to Wembley.

I woke up on the Saturday morning with little idea as to what had happened the night before. All I knew was that it was 9 am, and I was still drunk, so I headed straight into the kitchen to get another can cracked open. I sat on my own in Mat's living room, drank lager, and felt totally and utterly euphoric.

In that moment, if I could have permanently signed up to live in a world in which Leeds United were in a play-off final every Sunday afternoon, I'd have done it. Every weekend would be spent in a perpetual state of excitement, and I'd drink my way towards the match, feeling nothing other than ecstasy with my best mates. It was an emotion that I wanted to bottle up and lock away, ready to be used when I needed it most. I guess that's the drug's purpose.

When the lads woke up, I forced a can into their hands and insisted they joined me in getting back on the beers. I wanted them all to be on my level, I wanted this feeling to last forever, and I was elated when they gladly obliged.

The weather was glorious, so we spent the day frequenting London parks and beer gardens, all the while discussing what it might be like to see us win a play-off final at Wembley. In one of the pubs we were in, they showed the Championship play-off final between Bristol City and Hull City, and as Dean Windass fired Hull ahead, I dreamed of celebrating the next day like I could see their fans doing.

We'd effectively been drinking for thirty hours when Saturday evening came around, but there wasn't an ounce of me that was starting to struggle. The anticipation of the match was constantly fuelling my body with adrenaline, and I genuinely felt like I could keep going right through until 3 pm the following day.

We partied in Clapham until 5 am, before finally deciding to call it a night with less than twelve hours to go until we faced Doncaster Rovers for a place in the Championship. When my alarm chimed at 10.30 am on the Sunday morning, I felt like I'd been hit by a bus. I was horrifically dehydrated, my head was banging, and I had to sit straight back down for my dizziness after I stood up to go to the toilet. I honestly think that I'd have spent the whole day in bed if this had been an ordinary Sunday, I was in that much of a state.

However, the instant my mind acknowledged that it was play-off final day, every aspect of my hangover dissipated. I packed my things, left the lads in bed, and was on my way to meet my dad and brother at Wembley.

I'd been to Wembley once before to see the Leeds Rhinos' 1999 Challenge Cup final victory over the London Broncos before it's renovation started a couple of years later. As we'd driven down and parked close by back then, I'd not managed to fulfil a lifelong ambition of mine to walk down Wembley Way.

Every time that I'd watched the FA Cup final as a kid, I'd seen streams of fans walking out of Wembley Park tube station, and along the straight pathway that leads right up to the stadium. It seemed magical to me and felt every bit as special as I'd hoped it would as I eventually disembarked at Wembley Park myself.

As I walked down the steps, having made my way off the platform, I followed a legion of Leeds United fans through a tunnel that I could only assume led to the stadium. I joined in with the 'Marching On Together' chant as it reverberated around the tunnel, and eventually saw something enormous coming into sight at the other end.

As the entirety of Wembley emerged in front of me, behind

the famous bridge that leads up to it, I experienced another overwhelming feeling of euphoria. I was living a lifelong dream.

Having not made it to the League Cup final in 1996, and having been in New Zealand for the Championship play-off final in 2006, I had arrived at a final involving Leeds United for the first time in my life after fifteen years as a fan. I breathed in the moment, relishing how high on life I was.

After I met my brother and my dad, both of whom were in their Leeds shirts, I dropped my bag and rustled around for my own. As I pulled out the yellow item of clothing with the Leeds United crest on it, I buried my face in my hands. I'd accidentally packed my Leeds shorts, not my Leeds shirt.

Out of control with excitement, I then decided to wear my shorts on my head, as we took in the festival atmosphere of the occasion. Unfortunately, security asked me to remove the shorts as we entered the hospitality area of the stadium, but I made a hat of them once more as soon as we got inside the ground.

The adrenaline drove me up what felt like a thousand flights of stairs before we reached a vast high-ceilinged function room. A lady greeted us with a clipboard like we were in a fancy restaurant, and she led us to our seats after scowling at the yellow material flopping off the top of me.

I sank a couple of beers with dinner to further accentuate the extremity of my emotions. I was usually the quietest of the three of us when spending time with my dad and my brother, but this was a completely different story. They'd enjoyed a relaxing drive down from Leeds just a few hours earlier, whereas I'd been pissed out of my mind for forty-eight hours.

As soon as we'd finished dinner, I started a couple of Leeds chants, even though it wasn't a remotely appropriate environment in which to do so. I was too fired up on both life and alcohol to care, and fortunately, hundreds of Leeds fans followed my lead as I conducted them. It was heaven.

Eventually, we made our way from the function room towards the area that we would be sitting. I can remember catching my first sight of the green pitch, and as we walked through the gangway to witness the stadium from the inside for the first time, I raised my hands to my short-clad head in astonishment. It was so much bigger and more spectacular than I'd remembered it from 1999, it was utterly incredible.

We made our way down to our perfect seats, almost pitchside and bang on the halfway line behind the dugouts. We sat and watched in amazement from about 2.15 pm as fans steadily streamed in and encompassed the stadium. The atmosphere built, and built, and built, as the Leeds end became filled by about 2.55 pm, with the only disappointment for me being the tinge of sadness that I felt for not being in there with the lads.

The Doncaster end remained half-empty, and you could even see a few pockets of Leeds fans appearing in the upper tiers. The stadium was Leeds-dominated, and the atmosphere that we created was as raucous as I'd always expect from us. It took the teams walking out for me to first think about the football itself.

Doncaster had developed a reputation for playing free-flowing attacking football, which they justified with a 5-1 hammering of Southend United in the second leg of their play-off semi-final. I'd been massively impressed with a host of their players when watching that match, and there was no doubt that we'd have to be at our best to beat them.

Rovers' major strength that season had been the consistency of their performances, which was not something that we could say about ourselves. At that time, there wasn't a single fan of ours that knew which Leeds United team was going to turn up. If it was the team from the first leg against Carlisle, I was certain that we'd lose. If it was the team from the second leg, I gave us every chance of prevailing. It was time to find out.

I don't know if this is because I was still drunk from a weekend's boozing, or because I remained overwhelmed with emotion by the whole occasion, but I remember literally nothing about the first half of the match. I don't think a great deal happened, but I can't recall a single incident. I can remember asking my brother which two of the four central midfielders that we'd lined up in midfield with would play out wide, but that was just before the game had kicked off. Regardless of that, it was 0-0, and it looked as though there was an agonising forty-five minutes to come.

At half-time, I dashed for a piss and grabbed a quick beer on my own. I wanted to take a second to gather my thoughts, as the enormity of what might have been on the brink of happening dawned on me. I may not be able to remember any of the first half's football, but I can remember what was going through my head in my moment of solitude with perfect clarity. If Leeds were to score in the second half, it might just lead to the greatest moment of my entire life.

I made my way back down just as the players had lined up again, and another clear memory that I have is of looking over at the Leeds half of the stadium. There were so many empty seats; clearly, a lot of them were finishing off their beers before returning. After the match, I discovered that Rob, Andy and Bill were three of those people, as they didn't see what happened in the 47th minute.

As the referee blew his whistle to begin the most important forty-five minutes of my life, Doncaster immediately surged forward and won themselves a corner. As the Rovers fans shouted cheers of encouragement for their players, my old man said 'here we go' to my brother and me, clearly fearing the worst.

To our right, as we looked, the ball was swung in from the near corner flag into a very dangerous area by the penalty spot. Both hoping and expecting to see the ball cleared by one of our defenders, I watched in horror as Rovers striker James Hayter connected perfectly with his head. The ball flew past Casper Ankergren, and nestled in the bottom corner of our net.

My head dropped into my hands in despair, before I looked up to see Hayter wheeling away in front of the delirious Doncaster fans. It was heartbreaking to watch, because in that moment, even with over forty minutes remaining, I was sure that the game was over.

Every game of football is different, and occasions that have come before with entirely different players and managers can't influence how a current game plays out. That's the rational perspective, but in my head, I knew exactly how the rest of the match was going to go. I'd seen this footage before. We would have plenty of the ball, pass it around in midfield, make little progress forward, and ultimately lack any of the quality that you need to get back into a game of this magnitude. We didn't turn up against Aston Villa in 1996, we didn't turn up against Watford in 2006, and we hadn't turned up against Doncaster in 2008. That wasn't going to change for going 1-0 down as far as I was concerned, and it didn't.

Urgency soon became desperation, and it looked like we

were merely hoping that something would fall our way, not believing in our ability to get back into the game. We needed luck, and as far as I was concerned, I wasn't the kind of person that luck would favour at such a critical moment.

We didn't create a chance during the rest of the match, and as the final whistle went, that sinking feeling that I'd experienced so often drowned all the hope, optimism and joy that I'd felt over the past couple of weeks. It had been such a long season, with so much drama, but all forty-nine games had been for nothing. In true Leeds United fashion, we'd not turned up when it had mattered the most.

It had been such an amazing weekend, so full of happiness and laughter with my friends in London. Yet, it was totally and utterly ruined by the one thing that was out of my control, the sport.

I didn't say a word as we left the ground and trudged back along Wembley Way to the tube station to head back to where my dad had parked his car. All I wanted to do was to get home and disappear into a place in which nobody would ever disturb me, but we had to queue for a tube for over an hour amid massive crowds of devastated Leeds fans. As the weekend's alcohol wore off, I slumped to a whole new low, in a state of all-encompassing misery.

I stared out of the window as we drove up the M1 that Sunday evening and contemplated how I'd deal with the latest bout of despair that had overcome me. I felt empty. There was no emotion inside; no anger, no sadness, just nothingness. Fortunately, my brother and my dad said nothing either, and as the journey wore on, I felt the warm embrace of self-pity returning to save me from the pure darkness.

22

The wrong crowd

Society has a very clear definition of what the wrong crowd is. The definition is actually in and of itself, as a wrong crowd is invariably defined by anti-social behaviour. A wrong crowd tends to be formed by individuals that have a propensity *for* anti-social behaviour, with a tendency to get in with a wrong crowd usually coming as a result of some kind of psychological or emotional instability.

For a person that comes from a background like mine, university students really should have been the right crowd. Intellectual, academic, social, adherent; these are all the kinds of traits that I'd be expected to blend in with and conform to. Part of the reason that I suffered psychological and emotional instability at university was because of the students themselves, which actually made them the wrong crowd for me. I found the right crowd just before I headed back to Newcastle for my final year, which was by definition, the wrong crowd.

I enjoyed the summer after my second year at uni. After the devastation of Leeds United's League One play-off final defeat, I'd headed back to finish my exams, before returning to Leeds for three months. I picked up a bit of work at my dad's office, a fair few of my best mates were kicking around, I got a lot of time to myself, and there was some magnificent sport on display.

After England's desperately embarrassing failure to qualify, I'd spent the seven months leading up to Euro 2008 expecting to hate every minute of it. I'd perceived that each game would be like a dagger to the heart, serving to do nothing other than remind me of England's spectacular underachievement. However, in our absence, I found that I could simply enjoy the football for what it was, with the quality on display as good as I'd seen at an international tournament for a long time. Having a few bets on the games while watching with the lads over a couple of pints helped too.

I got down to Headingley Stadium for the first time in years to watch Yorkshire play in the cricket. There was something very therapeutic about sitting in the north-east upper stand, completely alone, and watching a few hours of slow-paced sport in the sun. It felt like the stadium was a fortress from the outside world when I was in there, nothing seemed to matter in the best possible way.

The undoubted highlight from a fandom point of view was the rise of Andy Murray. I had Wimbledon on in my bedroom whenever I was at home, and Murray's victory over eighth seed Richard Gasquet in the fourth round was the best comeback victory I'd seen from a British player. Murray showed an incredible combination of technical, mental, and physical strength to outlast the more experienced Gasquet over five sets. Eventual champion Rafael Nadal proved too strong for him in their quarter-final, but dramatically, that wasn't to be the case at the US Open.

As much as I'd watched of Murray, and as much as I believed that he had the potential to challenge for Grand Slams, I hadn't expected it to happen so quickly. The hard courts of

Flushing Meadows had long been touted as Murray's favourite surface, but it was still remarkable to see him battle his way through to the semi-finals at just twenty-one years old. His run included another incredible comeback win, this time over Austrian Jurgen Melzer, before victories over the highly-regarded Stanislas Wawrinka and Juan-Martin del Potro, which set up a last-four clash with Nadal.

I couldn't believe what I was watching as Murray completely outclassed Nadal to take the first set 6-2. He then nicked the second set on a tie-break, and although many thought that Nadal would mount a trademark comeback after he took the third 6-4, Murray closed the match out in the fourth to reach his first-ever Slam final. It was a performance that made the world of tennis sit up and take notice for the first time.

I was so in awe of Murray's brilliance that I got myself well and truly fired up for the final. With New York being five hours ahead, I got a few beers in and planned for a late night, all in the hope that our man could somehow repeat what he'd done to Nadal against the imperious Roger Federer.

As Federer ripped Murray to bits in three lightning-quick sets, I lambasted myself for forgetting that I didn't get to experience joy as a sports fan. Who on earth was I to think that somebody that I supported would win something? It was like I was watching one of Leeds United's 3-0 cup final defeats again, I felt so down in the aftermath, and couldn't help but assign partial responsibility to myself for the outcome.

A rational man would have taken Murray's brilliant overall performance to represent a hugely successful tournament, but that meant nothing to me. I was far happier resenting the world for denying me fandom glory, even if I was grateful to have another sporting entity through which to channel my erratic emotions.

A few weeks into the 2008/09 football season, I got chatting to a lad that worked in the warehouse at my dad's work. My old man was the IT manager, and I was there to provide basic support in the offices upstairs, although I quite often found myself talking to the warehouse staff about football when I was down in the shared canteen. It was my last week there before heading back to Newcastle for my final uni year, and I told this chap that I was going to Swindon for Leeds' match that weekend.

I'd signed up for club membership for the second successive season, and after enjoying being at Headingley on my own so much watching the cricket, I decided that I wanted to take a few trips around the country to watch Leeds on my own too. However, when I mentioned that I was getting to Swindon via a bus and a train to this lad, he told me that I should go with him.

He was a friendly, personable bloke, but was pretty aggressive with it, and if I'm honest, I didn't know how to turn him down. Without me even saying 'yes', he got straight on the phone to the guy who arranged the coach travel for him and his mates and asked if there was a spare seat for me. The guy on the other end of the phone confirmed, and suddenly, I was off to Swindon with a group of people about whom I knew nothing.

When the Friday rocked around, he popped up to the office and told me that the coach would be departing from outside a particular Leeds city centre pub at 5 am. With our game kicking off at 3 pm, I had no idea why we were leaving so early, but this wasn't my operation. All my new mate instructed was to be there on time with a fair few beers.

I met some of the lads at the pub that night intending to have a quiet couple. I'd stocked up my dad's fridge with eight cans ready to take to town with me at 4.30 am, and intended on having two or three pints before sloping off for an early night. The next thing I knew, my 4.20 am alarm was going off.

In the absence of all coordination and coherence, I stood up, before falling straight back over. I was still completely pissed and could barely stand up. I sat down for a moment to try and gather my thoughts, at which point a few vague memories started to fall in to place. The lads and I had unsurprisingly got carried away, headed into town, made the somewhat out of character decision to go to a club, before I'd rolled in at 3 am.

If I'd have slept for a little longer I might have been in big trouble, but the fact that I'd only had eighty minutes kip worked in my favour. Within a few minutes, I felt fantastic again, and I grabbed the eight cans of lager that I'd bought the night before and headed out into the early morning to catch my taxi.

When I turned up at the meeting point at 4.55 am to see the bus waiting for me, I jumped on before my new mate shouted my name from the back of the bus. He beckoned me down, and I joined him and a couple of his young pals, having walked past a very interesting-looking crowd of men in the process.

Making me feel instantly at home, he introduced me to the other chaps, and informed them that I was 'a top lad, pure Leeds this one'. Having cracked open a can to essentially continue my night out, an enormous bald man soon made his way to the back of the bus and demanded that we all opened our mouths. He subsequently poured far too much Jagermeister in, at which point I realised what to expect.

As we commenced the estimated four-hour journey, I mostly sat in silence while the other lads on the bus gave each other constant shit. The majority of them skinheads, and all of them with broad Yorkshire accents, I was entirely out of place but delighted to be so.

After one of the younger lads discovered that I was at university, I was soon christened with the nickname 'student', and was slandered for being a cheapskate, posh, and for robbing everyone else on the bus of their taxes. I decided against informing one bloke that the state did not fund university in England, never mind that mummy was paying my tuition fees.

Within a couple of hours, I was a lovely, warm drunk again, and felt like I was already part of the furniture. I had a nickname, everyone was incredibly welcoming and nice to me, and I could hold my own with anybody that wanted to talk Leeds United. I even found it endearing that most conversations ended up with me being called a 'posh cunt' due to my relatively neutral accent.

I got into some fascinating conversations with some of the older lads on the bus, who freely told me stories about their personal lives, while also regaling tales of bygone away-days. One guy explained that he'd been good friends with one of the Leeds fans that were tragically killed in Istanbul back in 2000, while another went into detail about some of the organised fights that he'd had with fans of other clubs during the 1980s. My mate had prompted him, which made me feel a little uncomfortable, but he opened up gladly. It was captivating.

I was due to head back to university a couple of days later, and couldn't help but see these guys as being far more interesting than the students that I'd met. It was just a group of working-class Yorkshiremen, but they had so much more to say for themselves, were far better at holding a conversation, and made me laugh more than I had done on any occasion at university.

There was an interesting occurrence just outside Birmingham, as we passed another bus full of Leeds fans. As we overtook them, the fans from the other bus starting doing the 'Leeds Salute' at us, expressing their unity as fellow fans. I was on the brink of doing the same back before every single man on our bus started shouting 'FUCK OFF', sticking 'two's' up at them, and aggressively banging on the windows. I didn't understand it, but one of the older lads that I'd befriended was quick to tell me that we weren't open to other fans, even if they were our own. 'It's us against the world on this bus; you need to learn that if you want to come with us again'.

Listening to those words from a scummy, angry Leeds fan from Wakefield was an incredibly poignant moment for me. I wasn't remotely like any of these blokes, but the phrase 'us against the world' resonated so powerfully that I instantly felt like a part of the tribe.

Having put a few cans away by now, I started to feel comfortable to join in with the aggressive behaviour on the bus. These blokes were coming out with some unimaginably horrific comments, but they'd say it in a bizarrely warm way, and would often follow up by hugging the guy next to them. It was a baffling environment to find myself immersed in, but I loved it.

At just after 9 am, we arrived into a small town called Abingdon, a short distance away from Swindon, where a pub had opened it's doors early just for us. I learned that the bus' organiser-in-chief called around the local establishments before every away game to find somewhere that was willing to open early for a group of rowdy Leeds United fans. I asked the man himself how he managed it, and he said the key was to find an independent pub or social club, in which the landlord recognised the opportunity to make a lot of money. We ended up staying there for about five hours, which will indeed have been well worth his while, even if we were a bit of a handful.

As I got back on the bus to head towards Swindon, a couple of the lads were shouting obscenities at some innocent locals on the Abingdon streets. The group of us were collectively so drunk that I started to doubt whether we'd be let into the ground. Apparently, they were like this every week, and stewards at football grounds would have one hell of a task on their hands if they wanted to reject large groups of Leeds fans for being drunk.

There were no problems getting in, and when I started to look at my ticket to see where we'd be sitting, my mate told me that I wouldn't need it. I'd been to a fair few away games before, but had always discreetly sat in the home end as it had been so hard to get tickets in the away end. I wasn't aware that it was an absolute free for all, but that was all part of why Swindon was my best stadium experience to date.

The raw noise that we were generating was reminiscent of a Premier League game against Manchester United at Elland Road, and any advantage that Swindon might ordinarily have had from their fans at the County Ground was rendered redundant. It was pure passion in every direction, everybody singing, everybody gesturing, everybody angry, but in the best possible way. As if I wasn't already fired up enough off the back of a night out and twelve beers, that moment took me into my absolute element.

After ten minutes of the game, I feared the worst, after left-back Alan Sheehan was sent off for a reckless challenge, leaving us to contend with ten men for eighty minutes. That only served to unify our players though, and we deservedly took the lead through Jermaine Beckford halfway through the first half. The celebrations with the lads were raucous to say the least.

When Swindon equalised on the stroke of half-time, we had every right to feel aggrieved, having been by far the better team. Manager Gary McAllister must have asked the players for more of the same during his team talk, as we came out in the second half and played brilliantly, with Neil Kilkenny and Beckford securing all three points for us. It was an outstanding team display, and the atmosphere on the bus as we got back onboard outside the ground was nothing short of phenomenal.

For the first half an hour of the journey back to Leeds, the chants were non-stop. The lads must have gone through every single Leeds United song going, and I was right in amongst all of it. It seemed like the perfect balance between joyful anger and just about staying within the parameters of acceptable behaviour, which was exactly where I wanted to be. Then, with a derogatory chant about Manchester United, things took a turn for the worse.

Having started with a song about the Munich air disaster, an incident in which several Manchester United players had died in the 1950s, the lads moved on to a slightly more innocent chant about 'shooting Chelsea scum', before singing about George Best's alcoholism. I joined in with all three chants, feeling slightly ashamed about the first one, although I did eventually cease my involvement as the songs moved away from football.

Somebody started a repetitive 'FUCK OFF TURKEY, FUCK OFF TURKEY' chant, which gained the full support of the bus as a show of unity for the Istanbul tragedy, before I started to feel very uncomfortable with what followed. 'I WOULD RATHER BE A P*** THAN A TURK, I WOULD RATHER BE A P*** THAN A TURK, I WOULD RATHER BE A P***, RATHER BE A P***, RATHER BE A P*** THAN A TURK'.

With one of my best friends being British-Pakistani, and having had many friends over the years of the same background, I swiftly sat down and muted myself. The line had been crossed, and I wanted no part of such vile chants. However, I take great shame in admitting that it did make me laugh, which I still feel horrifically guilty about to this day.

The only defence that I have for myself is that I didn't perceive this chant to be a sign of actual racism. I just thought it was throwaway, stupid nonsense, solely designed to either make people laugh or cause offence without genuine racist intent. Clearly, I was very naive to believe that none of the lads held anything concrete against either Pakistani or Turkish people.

Despite that considerable blip, we stopped off at a service station to pick up a few more cans, and the journey home was one of glorious triumph. By the end, I had many blokes proclaiming that I was 'alright for a student', and was encouraged to join them for every away game.

I headed back to university a couple of days later, and within a week, I knew that the students there really weren't the right crowd for me. I made the decision that I *would* go back on their bus, and things would get a hell of a lot worse than what I'd already witnessed.

23

Anti-socialism

I lived a polarised existence during my final year of university; the only socialising that I did was anti-social, and I became anti-social to the point at which I barely socialised.

Within ten minutes of my first Psychology lecture of the year, I walked out of the lecture hall and never went back. All of the material that we needed for our coursework and exams was online, so aside from the fact that I might have learned a few bits and pieces with more ease, I didn't need to be there. I had more than enough faith in my intelligence to be able to teach myself what I needed to know, and not going in meant that I didn't have to be around so many mundane people.

On top of that, I pretty much stopped going on nights out altogether. I didn't enjoy anything about being out with other students, and having done OK with girls in my first couple of years, I felt relieved of the ridiculous pressure that I'd been putting on myself to keep trying to get with them. In two years, I hadn't met a single girl that I'd been attracted to enough to make me want to make more effort, and without that, I felt no desire to socialise at all.

With three of the six lads that I'd been living with the previous year having moved home after finishing their courses, the three of us that remained got a smaller flat between us. My good friend Rout, one of the Leeds lads, had also finished uni but had stayed on in Newcastle to work with it being his spiritual home. The other lad, a bloke called Joel who Rout had met in first year, was a very introverted chap, and if he wasn't at uni, he'd usually be in his room doing his own thing.

With Rout being out at work most of the time, and Joel often keeping to himself, I effectively had the flat to myself for most of each week. It was incredibly liberating, as I was able to watch whatever sport was on TV whenever I pleased, I had plenty of space to do my uni work, and never at any time did I feel like I was going to be interrupted.

I also used the newfound time and space that I had to start playing and writing a lot of music, which I'd done bits and pieces of during high school. I treated myself to a new guitar and keyboard and found the writing process to be a very therapeutic method for channelling the various dark thoughts and feelings that I continued to have. On the whole, it was a very peaceful existence, and the only time that I'd be in social situations was at work, or on Leeds United away days with the lads I'd been to Swindon with.

In a way that couldn't have been more different, travelling around the country with these angry, aggressive football fans was also therapeutic. If I wasn't in my flat very slowly allowing my internal conflict to filter its way out of my body and mind, I was shouting, chanting, and screaming with a load of volatile blokes. The two methods were equally effective, even if they were polarised in how constructive and destructive they were.

Before Christmas, I travelled to Peterborough United, Millwall, Southend United, and Tranmere Rovers with them. As I continued to fume with the world at large without having any idea as to why, I felt like I could relate to anti-social behaviour more than social behaviour. Ironically, the irrational seemed to make a lot more sense.

Before Peterborough, we stopped at a social club a few miles out of town for our big pre-match drinking session. When I nipped to the toilet for a piss just before we were heading to the ground, I found one of the lads trying to rip one of the urinals off its hinges. 'FUCKING STUPID THING, GET THE FUCK OUT YOU CUNT'. I didn't see it happen as I was in one of the cubicles at the time, but I heard a huge crack and a thud, before opening the door to find the urinal on the ground and a massive hole in the wall. The bloke then strutted out of there as though he'd taken care of some serious business in a very professional manner.

En-route to Tranmere, I'd popped out the back of the pub that we were in to have a chat with one of the lads while he had a cigarette to find that two of the other lads had started a fire in a dumpster. They had no explanation for their behaviour at all, but I couldn't help but oblige when they encouraged me to pour some of my drink in to get the flames going a little more.

We eventually had to go inside and ask for a bucket of water as it got a bit out of control, under the ruse that it had started accidentally via a finished cigarette. All was well that ended well when we managed to put it out, but had we not, we could have been looking at an arson charge, or possibly even worse.

Neither of these compared to Millwall though, as any football fans reading might expect. By 1.30 pm in London, it had already been a chaotic day, as we'd set off from Leeds at 4 am, eleven hours before kick-off. We'd had to leave our pub stop a bit earlier than usual to head to the ground, and were told by the driver to remove every ounce of booze from the coach. We then drove for fifteen minutes or so, before being met by the police about five miles from the ground.

An officer got on the coach to check it for alcohol while scanning every one of us with vindicated mistrust. After seeing that we were clean, even if we were all incredibly fired up, he then disembarked the coach, before getting into one of four police cars at the side of the road in front of us. I then watched in amazement as the four vehicles flanked us, two in front, and two behind, with the lead car even having its lights flashing.

As we slowly made our way towards the ground, a strange kind of tension started to build among the lads that I couldn't put my finger on. Everybody had gone a little quieter, some of them were rubbing their hands together, while others looked a little nervous. It felt like being among a group of soldiers about to go into battle during a war.

As we got to within a mile of the ground, we saw a couple of groups of men with blue Millwall scarves heading for the match. As we passed them, one of our lads banged on the window and started shouting and screaming in their general direction. It prompted an angry response from our adversaries, which then led to almost every man on our bus charging to that side, banging on the windows, and shouting furious obscenities.

The closer we got, the more groups we passed, and our lads got progressively louder, angrier, and more abusive. 'I'LL FUCKING KILL YOU WHEN I GET OFF THIS BUS, I'LL FUCKING KILL YOU', I remember one of the lads shouting, as one of the Millwall fans threw a cigarette lighter at the window. The police presence wasn't making a jot of difference.

I spent most of the final mile of the journey sitting in a

kind of shocked state of paralysis, unable to comprehend what was happening. However, I was soon banging on the windows myself, trying to catch the eye of any Millwall fan that I could, and shouting things like 'FUCKING COME ON THEN, FUCKING COME ON'. I was no fighter, I'd barely punched someone in my life up to that point, but the mob mentality had totally consumed me. In that very moment, I was ready to get off the bus and head out on to the battlefield with all of my comrades.

Just as the bus pulled in alongside the ground, a stone thrown at the bus cracked one of the window panes. It sent the lads to the next level in terms of their animated aggression. Before they had a chance to try and get off, which a few had in mind, we drove through into a car park that was cordoned off by police to keep the fans separated.

With all the lads now looking out of the back window, we saw two police officers dragging away the man that had thrown the stone. Remarkably, this entirely changed the mood among the lads to one of ecstatic jubilation, and the group broke out into a chorus of 'WE ARE LEEDS, WE ARE LEEDS, WE ARE LEEDS'. That five-mile coach ride was genuinely one of the biggest thrills of my life up to that point.

Sadly, things on the pitch weren't going so well. We lost all four of the away games that I attended before Christmas, and also suffered a humiliating FA Cup second-round exit at the hands of non-league Histon FC. Eventually, after a 3-1 defeat at Milton Keynes Dons made it five defeats on the bounce in all competitions, chairman Ken Bates sacked Gary McAllister.

McAllister had tried to encourage us to play an attacking brand of football during his time in charge, but we'd never really looked like becoming a good team under him. He'd managed to get a lot out of a couple of players, and he deserved credit for throwing exciting young prospect Fabian Delph into the first team. Still, nine League One defeats before Christmas was unsustainable for a club that expected automatic promotion, and it was no surprise that Bates wielded the axe with us not even in the play-off picture.

There was a lot of optimism around when we appointed former Blackpool coach Simon Grayson as our new manager. Grayson was born in Ripon, was a lifelong fan of the club, had been on the books as a player for a few years in the late 80s and early 90s, and had guided Blackpool to promotion from League One a couple of years earlier. He knew the club inside out, he knew what the fans would want to see, and he knew how to get a team out of that division. It seemed like the perfect fit.

Grayson started with a well-earned point against high-flying Leicester City on Boxing Day, before guiding us to five wins from the next seven games to get us right back in the play-off mix. However, it soon transpired that my belief that we'd turned the corner had been naive, as I experienced one of the worst twenty-four hours of my life on Tuesday 17th February 2009.

After travelling down to watch our 1-0 defeat at Walsall at the end of January, I went into our trip to Hereford United coming off the back of five straight away-day losses. It had all started so well against Swindon Town back in September for me, but I'd had no luck whatsoever since then. With Hereford being bottom of League One, I was extremely confident that my curse was about to be broken.

I took the train from Newcastle at 8 am with the coach

leaving from the usual spot at 10 am. After I arrived in Leeds, I picked up eight cans, jumped on the coach, and started to get fired up for another massive game of football. We'd been beaten at local rivals Huddersfield Town three days earlier, which meant that nothing short of three points would suffice to keep us in the hunt for the top six.

The journey down was far more subdued than usual, with many of the younger lads that I usually sat with not able to make it because of work. There were still plenty of folk on the beers, but the bus was pretty tame, which made the long journey south-west seem even longer. The fact that I had alcohol meant that a situation like that was never going to bother me, though.

When we eventually arrived in Hereford at about 2.30 pm, things started to liven up a little. We set up shop in a social club just outside the city, and when a couple of regulars vacated the pool table, a group of four of us decided to have a tournament.

By way of me being 'student', I was tasked with setting up the tournament as a result of me being 'the only cunt 'ere wi' brains', and I even called myself 'student' on the darts blackboard I used to display the format. It was a simple round-robin, everybody played each other once with the top two facing off in the final.

I won two of my three games, while a quiet, but strongly-built bald bloke won all three of his, which left the two of us to play the final. A bit of a crowd gathered for it, adding pride to the £20 prize at stake with each player having put down a fiver at the start.

I played one of the best games of pool I'd ever played to pot the black with my opponent still having five balls remaining on the table, to which I received a warm round of applause. However, as I walked around the table to shake my adversary's hand, I picked up the £20 from atop the table first, which sparked a furious reaction from him.

He refused to shake my hand, before squaring up to me in demand of a rematch. He claimed that I'd disrespected him by picking up the money first, which on reflection I agree is quite an annoying thing to have done, but his reaction was way overboard. Out of the corner of my eye, I saw a couple of the other lads looking concerned as this bloke got right in my face, which suggested to me that everybody knew that he was trouble, and didn't know how to deal with him.

I'd always struggled with social disharmony, which had made me quite good at diffusing conflict over the years, so I kept calm even as I appeared to be on the brink of getting a smack. As the bloke insisted on a rematch for another £20, I told him that I wouldn't play him for money, but that I'd give him his rematch and buy us each a pint instead. It was the perfect solution, as clearly all that mattered to him was the pride, and I went and grabbed a couple of beers before allowing him to break.

To be fair to him, he was a good player, and he eventually beat me with two balls to spare. Hoping to maintain the peace once more, I went over to shake his hand, to which he said, 'you can fuck off with your handshake you student cunt'.

It was a bizarre turn of events and one that left me feeling pretty angry, bearing in mind that I'd just bought him a pint and shown grace in both victory and defeat. However, I knew better than to express my displeasure, as there was absolutely nothing in it for me. He obviously had major anger issues himself, and by way of him calling me a 'student cunt', I wondered whether he had a bit of an inferiority complex too. One of the older lads came over and told me to ignore him, and I thought little more of it and cracked on with my day.

For the first time during an away-day experience for me, we walked to the ground from the place at which we'd stopped pre-match. It wasn't great timing to do that either, as the weather was utterly horrendous. The February hail and snow was interchangeable amid a blowing gale, and as the ground came in to view, I realised that we would have little protection from the elements.

The capacity of Hereford's Edgar Street stadium was only about 5000, and, there must have been 2000 Leeds fans there. For the first time in my life, I found myself in a standing area of a stadium for a competitive Leeds United match, although that delighted me. The weather was awful, I was on the terraces, I was 300 miles from where I lived on a Tuesday night, the pitch was an absolute state; this was League One.

We made a solid start to the game and won a penalty when winger Andy Robinson was brought down in the box. However, loan signing Lee Trundle, who came with a reputation of technical excellence, trickery, and goalscoring prowess, didn't have it in his armoury to beat Hereford United's goalkeeper from twelve yards.

Just before half-time, with the winter weather unrelenting, Dennison Myrie-Williams fired past our goalkeeper Casper Ankergren to give the 24th-placed side the lead. It seemed to come out of nowhere, but I don't think that anybody begrudged Hereford their lead, as we'd been horrendous since Trundle's penalty miss.

With the indoor area of our stand providing zero protection

from the cold at half-time, I bought myself a pint to try and warm myself through. Unfortunately, I could barely drink it because my hands were so cold, and after downing about half of it, I threw the rest away. It was reaching the point at which every little detail of the day was going horribly wrong, and I could feel a rage building up inside of me. I needed my football team to do something.

As the second half started, the wind appeared to have changed direction, and it kept blowing my hood from over my head. My ears and hands were perishing, Leeds were losing at Hereford, and unless we could turn the match around, I had one hell of an overnight journey back to the opposite side of the country to stew over the likelihood of another season in the third tier of English football.

The next twenty minutes was as bad as anything that I've ever seen at a live football match. Neither side had a clue what they were doing, there wasn't even an attempt to string a couple of passes together, long balls were being aimlessly pumped forward in the howling wind, and I felt like they could have played for days without scoring another goal between them. I was wrong about the last part.

When former Manchester United striker Febian Brandy made it 2-0 to Hereford, I felt like I'd experienced some kind of internal explosion. Feeling more anger than ever before in my life, I screamed 'YOU SET OF FUCKING MORONS, WHAT THE FUCK IS WRONG WITH YA LEEDS? WHAT THE FUCK IS THIS?', which yielded a couple of surprised looks from the people around me.

I stormed away from the terrace, not knowing where I was going, all the while feeling an overwhelming desire to run away from my entire life. However, as I charged around the back area of the stadium, I realised that I couldn't even run away from that football match, as I was 300 miles from where I lived, and my only route home was on a bus full of people that I barely knew. I was all revved up with no place to go; something was going to have to give.

As I strode purposefully into the toilets, I walked straight up to the cubicle in front of me and booted the door as hard as I could. The top hinge came loose, and the door rested against one of the walls of the cubicle, barely being held up by the bottom hinge.

As I took a step back from my destruction, I saw two blokes taking a piss that I'd not even noticed when I'd marched in there. One of them was a young lad of a similar age to me, who laughed, while the other was an older, softer looking man, who looked at me like I was the most disgusting piece of dirt that he'd ever seen in his life. It felt like he'd stared deep into my soul and seen the devil; it made me feel awful.

I got out of there as quickly as I could and saw a couple of stewards heading towards the toilet as I immersed myself back among the fans in the terrace. I held my hood up over my head to hide my face and submitted to the shame and anxiety that had instantly encompassed me. I was typical football scum.

Soon after, the Leeds fans started singing 'WE'RE SHIT, AND WE'RE SICK OF IT', a chant that resonated so deeply with me. I was so sick of Leeds being shit, and I was so sick of life being shit. I hated everything in the world, with the number one thing on that list being myself.

The game finished 2-0, but the day's events hadn't finished just yet. The bus was the most subdued I'd ever known it after a match, with everybody freezing cold, feeling a bit hungover from the day's drinking, and staring down the barrel of an awful journey home. The level of quiet only served to accentuate what followed.

'OI, YOU! ARE YOU A P***?' shouted my adversary from the pool tournament, in the direction of a dark-haired bloke a few rows in front of him. As everybody turned around, the young lad that he was targeting asked if he was talking to him, to which the madman replied, 'YEAH I'M TALKING TO YOU, DO YOU SEE ANY OTHER FUCKING P**** ON THIS BUS?'.

The guy had quite a tanned complexion but was very obviously white. It would have been horrendous enough had it actually been a Pakistani person, but you could argue that how bizarre it was made it even worse for the young lad on the receiving end. He had no idea what to say.

Attempting to defuse the situation, he replied by saying 'I'm not a p***, no', and then gave his name, which was a typically caucasian British name. At this point, the madman yelled, 'THERE IS ONE THING THAT WE WILL NEVER HAVE ON THIS BUS, AND THAT'S P**** AND N******, SO YOU BETTER PROMISE ME RIGHT NOW THAT YOU'RE NOT A FUCKING P***'.

He was disgusting, vile, beastly; any word that describes the pits of humanity. I couldn't help but be grateful for having lost that final game of pool against this bloke, as, by this evidence, it would have ended very, very badly. I'd been right to intuit that there was something very wrong with him, and my angry outburst at a cubicle door suddenly didn't seem so anti-social. That was a sign of the calibre of people that I was associating with; I'd just kicked a door off it's hinges, and it was by no means the worst behaviour of the day, not by a long shot.

I couldn't sleep at all on the journey back and had all sorts of thoughts running through my head. *What if they had CCTV in those toilets at Hereford, what if I got arrested, what if I got banned from attending all Leeds United games.* At least the last thought wouldn't have been so bad, bearing in mind that I supported the worst team in the country when comparing expectation to achievement.

After arriving back into Leeds at about 2.30 am, I walked to the train station to discover that I'd have to wait three hours for the next train to Newcastle. I'd not done my research for the northbound journey, having simply purchased an open return, and I sat in the wide-open, perishing train station, slipping in and out of shivering, hungover sleep for three long hours.

I eventually got to bed in Newcastle at 8 am, having left at 8 am the previous day. The only thing that I could claim to have achieved in that twenty-four hours was that I'd visited a new football stadium, although I wasn't sure that Edgar Street even classified as that.

When I woke up that afternoon after a few hours kip, I promised myself that I'd never go on that bus again.

24

Positive self-destruction

The weekend after the Hereford debacle, Rodney and I went to Manchester for a lad called Craig's (one of my few university friends) 21st birthday party. He was a huge Scum fan, as were his family, and we spent the Saturday afternoon in their living room watching Soccer Saturday.

With Leeds drawing 0-0 at home to Cheltenham Town at half-time, I experienced another poignant moment in my sport-supporting life, as a family of Manchester United fans started telling Rodney and me how sorry they felt for us. A failure to beat Cheltenham at home while in the presence of Manchester United fans may have been the end of the road for me.

At the start of the day, there'd been a few friendly jibes fired at us by the Scum contingent, jibes that I'd received well enough, but to which I had no response. The jokes were all very obvious, we'd had arguably the biggest fall from grace in football history, had recently been knocked out of the FA Cup by a non-league team, and thousands of our fans were still stupid enough to take a Tuesday off work to travel to places like Hereford to watch us lose to a team with about 1000 fans.

Scum, on the other hand, were well on their way to a third straight Premier League title, were current European

Champions, and had won everything there was to win on multiple occasions during my lifetime. What joke could I have possibly made back to them? One about the Munich air disaster? I would never have done this to a lovely family whose home I was in, of course, not to mention that my recent horror at some of the coach lads had moved me away from that kind of behaviour forever.

Just as I started to accept that another embarrassing low point was impending, Jonny Howson popped up with a goal early in the second half, which led me to run around the living room cheering and screaming raucously. It was one of my biggest ever releases of aggression and anger, and I think it took the room a little by surprise. In the immediate aftermath, it drew a comment from one of Craig's mates, who was an Arsenal fan.

'Fucking hell mate, it's only Cheltenham', he said, in a calm and measured, but judgemental tone of voice. However, when the words left his lips, the burning desire inside me was to look him straight in the eye and scream, *HAVE YOU GOT ANY FUCKING CLUE WHAT I'VE BEEN THROUGH AS A FAN? HAVE YOU EVER TAKEN TWENTY-FOUR HOURS TO TRAVEL TO AND FROM HEREFORD TO WATCH YOUR TEAM LOSE COMFORTABLY TO BOTTOM OF THE LEAGUE? DO YOU KNOW WHAT IT'S LIKE TO SUPPORT A TEAM THAT'S NEVER WON ANYTHING? DO YOU KNOW WHAT IT'S LIKE TO SUPPORT A TEAM THAT'S NEVER ACHIEVED ANYTHING? FUCK YOU, AND YOUR ENTITLED ARSENAL BULLSHIT, YOU'VE GOT NO FUCKING IDEA WHAT IT'S LIKE TO BE A REAL FOOTBALL FAN!.*

Fortunately, I was in control of my ethics enough to be able to keep my reaction in order. I turned to him and calmly stated, 'Come back and tell me how to react when you're scrapping away in League One mid-table mate'. I gave him a little smile afterwards, and he returned the favour before offering me a 'cheers' toast with his beer. I appreciated the gesture.

Soon after, Howson bagged his second to make it 2-0, yielding a more relieved angry-aggressive response from me. However, on this occasion, I was particularly appreciative of just how animated Rodney was. As one of my very best mates, I think Rodney must have seen that I needed some support after that mini-altercation, and although he wasn't usually as emotional as me, he was right by my side on that occasion.

After the final whistle went, Craig's dad, who had been a season ticket holder at Old Trafford for decades, asked if he could have a quick word with me in the kitchen. I'd thought he was going to tell me to calm down a little or ask me for some help with something relating to Craig, but he instead said something that caught me totally off-guard. 'As much as it pains me to say it as a United fan, I hope Leeds get promoted for your sake, I've never seen a football team mean as much to someone as Leeds do to you'.

The words pierced me in the same way that my new manager's effort to sort my tax situation out had done the previous year; it warmed me through to know that somebody wanted the best for me. It was as though he'd seen the desperation in my celebration; like he knew something about me that I'd not known about myself. The reality was that every one of those over-emotional goal celebrations had been a subconscious cry for help, and although I barely knew him, Craig's dad had answered my call on that occasion.

As a result of the retrospective understanding that I'd received from that Arsenal fan, alongside those shows of support from Rodney and Craig's dad, I went out that night in a very positive mindset. I was still all over the place emotionally and had uncontainable energy inside of me that I somehow needed to release. I wasn't going to do that by trying to get with a girl, as I was far too erratic to even come across as attractive at that stage, so I decided to take a different approach.

I was incredibly drunk as the clock reached about 2 am, and with the night drawing to an end, I told Craig and the people that we were with that I needed them to come out on to the bar's balcony. We were on the Deansgate Locks in Manchester city centre, and as the group joined me outside, I simply stated, 'Happy 21st Craig'.

I then proceeded to climb on to the barrier that separated the balcony from the Bridgewater canal, which wasn't high with it being the ground floor, at which point a bouncer caught sight of what I was about to do. He started pushing the crowd out of the way and charging towards me to stop my act of stupidity, which only served to encourage me. As he closed to within a few metres, I shot him a confirmatory grin, before leaping ungracefully into the filthy water below.

I was so drunk that I didn't feel the cold, and as my head came out of the water, I received a hero's response of laughter and applause. I lapped up the adulation, before clambering out the other side and finding some shelter to try and dry off my sodden clothes. Fortunately, a couple of the other lads that were staying at Craig's came out soon after, and I was in a taxi back to a warm home before long. I still look back on the moment fondly with Craig to this day.

That was the start of a new phase of self-destructive behaviour for me, what I classed as being a positive, fun kind. I'd get ludicrously drunk, and do some of the most obscene things imaginable in an attempt to gain positive attention from whoever would give it to me. I genuinely don't think that it was a coincidence that this happened alongside an incredible upturn in form from Leeds United.

After beating Cheltenham Town, we lost only one of our final fifteen games, which was at table-topping Leicester City in the 92nd minute, a game from which we at least deserved a point. We managed eleven wins, and three draws to finish fourth and played the best football that I'd seen from a Leeds United team since the David O'Leary days.

When I was back home during the Easter break from uni, Andy, Rodney and I met up in Headingley at midday and walked to Elland Road with a couple of beers in the glorious sunshine. I felt euphoric en route to the ground, partly because of the weather and being with two of my best mates, but also feeling like I knew that Leeds were going to win. Yes, we were only playing Tranmere Rovers, but there'd been so many times in recent years that I'd had absolutely no faith in us as a team whatsoever. Feeling confident that we could beat any team was strangely empowering, and we subsequently strolled to a 3-1 victory.

After the match, the three of us went out in town and got riotously drunk. As part of the ridiculous nature of my behaviour at the time, Rodney and I played multiple games of 'rock, paper, scissors' for who had to buy two pints for themselves from the bar, one to drink, and one to pour on your head. I lost on three straight occasions and was delighted to have done so. Andy's contribution was to run home from town after fourteen hours on the booze, which led to him tripping up and smashing his face to pieces on the concrete. It turned out that he was OK, which left me happy to ponder how much I'd have given to have seen CCTV footage of his fall.

So, it was the play-offs once more, and who better to be pitted against than everybody's favourite team to hate, Millwall. They'd become a very solid side in 2008/09, hard to beat, physically imposing, with strikers that were always likely to score at some point during any given match. Still, we were the form team, and the only thing that made me doubt whether we could beat them over two legs was how badly scarred I was from our inability to perform in big matches historically.

I'd tried, and failed, to get tickets to the away leg, but decided to come back to Leeds from uni for the full week of the two matches to watch the first game with Rodney, before going to Elland Road for the second. With the away leg coming first, I believed that any result would be enough for us, as I had total belief that we could win with our home crowd behind us.

I met Rodney at 11 am at one of our favourite Headingley pubs for the first leg, which turned out to be a cagey affair. There was nothing to choose between the two teams, but Neil Harris nicked a goal for Millwall in the second half to give the Lions the edge going into Thursday's match. It was a tough defeat to take, but Rodney and I still felt confident going into the second leg.

We spent that Saturday hammering the lagers, even though Rodney was running the Leeds half-marathon the following day. His girlfriend Ruth turned up to the pub late in the afternoon to find us smashing the pies that we'd ordered into each other's faces, and challenging each other to see who could stuff the most peas inside their nostrils. I say challenging each other, Rodney was encouraging me, and I managed to win in a battle against myself with fourteen peas. Ruth was a great sport before she rightly implied that it might be time to go home.

I spent the four days between the two Millwall games getting prepared for my final exams, as I only had a couple of weeks at university left to navigate. It had been an awful experience for me, and I was utterly delighted to be getting out, and discussions that I'd been having with my pals Mel and Neil about going travelling again only made things better. The plan was to work in any old job for a year to save up, and then take off on an unplanned adventure to see where the world took us. It was a hugely exciting prospect.

Amid all this, it took what seemed like an eternity for the second leg to arrive, but when it finally did, the atmosphere at Elland Road was electric. We were right in amongst the hard-core supporters in the Kop, a far cry from the Family Stand upper tier for the home game against Carlisle the previous year.

The atmosphere had been extremely mixed that night, primarily because of the unpredictable nature of the team under Gary McAllister, which made even his most ardent of supporters have their doubts. This year, under Simon Grayson, every fan in the stadium knew that we were a quality side that had every chance of turning the tie around.

We didn't have too many chances in the first half but were undoubtedly the better side, and probably should have been a goal up. As it was, there were no goals after forty-five minutes, and the tie was still Millwall's to lose.

There'd been many Elland Road occasions on which our fans had attempted to show their support by being vocal, but had only served to create an intense and pressurised atmosphere for our players. However, it was pure support on this occasion, with no anxiety, and no overbearing weight of expectation; it was a beautiful outpouring of hope and belief.

Responding to the energy inside the ground, we won a corner straight away, which dramatically led to a penalty after a foul on centre-half Sam Sodje. Free-scoring Jermaine Beckford stepped up, but his spot-kick was saved by Millwall' keeper David Forde, in a moment that made you think that it might not be our year once again.

However, with the fans refusing to be defeated, we were soon on the attack again, and an inch-perfect cross from Ben Parker found Luciano Becchio sliding in between Millwall's centre-halves to tap into an empty net. The celebrations were out of this world. We'd scored, we were level, we were no longer losing the tie, and now there would surely only be one winner with thirty-five Elland Road minutes to go.

We were well in the ascendancy for the next fifteen minutes, but Millwall did brilliantly to weather the storm. As the game entered it's final quarter, the away team started to creep back into it, and the game opened up for the first time over the course of the two legs. I could sense that the scoring wasn't over and that one goal would likely send it's scorer to Wembley.

When Djimi Abdou poked in Millwall's equaliser in front of the Kop with fifteen minutes remaining, our fans still responded with pure positivity and encouragement. There was no giving up, no belief that we'd thrown it away again in spite of all of our shortcomings in recent years. Elland Road remained unified behind their Leeds United team despite how difficult it would now be to find a way to Wembley.

As it was, we huffed and puffed, going close on a couple of occasions, but just couldn't find a way past Millwall's resolute rearguard. When the final whistle went to end our season, it was a devastating, brutal sinking feeling for the fourth consecutive year.

As I turned to the lads, Rodney was in floods of tears, just as he had been when Alan Lee had scored for Ipswich Town to relegate us from the Championship, but on this occasion, he was also clapping and singing with immense pride. Bill kept singing even though he'd already lost his voice from displaying such vociferous support throughout the match.

I joined my friends, and the many other thousands of fans, in applauding our players as they lay defeated on the pitch, while the Millwall contingent celebrated in front of the few away fans that had been allowed to travel by the Football League. Our players responded, applauding back and throwing their shirts into the crowd to show their appreciation for the immense support that we'd given them. It was another desperately pain-ful night, but I experienced glory in defeat for the first time in my football-supporting tenure that evening in May 2009.

As I walked away from Elland Road, I felt as though my life had reached a turning point. I was on the brink of finishing university after three awful years, and I knew that I'd be able to take pride in earning a degree despite the challenges I'd faced psychologically. I was about to come back to Leeds to save for another travelling adventure, while my football team were showing signs of real progress for the first time since our spectacular demise. Both of these things gave me the direction, focus, and purpose that I needed to find positivity in the world again. I just needed to channel my self-destructive behaviours in the most positive ways possible.

25

No high without a low

One thing that I can proudly say about myself as a gambler is that I've never lost money that isn't mine. I've never placed a bet that has left me in debt, which I commend myself for to a degree, although it doesn't mean that I've not been addicted.

University may have been an awful experience for me, but I rounded it off in style on the final weekend of the 2008/09 Premier League season. I'd had a very productive year of football betting, with my online account £450 up by the time I reached the end of the campaign, and I decided that I would have one big bet to sign off for the summer.

In the aftermath of Leeds United's tragic, but inspiring end to 08/09, I decided that I was going to get a season ticket for 2009/10. With Simon Grayson appearing to have galvanised the club, my take was that next season would finally provide the glory that I'd waited seventeen long years for, and as I would be back living in Leeds for the first time in three years, all the pieces fitted. If I was going to be working a mundane job for a year to save for travelling, having Saturday at 3 pm to look forward to every week would undoubtedly provide the thrill that I would need.

I did know that it would cost in the region of £500-£600

though, which is why I thought I'd have a crack at winning that cost in one fell swoop. Hull City and Newcastle United were battling it out for survival on the last day, with Newcastle needing to better Hull's result to stay up. Having watched plenty of each team over the previous few weeks, particularly Newcastle with me living there, my take was that both sides would lose, even though they were playing against teams whose seasons were essentially over.

Hull were expected to face Manchester United's second team with a Champions League final to come for Scum the following Wednesday. Newcastle meanwhile, travelled to Aston Villa knowing that their hosts could do no better than the UEFA Cup spot that they'd already confirmed.

My hunch was that even though Hull and Newcastle were so desperate for the points, they were both so bad that they would lose anyway. I followed my hunch and stuck an outlandish £100 on the Manchester United-Aston Villa double. Ordinarily, the price would have been about EVS, bearing in mind the teams' respective league positions, but in the present circumstances, it was 5/1.

Dramatically, both Villa and Scum won 1-0, which earned me my biggest ever gambling victory by some margin of £500. I couldn't help but feel guilty about my good friend and flatmate Rout, who was a massive Newcastle fan, as I knew only too well how relegation felt. Had he been there that weekend, I probably wouldn't have put the bet on, and I might not have confirmed my 2009/10 Leeds United season ticket with my dad either.

As I packed my things to leave university, I couldn't help but wonder how different things could have been for me. Various family members had told me multiple times that it would be the best time of my life, but it couldn't have worked out any differently. Everything about it had been miserable, which was exemplified by the drastic sporting misfortune that I'd experienced.

Between September 2006 and May 2009, Leeds United were relegated and suffered two play-off losses. England failed to qualify for a major football tournament for the first time in fourteen years. Our national rugby team lost a Rugby World Cup final. Our cricketers suffered a 5-0 Ashes whitewash and endured a terrible World Cup campaign. The USA defeated Europe in the Ryder Cup for the first time in nine years. Britain's number one boxer Ricky Hatton suffered the only two defeats of his career to that point, and emerging tennis star Andy Murray lost his first major final at the US Open. There'd been a lot of pain, and the way I saw it, the sporting world owed me big.

I got back to Leeds to find that Neil had made arrangements for us to live at a house that his dad owned in Headingley. The rent was next to nothing, and bills were expected to be cheap enough for us to be able to afford Sky Sports, which we knew would be ideal for getting us through those long working weeks over the winter. We made plans to spend every weekend sitting in and watching every sporting event imaginable to ensure that we could avoid splashing our cash on big nights out in town, which was a plan that suited me down to the ground.

While Neil arranged a transfer from his job working at a bookies at university, I eventually found something after six weeks of trying, and even then I was told I wouldn't start until mid-August. Pre-uni in 2005, I'd applied for one job and was successful, but apparently finding work had become more challenging after some financial crash had occurred in 2008.

The upside to me having to wait to start working was that I could spend the whole summer watching sport. I took in each Test of the British and Irish Lions' tour of South Africa with my dad and Neil, and loved every second of the most compelling rugby union I'd ever seen, even though we lost the series 2-1. I experienced my first feeling of sporting triumph in years as England beat Australia to regain the Ashes in a thrilling 2-1 series victory that had echoes of 2005. Murray broke new barriers at Wimbledon by reaching a first semi-final at his home Grand Slam, where he fell in four tight sets to Andy Roddick. And, amid all this, I spent many a day alone at Headingley Stadium watching Yorkshire in total peace; it was glorious.

My starting work at a basic administrative job coincided perfectly with the new League One season, as Leeds opened up with a 2-1 victory over Exeter City after my first week on the job. It felt fantastic to be back at Elland Road as a season ticket holder for the first time in seven years, and within a few weeks, it appeared that signing up had been an excellent decision.

Eleven wins, three draws, and just one defeat from our first fifteen games of the 09/10 campaign was an exact replica of how we finished 08/09. We weren't playing quite as well as we had earlier in the year, but looked incredibly efficient, and were clear atop the table going into the November international break. We should have been playing that weekend, but our match had to be rescheduled after three of our players received call-ups from their respective countries.

I'd managed to save about £1000 towards my travelling fund, I was living a quiet, peaceful existence, and Leeds United were odds-on to win something for the first time in my life;

everything appeared to be in its right place. Most importantly, it had been a long time since I'd self-destructed, too long a time as it transpired.

With Andy, Neil and me working hard in our first post-university jobs, we decided that we'd earned a big weekend away. Rodney was still in Newcastle as part of his four-year degree, and we perceived that having free accommodation and student nights out to go on would represent a nice, cheap break. As we saw it, the whole thing would cost us about £150, which wasn't at all damaging for mine and Neil's travelling budget, and with Leeds not playing, I couldn't think of a reason not to go.

I knew exactly how the weekend was going to pan out, largely because I was a chief orchestrator on such occasions. Big night out on Friday night; get up on Saturday and go to the pub all day; big night out on Saturday; go home on Sunday in absolute ruin. Get there, act like a clown for forty-eight hours, have a pleasant time with your mates, and get out relatively unscathed.

Having rolled in at 4 am after the expected huge Friday night out, I woke up on Rodney's living room couch, still totally pissed, at 8.30 on Saturday morning. Since that incredible, yet devastating weekend in London for the 2008 play-final, I'd developed an interesting habit of getting straight back on the beers whenever I'd woken up still drunk, and that Saturday was to be no exception. I strolled round to the local shop and picked up a crate, and sunk cans over some Saturday morning television as I waited for the other lads to wake up.

When they finally joined me, I forced a lager into each of their hands to get the day started in earnest. I could tell that none of the three of them wanted a drink, but I made it abundantly clear that they didn't have a choice. It only takes one man to dictate terms in that kind of situation, and I was that wanker.

Ordinarily, mid-morning would be the time that we would get our football bets lined up for the day, with Soccer Saturday gambling having become the cornerstone of our weeks since we'd moved back to Leeds. However, with the international weekend scuppering that plan, we decided to take a trip to the bookies.

Andy, Neil, Rodney and I had all been partial to a spin on the virtual roulette games that you find in any decent bookies over the years. Although we'd never openly admitted it to each other, or ourselves, we'd all probably had minor addictions at some point between the ages of sixteen and twenty-three, although I think we believed those days to be behind us. I'd had genuine success with football betting in 2009, and I now perceived myself to be a measured, effective gambler.

We did what we called an 'old fashioned twenties in' on the virtual Roulette, where each of us put £20 into the Itbox machine, in the hope of achieving plenty of gaming time. The goal of playing wasn't necessarily to win, more just to have fun and feel the incredible rush of excitement that comes with placing your entire emotional state in the hands of a random number generator.

We played for about an hour, with the thrill of the game taking us to some dizzying highs and some crushing lows, before eventually losing our £80. It had been great fun, and everyone had enjoyed it immensely; the line should have been drawn there.

I could feel the temptation of just one more 'twenties in'

burning intensely inside me, although Rodney insisted that our time was up. Rodney had always had this annoyingly admirable maturity upon which he could draw to intervene before he made any reckless decisions, which the other gamblers among us hadn't. At that point, he, Andy and Neil all stopped, whereas I slipped another £20 into the machine.

I stuck four £5 singles on the thirty-seven-number board, leaving me with less than a one in nine chance of winning. I pressed start and watched the exhilarating game spin it's wheel, with the little ball starting its journey in the opposite direction around the edge of the numbers. I can remember the numbers that I'd covered to this day; zero, nine, twenty-eight, and thirty-six, and the closer that the ball got to dropping into one of the slots, the more intense my excitement became. As the ball bounced in, it momentarily appeared as though it was going to land in zero, before falling into its neighbour thirty-two. £20 lost in the blink of an eye, but at that point, I managed to walk away.

£40 down and four beers deep by 11.30 am, I then left the lads to it for a little while as I had planned to go and visit my sister Claire, who was also at university in Newcastle. I called her to let her know that I was on my way, and picked up a pint can of Stella en route to ensure that the buzz of the booze didn't wear off. As she answered the door, Claire gave me a slightly confused look after seeing the can, but after a brief rolling of the eyes and a smile, she hugged me and invited me into her house.

I can remember being a little all over the place as we sat and chatted, but having a lovely time. I'd not seen Claire for a couple of months, so we caught up on all sorts over a late morning cup of tea/can of lager before she very nicely made me a fish finger sandwich. It's fascinating how the details become so clear when you access a memory that you've most likely repressed from your conscious mind.

As I look back, it devastates me that I wasn't in the psychological place to have been able to think to take my little sister out for lunch when dropping in to see her at university. I was working and earning money, and she will have had next to none as students do, yet she made me a fish finger sandwich while I drank a beer that I'd bought from the shop beforehand, without having even asked if I could pick anything up for her. As painful as that is to recite, I think we both enjoyed ourselves before I took off to go and rejoin the lads for the rest of the day.

When I got back to Rodney's, I found the lads gambling on Roulette using their online accounts. They were only doing small stakes, and were in complete control, but seeing them play piqued my interest once more. After impatiently waiting for them to finish, I logged in to my account and decided to have a little play myself.

I put £20 in, and placed £10 on the board, spreading my chips across an array of different numbers. Then, in the click of a mouse, the £10 was gone. Instantaneously, I pressed *repeat bet*, and clicked *spin* again; same outcome, £0 returns.

Without a second's thought, I threw another £20 into my online account, and spun all £20 on this occasion, with the identical outcome. £40 gone in the space of a minute.

The lads had left me alone on the computer in Rodney's bedroom at this point, and I could hear them chatting in the living room from where I was. I was desperate for them not to know how much money I'd just lost, but I was also desperate not to stop. I loaded £100 more into the online casino.

By the time that Rodney came back into the room to see how I was getting on, I'd lost nearly £400. Just like that, with a few clicks of a mouse, I was £400 worse off, and I felt sick beyond belief. The guilt that I was feeling overwhelmed me, and I had to tell him what had happened, at which point he dragged me out of the room and insisted that we go out to the pub to ensure we were in a safe environment, as far away from gambling as we could be.

That afternoon is a blur to me as I look back. I'd already been blind drunk by the time that Rodney had dragged me away from his computer, and I'm pretty sure that I spent the afternoon saying little as we all drank in various pubs. Maybe I'd spent the time contemplating what a mess I was while the other lads chatted away, although when I think about what happened later, I must still have had my mind on gambling.

I'd known that Ireland were playing France in the 2010 World Cup Qualifying play-offs at 5.30 pm, and I'd recently watched each team play during their campaign. France were enduring a torrid time as a team despite the wealth of talent that they had at their disposal, while Ireland based their entire foot-balling philosophy around being solid at the back, and hoping to nick a goal through Robbie Keane at some point. I was adamant that the game would be 0-0, with both teams likely to play for it bearing in mind their respective circumstances.

When we returned to Rodney's house later on in the afternoon to get ourselves ready to go for a meal, I slipped on to his computer, and placed £72 on *Ireland 0-0 France* at 7/1, in an attempt to leave myself ever so slightly up for the day. I knew that I wasn't going to be watching the game, but I saw this as being too good an opportunity to miss to win my money back.

I barely said a word throughout the meal, not because of nerves about my ludicrous bet that was currently playing out, but because I was too drunk to be able to adequately communicate with people that I didn't know all that well. I allowed the whole conversation to pass me by, occasionally asking Rodney to check the Ireland-France score on his phone for me.

After dinner, and with the game still at 0-0 with twenty-five minutes remaining, we popped in for a drink at a close-by bar, which just so happened to be showing the game. If a match is 0-0 after sixty-five minutes, any good football fan will tell you that there is every chance that the score will still be goalless after ninety minutes. While everybody else settled in at a suitable table to continue their conversations, I turned my back to the group to follow the match.

I can so clearly remember the rush of fear that flowed through me as I watched Patrice Evra go down in the penalty area under a challenge from Ireland 'keeper Shay Given. It looked like a penalty on first viewing, so when the referee waved the French appeals away, I started to believe that I might be on the way to recovering all of my roulette losses, with a little extra to buy myself a couple of drinks.

Within moments, Nicolas Anelka struck a shot from twenty-five yards out, that took the most wicked of deflections off Irish defender Sean St Ledger. The effort would have been harmless had it not hit St Ledger, but as it was, the ball span up and away from Given in the Ireland goal. Agonisingly, it hit the inside of the post, before nestling in the back of the net.

I'd barely suffered a sinking feeling throughout the day despite the hundreds of pounds that I'd lost. However, the feeling that encompassed me as that £72 football bet fell at a

72nd-minute hurdle in such horrific fashion was almost indescribable; I felt physically sick.

I don't even think that I felt sick about the money. As I reflect, I genuinely believe that I was just devastated to face up to the fact that my day's gambling was over. There was no more sport available to bet on, and I knew for a fact that we weren't going back to the house to allow for online gaming before we headed into Newcastle city centre for our Saturday night out.

I was almost £500 down, but the alcohol masked how awful that reality was. Aware of my financial implosion, the lads dragged me out of the desperate mood that I was in and bought my drinks throughout the night in an attempt to soften the blow. I tried my best to enjoy the night as a result of their generosity, but I felt nothing but emptiness. The worst was yet to come.

The next day, I lost another £300 on online Roulette trying to recover my losses. I only stopped when I recognised that more betting would have taken me into an overdraft of some kind, and I stuck to my principle of never gambling money that wasn't mine. I had £185 in there, which I hoped would see me through until the end of the month. All the money that I'd saved up to that point for my big travelling trip was gone.

Never in my life had one of my friends expressed concern about me up to that point, but Andy and Rodney made it clear to me that I needed to take a very long break from gambling. I knew that they were right, but was too disorientated to be able to process the information in that moment.

The coach journey back to Leeds that evening was brutal. I had the same sinking feeling that I'd had after Leeds lost to Doncaster in that 2008 League One play-off final, but on that occasion, I'd had Leeds United to blame for my horrific mood state. I couldn't even call upon the warm embrace of my old friend self-pity; I just had to search my soul to try and fathom how I was capable of such astonishingly reckless behaviour. Bearing in mind the upbringing that I'd had, and all the privileges that I'd been afforded, I was acting extraordinarily.

I thought about my sister, and how lovely she'd been to have looked after me when I'd gone to visit, even when it should have been the other way round. I can remember trying to imagine what she'd have thought of me if she'd have known how much money I'd just thrown away. Deep down, I knew that she would have just wanted to try and support me in any way that she could, which made it even worse.

The thought of somebody acting nicely towards me when it was the last thing that I deserved was unbearable. The only thing that made me feel better was the demand that I made upon myself not to gamble moving forward.

The following weekend, after another mundane week at work, I reached Saturday in the knowledge that I'd be watching the football all day without being able to have a bet. The thought made me feel so uninterested in watching Soccer Saturday, that I instantaneously jumped on to my online account. I put £100 on to a football treble and watched alone as two of my three teams won, while the other drew. Another £100 gone.

It took me breaking a rule that I'd set myself just a week after suffering such horrendous losses to recognise the scale of my problem. It occurred to me that I couldn't enjoy football, or a weekend away with my mates for that matter, without having the thrill of a bet to keep me company; I was addicted to gambling.

Only six months after my fantastic £500 betting victory, which I used to buy my season ticket, I'd lost all that, and £300 more, in one weekend, and a further £100 the following week. I'd always bitten back against the phrase *the bookie always wins*, but I had a bona fide example of it being true beyond measure.

The good news was that I didn't place another bet all season after that, and went out and found a second job to help with the process of recouping my losses, instead of trying to win it back. It was one more self-destructive behaviour off the list.

26

3rd January 2010

' I hope all you Leeds United 'fans' enjoyed your day in the sun. Now, get back in your closets for the Wycombe and Exeter games, and we'll see you again for the Spurs match, if that's big enough for you.'

On my last Sunday night of freedom before I started working it every week at my new bar job, I watched the FA Cup third-round draw. For the first time since our relegation from the Championship had dictated that we had to qualify for it, Leeds United were in the hat for the stage at which the Premier League teams entered the competition. We'd been on the brink of suffering another humiliating second-round defeat to a non-league side earlier that day when Kettering Town had taken a second-half lead. Fortunately, Jermaine Beckford did what he was doing most weeks at that time, and grabbed a goal to ensure that there would be a replay back at Elland Road.

Entering the draw as Kettering Town or Leeds United, we knew that we weren't absolutely guaranteed a place in the third round. However, I watched on in the hope that we would be pitted against a big side, safe in the knowledge that we'd beat Kettering should there be a worthwhile prize at stake.

As the draw was whittled down to eight balls, with fifty-six already having been drawn, I couldn't have been more aware of the fact that both our ball, and that of Manchester United's, hadn't yet come out. Eight balls became six, and then six balls became four, with both key balls remaining in play, alongside Accrington Stanley or Barnet, and Gillingham. I'd seen my team play Manchester United many times over the years, and I still expected us to compete against them in the league at some point in the not too distant future. None of Kettering, Accrington, Barnet or Gillingham could say the same, but I still think that your average Leeds fan was more excited by the thought of facing them than any fan of those considerably smaller clubs.

When Accrington or Barnet was the first of the last four balls to be pulled out, there was still only a one in three chance that we would draw the current English champions. This was a marked improvement on the one in sixty-three chance that we'd had at the start, of course, but the still-present gambler in me recognised that the odds remained against us. If any other ball than Gillingham was to follow Accrington or Barnet, the dream that had increasingly threatened to become a reality would be vanquished.

As the number was revealed, and Gillingham the name of the team announced, I took off sprinting around the house, screaming deliriously in the process. It was only when I came back downstairs to find Neil (a Liverpool fan) in fits of laughter at mine and Andy's joy that I discovered that the tie would be played at Old Trafford.

My first action after I'd sufficiently calmed down was to call my dad to celebrate that we were going to Old Trafford. My second was to call the job at which I'd not even started to ask them for the weekend of 2nd/3rd January 2010 off work.

The compromise was that I had to work New Year's Day, and that was fine by me; I'd have done every other day of 2010 if they'd have asked me to, even if the Scum match wasn't yet guaranteed.

I was given four weekly evening shifts at my new job, totalling twenty-four hours, to go alongside the forty-eight hours I was working at my day job. I didn't know how long I intended to maintain both positions, but it quickly became apparent to me that the act of saving wasn't the most crucial part. It was the lack of available time I'd have to spend money that mattered for a liability like me.

My first feeling of regret at what I'd taken on came when I couldn't get down to Elland Road for our replay with Kettering. Fortunately, I was able to listen to the radio at work but feared the worst when the part-timers dramatically pinched a 1-1 draw in normal time. Thankfully, they ran out of steam in extra time, and we saw them off 5-1 in the end, but we'd suffered one almighty scare. None of that really mattered though, as it was we that were heading for a grand day out.

The following day, I successfully applied for tickets for the old man and me to go to Old Trafford for the first time in my life, the thought of which excited me beyond all measure. After such a long absence from the Premier League, I'd started to accept that I might never get to see Leeds play there, but my dream was about to come true.

A month or so into my crazy seventy-two-hour working weeks, and four days before the big match, my grandad called a meeting with my brother, my sister and me. With Claire having just turned twenty-one, he said that he had something that he needed to discuss with us now that we were all of that age, which sounded both curious and ominous.

While out at a local restaurant, my grandad passed us each an envelope, which we opened sheepishly beyond his straight-faced gaze. Inside there was a cheque, that he informed us was from our great grandparents as part of their will. Although I'd been very fortunate to have known both of them well, with my great-grandad having died when I was thirteen and my great-granny when I was nineteen (at the ripe old age of 100), I hadn't been expecting any money at all from them. As it was, they'd left me enough to be able to jump on the next plane out of the UK and be away for a long, long time.

Having so recently displayed such a flagrant disregard for cash during my gambling episode in Newcastle, I felt hugely conflicted as I stared at the cheque. There'd been a few occasions in recent times on which a gesture had emotionally moved me, but this was on a whole new level. It was life-changing for me, it was a chance to be free, yet my overriding emotion was to feel riddled with guilt.

How could somebody so undeserving be the recipient of such an incredible gesture? I was an absolute reprobate who cared solely about himself. How was it just that I receive something so substantial having done absolutely nothing to have earned it?

So many thoughts rushed through my head as I left the restaurant that night. I could practically do whatever I wanted and go wherever I wanted, with the mere thought of that inducing more excitement in me than I'd ever felt. However, wherever my mind tried to drag me to, the core of my emotions told me that I first had to do something that would make my great-grandparents proud of me. It was the only way that I might be able to feel worthy of their gesture.

I decided that I would continue to work both of my jobs for twelve months. I didn't need to work seventy-two-hour weeks now, but my take was that if I could earn the money I'd require for a spectacular travelling trip in my own right, I could rest easy in the knowledge that the gift I'd received had yielded a positive behaviour in me. It felt like both the right and an incredibly important thing to do.

With the FA Cup third-round clash between Manchester United and Leeds United taking place on Sunday 3rd January 2010, I decided to work both the 1st and the 2nd to get the year off to a positive start. I had a feeling that 2010 was going to be a good year, with my travelling trip to come, and Leeds looking extremely well set for promotion to the Championship.

Going into the Old Trafford showpiece, we lay eight points clear of second-placed Charlton Athletic and eleven points clear of third-placed Norwich City in League One. In forty-six league games under Simon Grayson in 2009, we'd managed thirty-two wins, eight draws, and six losses. In a typical forty-six-game League One season, 104 points would likely see a team win the league by a fifteen-point margin. It had been an extraordinary year, although it would mean nothing if we couldn't get the job done in the new one.

I was partly looking forward to Old Trafford as it could serve as an occasion that we could embrace for what it was, without feeling such pressure to win the game. I'd felt so expectant before every Leeds United match for such a long time, and it was incredibly liberating to be able to approach one with no expectations at all.

The old man and I cruised over to Manchester that morning

with excitement coursing through our veins. Scum were top of the Premier League, and coming off the back of three successive titles, while little old Leeds lay forty-eight places below them in the English football hierarchy. I exchanged some light-hearted messages with my pal Craig, who had a ticket in the Stretford End, and I loved reading his comments about how much all Scum fans had missed these matches.

After we'd parked up, it felt magical to be strolling towards the stadium and evoked memories of my first authentic match-day experience when the two sides had met at Elland Road back in April 1994. With an intense hatred existing between the two sets of fans, my dad and I kept our heads down as we made our way towards the away stand, readying ourselves to enter the so-called Theatre Of Dreams.

I'd been able to hear our fans belting out a rendition of our anthem *Marching On Together* from some distance away, and my dad and I joined in at the exact moment that we made it through the turnstiles. I got goosebumps as I made my way up the steps, with the noise ever increasing as we approached the upper tier.

As the gangway appeared in front of us, we caught our first sight of the Old Trafford turf, which caused me to jump on my dad in excitement. As the entire stadium opened out in front of us, the beautiful hostility pierced me for the first time. It felt like every possible emotion was encircling the place; it was delectable.

We located our seats, which were only two rows from being as high up as you can be in the biggest club ground in English football, and although it seemed like we were a million miles from the pitch, the view was still incredible. As the players walked out, the magnitude of the occasion sank in, and a pulsating rush of adrenaline surged through my body.

I immediately looked through the Manchester United line-up as their players strode towards the halfway line. Dimitar Berbatov, one of the best technical players I'd ever seen, was in there, undoubtedly my favourite ever English player and now one of the world's best, Wayne Rooney, was among them too. However, it was a far less eye-catching player that most caught *my* eye.

It was nine years and ten months to the day since centre-half Wes Brown had scored a dramatic own goal in stoppage time at Elland Road. The goal was incorrectly disallowed for offside against our striker Mark Viduka but had it stood, we'd have won the game, and had an extra two points to our Premiership points tally.

Those two points would have seen us finish a point ahead of Liverpool at the end of the 00/01 season, which would have taken us into the Champions League for the following season. Had that happened, the total and utter chaos that Leeds United had been through over the previous nine years and ten months might not have happened. I know that this is all hypothetical, and I'm clutching at the very finest of straws, but maybe we'd have won the top-tier title on one of the five occasions that our Lancastrian adversaries had since that day.

As I saw Sir Alex Ferguson walking up the touchline, I felt a shiver go down my spine. At first, I thought it was a combination of awe and disdain as a result of how much I simultaneously appreciated and resented him for what he'd achieved as a manager. However, even though I was simply a fan of an opposing club who would never come in to contact with him, I felt genuinely intimidated just by being inside the same stadium as him.

I'd seen him in the flesh on plenty of occasions at Elland Road, but now, a little older and wiser, I recognised that he probably commanded more respect than anybody else in world football. As a team, we had to ensure that we didn't show that to Manchester United.

The first fifteen minutes of the game flew by. Little happened in terms of the football, but 9000 men and women from Yorkshire were having the absolute time of their lives behind enemy lines. It felt like we'd turned up to a house party at which we'd not been welcome, but we were so overbearing that the host'd had no choice but to let us in. The idea was that we'd be allowed to stay provided that we promised not to spoil it for everyone else, but very few unwelcome guests don't at least try to crash a party.

With nineteen minutes on the clock, one Leeds-born, life-long fan, centre-half Richard Naylor, bustled Berbatov off the ball just outside our penalty area, which resulted in another, midfielder Jonny Howson, picking up the pieces. Howson did well to wriggle clear of a couple of challenges and move into space, before picking his head up to assess his options.

Instead of looking for an easy sideways pass, like most players in his position would have done, Howson looked forward. Trusting in his teammate's vision and ability, our lightning-quick number nine Beckford peeled off the back of that man Wes Brown around the halfway line, which Howson responded to by playing an inch-perfect diagonal pass.

As I watched the ball falling towards Beckford around the edge of Scum's penalty area, I grabbed my old man's arm, realising that a good touch would have him in on goal. My dad responded by uttering the words 'come on Jermaine' intently, before our star striker's touch appeared to have taken him too wide.

Home goalkeeper Tomas Kuszczak hesitated as the ball slightly got away from Beckford, before eventually deciding to close our striker down in an attempt to narrow the angle. With Brown now sliding in from behind Beckford to try and atone for the error of losing his man, it looked an impossible task for the former-Wealdstone man to score from where we were. Brown may have been reprieved on 3rd March 2001, but he was not to be reprieved on 3rd January 2010.

We watched in astonishment as Beckford squirmed the ball beyond Kuszczak before time seemed to stand still. I stared in total disbelief as the ball trickled into the six-yard box, and then crept towards the Manchester United goalline at the slowest speed imaginable. I willed the goalposts to start gravitating towards the ball, as the two grew closer, and closer, and closer. Then, it was total and utter pandemonium.

I'd gone wilder than most in response to my team scoring in recent years, but it was as though there were 9000 of me as Beckford's effort nestled in the back of the Stretford End net. It was like being in a moshpit; guys were jumping on my head from behind me, people throwing elbows in front of me, folk punching me repeatedly. I even got head-locked by the enormous bloke that was on the other side of me to my dad. It was pure delirium.

Whatever happened in the rest of the match didn't matter; nobody could take that moment away from every Leeds United fan that had made the journey to the wrong side of the Pennines that morning. I'd dreamt of going to Old Trafford as a Leeds United fan since I was about seven-years-old, and had fantasised about how it would feel to celebrate us scoring in the back yard of our biggest rivals. Never could I have imagined that I would fulfil that dream with my team in the third tier of English football, in the FA Cup, against a Manchester United team that had won three straight Premier League titles, and a Champions League less than twenty months earlier.

Scum responded well, putting us under pressure as their fans dealt with the shock of falling a goal behind by getting behind their team. Our backline looked so determined though, defending resolutely with the help of holding midfielders Michael Doyle and Neil Kilkenny in front of them. I must have looked at the clock on the Old Trafford big screen about a hundred times during that half, as time seemed to have slowed down just as it had in the 19th minute. Eventually, the referee blew his whistle to bring it to a close.

My dad and I, as well almost everyone in our immediate vicinity, could do nothing other than laugh for the next fifteen minutes. *Who the hell did we think we were to be leading at half-time?* There wasn't a single person that was getting carried away. It was all just about embracing the moment, as the reality was that Ferguson would likely get them in at half-time, give his players the infamous hairdryer treatment, and send them back out to overwhelm us in the second half.

As the players came back out, some nastiness surfaced between the two sets of fans. We were quite close to a barrier of stewards that were separating the white-shirted fans from the red, but a couple of stabbing gestures from some kids on their side sent our fans wild.

As I'd known a good friend of one of the Leeds fans that was stabbed to death in Istanbul back in 2000, it touched a nerve with me too, although I was determined not to stoop to their level. Many of our lot thought differently, with some responding by doing flying actions as a reference to the Munich Air Disaster, while others started chants about it. It was a vile back and forth, and one that conveyed precisely how bad an impact football can have on people. What happened on the field was all that mattered to me.

We started the second half well, limiting our esteemed opponents to possession in unthreatening areas, while also passing the ball around extremely well ourselves. They managed a couple of half-chances, but it didn't take long for Ferguson to call for the cavalry, as in-form Ecuadorian Antonio Valencia was thrown on, along with a player of whom I had an acute memory.

I'd first seen Ryan Giggs play almost sixteen years prior to that day, back on my first truly memorable occasion as a Leeds United fan. Giggs had transformed himself in that time from being a flying winger to an accomplished, scheming central-midfielder, but he still carried the same level of importance and influence as he always had. I was seven-years-old, and Giggs twenty, back on that evening in April 1994, yet here I was at twenty-three watching a thirty-six-year-old Giggs in January 2010. It was no surprise that I was still supporting my team, but it was remarkable that Giggs was still playing for his.

Scum became a lot more composed at that point and started to create chances. However, their shooting was wayward, and as the clock ticked away ever more alarmingly for the English champions, Ferguson introduced another veteran, Michael Owen, in the hope that one of those chances would find the back of our net.

With only twenty minutes now remaining, it was almost impossible not to start to dream of *the* impossible. They may finally have taken the ascendancy, but we still looked incredibly well organised, and we even fashioned a couple of chances of our own. With the home side pushing ever further forward, Beckford almost got in on goal on the break for a second time, before substitute Robert Snodgrass smacked a rare attacking free-kick against the crossbar.

It didn't feel that much like a cup tie between a top-tier and a third-tier team. We were more than holding our own, with our players showing great aptitude and professionalism to win fouls and waste time wherever they possibly could.

Only when I saw that only five minutes were remaining did I contemplate that we might actually be able to beat Manchester United at Old Trafford. I tried to calm myself down by saying that if they equalised, we would have a replay at Elland Road, which would be worth celebrating in itself, but that was undoubtedly a defence mechanism to protect my emotions from what would be a devastating outcome.

As stoppage time approached, Scum started to take a more direct approach, launching the ball into the box or getting it to the wide areas whenever possible. There were a couple of goalmouth scrambles, in which our heroic defenders had to throw themselves in front of shots towards goal, but we never really looked like we were going to concede.

The clock ticked past the ninety-minute mark, and the only thing that stood between us and one of the most famous victories in our club's history was 'Fergie Time'. Over the years, I'd seen Manchester United score countless goals after the full-time whistle should have been blown to earn a result that they shouldn't have earned. What made them so brilliant of course was that if they got any luck, they always capitalised upon it, and with predators like Berbatov, Owen, and Rooney on the pitch, we had no margin for error.

Still, we held firm, and our heroes even managed to string a few passes together despite the tremendous pressure they were under, wasting critical seconds in the process. It had been a flawless away performance, and there can't have been a football fan watching that believed that we didn't deserve our victory from there. Then, as I saw our gutsy midfielder Michael Doyle jump into the air with his arms aloft, I knew.

We couldn't hear the full-time whistle from where we were, and the noise in the stadium had been so loud throughout the match that I don't think anybody else could either. However, all we needed to see was eleven heroes in white jubilantly sprinting around the Old Trafford turf to know that we'd beaten the Premier League champions, and our most bitter rivals, on their own patch.

I'd been a fan of my club for nearly seventeen years by the time Leeds United had won a match at Manchester United, but this was the best possible manner in which to have done it. With everything that had happened to us in recent times, this was the most seminal of moments, and every single one of our supporters knew it.

The celebrations were even more emotional than they'd been after Beckford's goal, with middle-aged men crying their eyes out, and lads younger than me on their haunches appearing to be praying to and thanking some kind of deity. We'd felt so much collective pain over the years, and it genuinely felt like a well-earned divine intervention had served us.

As the home fans evaporated from view, our players and coaching staff remained on the pitch for fifteen minutes after the game to celebrate with us. We chanted the name of each individual and lapped up their applause in response. It was pure unity, and we'd made a statement to every fan, club and body of English football; we were back.

We were kept in the ground for forty-five minutes after the game to ensure that the police could keep all the fans separated, something that I secretly enjoyed. We'd done such a job on our enemies that our supporters needed protecting from the 70,000 or so furious Mancunians outside. In reality, I'm sure plenty of the folk around me would have relished a fight.

Craig messaged me soon afterwards to say that the atmosphere was toxic outside the ground. He warned us to be careful when we made our way back as he thought that he'd seen a bloke with a knife. That levelled me out a little, and the old man and I warily jogged back to his car after we were finally released.

I got home a couple of hours later and jumped on to my laptop to start reading all the online match reports, and not only had we won the game, we'd had a remarkable fifty-four percent possession in doing so; we'd outplayed Scum. I then watched a replay of Beckford's goal, which was when it all truly started to sink in.

The last few hours had felt like some crazy dream, and the emotion of the experience just started to pour out of me. I wasn't one for crying, having not done so for ten years by this point, but I found myself pacing around the house furiously, unable to contain the energy inside of me. I was so, so happy for the first time in as long as I could remember.

I logged on to social media to check the reactions of all the people that I knew. There were friends and family that I didn't even know were Leeds fans posting about the game, which was a sign that our football club had brought the entire city together. I also learned that we'd been drawn away at Tottenham Hotspur in the fourth round; my dad and I would have another huge away day to embark upon in a couple of weeks' time.

I couldn't help but revel in a great sense of warmth for the unity between absolutely everyone involved. It was something that I felt supremely grateful to be such a big part of, and all I wanted was for the feeling to continue forever. Sadly, when I recognised that it couldn't, I took a considerable turn for the worse.

My consciousness of the high's shelf life brought me crashing back down to earth. Slowly but surely, the reality of my every-day life seeped back into my mind, and every ounce of such long-coveted happiness was cruelly torn away in an instant.

I felt so desperate as that joy vanished, that an all-encompassing rage started to consume me. I can remember going up to my bedroom and screaming into my pillow, so angry was I that I couldn't feel that good forever.

I went for a run to try and blow off some steam and ended up being out for well over an hour. I can remember it being freezing cold, but I must have done almost ten miles. It turned out to be an excellent decision, as I managed to dispel virtually all of that overwhelming negative energy, which just left solemn darkness hanging over me as I sat down in the living room after taking a shower.

I was relieved that Neil wasn't in, as I needed the time alone to process the insane emotional experience that my day out at Old Trafford had been. It had brought out the very best in me but had also brought out a side darker than I'd ever imagined myself to have had.

A couple of hours later, my thoughts and feelings about the people that had posted about our victory on social media changed dramatically. *Where had they been when we'd been relegated from the Premiership? Where had they been when we'd lost in the Championship play-off final? Where had they been when we'd been relegated from the Championship? Where had they been during our League One play-off final defeat? Where had they been for last season's League One play-off semi-final defeat?*

The next thing I knew, I'd taken to my laptop and delivered a rare post of my own. 'I hope all you Leeds United 'fans' enjoyed your day in the sun. Now, get back in your closets for the Wycombe and Exeter games, and we'll see you again for the Spurs match, if that's big enough for you.'

Within a couple of minutes, a fair few comments had appeared below, one of which was from my sister. 'So much hate' is all she wrote. Never have three words described me more accurately.

27

Clinging to another cliff-edge

During the first three months of 2010, I started to spend some time with a girl that I actually liked for the first time in my life. I met her at my day job's Christmas party, and we got chatting over various common interests that we shared.

I didn't see very much of her at first, and we didn't even share messages that often, but the rare contact that we did have was compelling, and it always felt exciting to meet eyes around the office. As time moved on, we started to go for the odd drink after work on a Tuesday, Wednesday, or Thursday, which were the only days that I had free from my evening job. I'd spend my entire week looking forward to it.

She had an incredible lust for life and an enthusiasm for everything that she came across in a way that I'd never seen in a person. Most importantly, from my perspective, she appeared to have a lust and an enthusiasm for *me*.

Due to my shift patterns and her circumstances, we never saw each other more than once a week during that three-month period. If we knew that we were seeing each other, we wouldn't message either. It was all at arm's length on a physical level, but I developed exceptionally strong feelings for her.

With every girl that I'd previously spent time with, I'd either not been able to engage with them on an emotional level or had found that I would very quickly lose interest if I saw them regularly. Regularly in my terms constituted as little as a couple of times per week, but that was more than enough for me to feel smothered.

Aside from the fact that we literally couldn't see each other often at all, what worked particularly well with this girl was our key common interest. She was desperate to ask questions about deep, philosophical issues, and I was desperate to venture my opinion about deep, philosophical issues. Ultimately, we both wanted me to talk.

After things started to get a little heavy between the two of us, the situation broke down for a number of reasons, none of which I feel the need to discuss. It hurt badly, and I felt as though I'd lost the one light that I had in my life at the time, amid my insane working schedule.

The funny thing was that as I dealt with the emotional pain that the situation caused me, I didn't mourn the feeling of what could have been between us. I didn't think about all the things that we could have done together, the places we could have gone, or the moments that we could have shared. Although I did want to be with her, the loss of the excitement of the whole situation hurt far more. The fact that I wouldn't have the immense buzz of having a beautiful woman who I had so much respect for giving me extremely positive attention.

I'm pretty sure that part of the reason that I subconsciously came to depend on the excitement of seeing her, or receiving a message from her, was because of another catastrophic collapse from Leeds United. Three months to the day from the glory of Old Trafford, Swindon Town came to Elland Road and thumped us 3-0, which was our fourth straight League

One loss. We'd won just three games in sixteen since beating Manchester United, and had dropped to fourth in the table, having had an eleven-point automatic promotion cushion back then.

There were just four days between the breakdown of my fleeting romance and the Swindon humbling. I can remember working alone on the upstairs bar that Sunday night and trying to think of one thing that had fallen in to place for me over the past four years.

All that I could conjure was the amazing inheritance that I'd received from my great-grandparents, which I couldn't have been more grateful for, although I remained adamant that I didn't yet want to see if money could buy me happiness.

Old Trafford had been special beyond measure, but I couldn't help but wonder whether that victory had somehow disrupted my team's mentality. The timing certainly suggested it had, and the reality was that I'd have switched it for promotion from League One in a heartbeat.

Going into the final seven games of the season, Swindon now occupied second place with seventy-three points, old foes Millwall were third with seventy-two points, we sat fourth with seventy-one points, while Charlton Athletic were level with us on seventy-one in fifth. Norwich City were as good as champions already and were out of the picture.

Despite our diabolical form, we did have a favourable run-in, having played many of the bigger sides in recent weeks. Away at Charlton did stand out as a potentially decisive fixture in our penultimate match, but we now had to depend on slip-ups from Swindon and Millwall for that even to be relevant.

With our rivals barely having been in the top two between

them throughout the season, I knew that having us breathing down their necks would present a very different kind of challenge for them. As we could so well attest to from experience, getting to where you want to be is difficult, but staying there is considerably harder. They may have chased us down, but could they hold us off?

We won our first game and scored our first goals in four weeks at Yeovil Town two days after the Swindon defeat. I watched the game on Sky, and the players looked somehow rejuvenated, despite how little time they'd had to prepare, and how long a journey they'd had to take. By no means was I getting carried away though, as Yeovil were poor, and all three of Swindon, Millwall and Charlton also won.

The following weekend, Swindon appeared to crack under the pressure, falling to a 3-0 defeat at Colchester United, while we beat Southend United 2-0, and Millwall hit Gillingham for four. With Charlton slipping to a narrow defeat at Southampton, Millwall were now in charge on seventy-eight points, we were third on seventy-seven points, Swindon were fourth on seventy-six points, with seventy-four-point Charlton's most likely destination now the play-offs.

Two days later, Swindon's challenge further faltered as they dropped two points at home to Exeter City, with the other three sides all in action the following day. I took the day off work to travel up to Carlisle with a guy who I played football with, and we outplayed a passive Carlisle United side to win 3-1. Former Leeds favourite from the David O'Leary era, Ian Harte, lined up against us that day; it was over nine years since his wand of a left foot had fired in a free-kick against Deportivo La Coruna in a Champions League quarter-final.

We may have reached a couple of major European semi-finals back then, but we hadn't *won* anything. When news filtered through that Millwall had only managed a draw at Yeovil, winning promotion from League One was back in our own hands. Charlton had managed to beat Colchester to keep themselves in the picture, which made that penultimate fixture look all the juicier.

There were more dramatic twists that weekend, as Millwall lost at Huddersfield Town on the Friday night, which left us knowing that we would be promoted even if we were to lose one of our final four games. Now feeling the pressure ourselves, we used that defeat up at Gillingham the following day, with both Swindon and Charlton also failing to capitalise.

Our penultimate home game against MK Dons has to go down as the most shambolic game of football that I've ever seen. We were awful, but won 4-1, with the match feeling more like a training match for the most part. The Dons had nothing to play for and ambled around the pitch like they were already on their summer holidays psychologically, but still managed to have three players sent off. I can remember walking away from Elland Road feeling a bit embarrassed by what I'd just seen, although it helped that events elsewhere had been significant.

With Swindon and Charlton both having drawn, it looked like it was now a two-horse race between us and Millwall, who had edged out Leyton Orient 2-1. The Lions were just a point behind us, with Swindon and Charlton now four and five back respectively, as my dad and I headed down to London a week later.

Just before half-time at The Valley, with our game locked at 0-0, I received a text message from Rodney to say that former

Leeds striker Ian Thomas-Moore had scored to give Tranmere Rovers the lead over Millwall. As it stood, if we could beat Charlton, we'd be promoted, and the whole away contingent and I were soon celebrating madly.

About thirty seconds later, I received two more text messages, from two lads that I knew loosely, both of whom claimed to have just seen me on TV. It turned out that they were both at Elland Road, where our match was being shown live on a big screen for the fans that couldn't get tickets. Later that night, I saw myself on The Football League Show, my first ever television appearance.

Early in the second half, with every Leeds fan at The Valley fuelled with anticipation, excitement, and nerves, I received another text message to say that on-loan Leeds midfielder Andy Robinson had just made it 2-0 to Tranmere. The picture was now clear, Millwall were as good as beaten, and if we scored, we were up.

Very little happened in the second half of our match, but there was an enthralling buzz of excitement among our fans as we pressed for a winner in the final minute of the game. There was plenty of effort from the players, although we seriously lacked quality, and created little other than the odd goalmouth scramble from long balls into the Charlton box.

Then, in yet another dramatic twist, Charlton went up the other end and scored through a deflected Akpo Sodje header, and we'd missed our chance. We still knew that another opportunity awaited the following week, but I couldn't help but be furious as the final whistle was blown.

I couldn't have imagined a better way to celebrate seeing Leeds United achieve something for the first time in my life than on a glorious May away day in London with my old man. From the moment that Millwall had slipped two goals behind, I'd spent the remainder of the game imagining the bedlam among our fans at the final whistle. It would have felt like we'd truly earned our promotion had we taken the chance that was presented to us, but it wasn't to be, and it would go to the final day.

With forty-five games now played, the League One automatic promotion equation could not have been more finely poised. Leeds United eighty-three points, Millwall eighty-two points, Swindon Town eighty-two points, Charlton Athletic eighty-one points. Even our local rivals Huddersfield Town had an outside chance on eighty points, although they would require a miracle considering the final day fixtures.

Our task was very straight forward; beat Bristol Rovers, and win promotion to the Championship. If we weren't to beat Bristol Rovers, Millwall and Swindon, who faced each other at The Den, were waiting to pinch second spot from us. Should we lose, and Millwall and Swindon draw, Charlton knew they could nick automatic promotion with a win at Oldham Athletic. If Leeds, Millwall, Swindon and Charlton were all to fail to win, Huddersfield could secure the most unlikely of promotions with a handsome win at Exeter City.

As I look back, I don't remember anything about the morning of 8th May 2010. I don't know whether I worked the early shift at the snooker hall, what I had for lunch, or the 23rd drive to Elland Road of what had been a rollercoaster of a season. I can't even recall if I was nervous; I genuinely don't know what I felt as I prepared to watch my team attempt to win something for the first time in my life. When I say win something, I mean promotion. How many sporting scenarios are there in which you are hoping to bask in the glory of finishing second?

I have vague memories of being amazed by the atmosphere at Elland Road just before the game kicked off, with over 38,000 fans packing into the stadium. My dad and I had become familiar with half that number throughout the season, but even I wasn't in the mood to criticise those that only turned out on the big occasion. This match was too important; we just *had* to get the job done.

As the players walked out to a raucous 'COME ON' from the crowd, I was surprised to see that Jermaine Beckford had been selected as captain. With there being Premier League interest in him, Beckford was expected to move on regardless of whether we won promotion or not, and there was no doubt that he'd been a brilliant servant for us. However, Simon Grayson's decision to make him skipper for what I believed to be the first time ever came as a major shock, as this was no time for sentiment. It almost hugely backfired on thirty-three minutes.

Although we were on top, little had happened in the first half an hour or so. As I'd experienced so many times over the years, the tension was rising inside Elland Road with the match still goalless. I think everybody had been hoping for and expecting an early goal to settle the nerves, but that was never going to happen with Leeds United.

In a moment that couldn't have been more characteristic of our football club, a melee broke out in back-play just outside of the Bristol Rovers box. As it was at the opposite end of the pitch, we couldn't see what had happened from the Kop. All we knew was that our winger Max Gradel had severely lost his cool, and a Rovers player was in a heap on the floor.

I'd never heard a collective groan around our stadium like the one that occurred as the referee showed Gradel a straight red card. He clearly couldn't believe what had happened, and subsequently tried to get at both the victim of his actions and the referee, which caused Beckford to try and interject as part of his new role as on-field leader.

When Gradel showed absolutely no regard for Beckford's intervention and tried to shove him out of the way, I honestly thought that the two of them were going to come to blows. Beckford had his finger in Gradel's face, who did nothing other than try to shove his captain out of the way; it was farcical. Fortunately, the experienced Michael Doyle managed to drag Gradel away, and we could battle on with ten men, not nine.

I'd never known the Kop to go as quiet as it did when the half-time whistle went. None of us had a clue what to say to each other, yet you sensed that the last thing that anybody was feeling was surprised.

Gradel's moment of madness had pretty much summed up what had happened to us since that incredible day at Old Trafford four months prior. The fans, the players, and the coaching staff were quite simply all over the place, and our only hope lay with how hard our players would be willing to fight in the second half, and whether lady luck was on our side.

Despite all this, the fans were incredible as the second half kicked off. It was reminiscent of the unity shown during our play-off semi-final with Millwall twelve months earlier; everyone in the stadium knew that our ten players needed us. If we were going to miss out on promotion, then it would not be because the Elland Road faithful hadn't been supportive enough; it was on us to inspire ten average blokes to claim

46th place in England's football hierarchy.

When Daryl Duffy put Rovers ahead three minutes later, a smile broke out across my face. Only Leeds United, *only Leeds United*. How many times would I have to say to myself, 'I've seen it all now', for me to realise what my football team was capable of? It was literally laughable.

I have to give my fellow fans tremendous credit from there, as they let out a deafening roar of encouragement, refusing to be deterred, somehow still believing. I wish I could have said the same about myself.

One of the clearest memories of what was going through my mind while we were 1-0 down that afternoon, involved me hoping that Millwall were winning against Swindon. I was convinced that we were now going to miss out on automatic promotion, and I actually wanted to see Millwall claim second spot. I couldn't bear the thought of facing them in the play-offs again.

There was a bloke with a radio a couple of rows back that informed us that Millwall and Swindon were drawing, while Charlton were winning. Dramatically, that meant that as it stood, Charlton would be promoted, with every result going exactly as they needed. There was still a long way to go yet, though.

Grayson threw on one of our own, Jonny Howson, to try and provide some much-needed energy, and the crowd responded with yet more reverberating support. Several fans were confused as to why Howson hadn't started, although his introduction didn't seem to have any immediate effect. As the hour-mark approached, we'd barely fashioned an opening.

Then, on fifty-nine minutes, a tame cross towards the edge of the Rovers box was sent over from the left. All I could see was one of our players taking a touch with his back to goal, with a couple of defenders obscuring my view from either side. The next thing I knew, Elland Road had erupted.

Seemingly from nowhere, the ball had flown past Rovers' goalkeeper Mikel Andersen and into the top left-hand corner as I was looking at it from the Kop. I'd not even seen Howson on the edge of the area in the build-up, but it was he that conducted the crowd after wheeling away in celebration. Game on.

Although there were four minutes between Howson's goal and that man Beckford completing a stunning turnaround, it felt like it all happened in one fluid moment. It was as though Andersen had picked the ball out of his net after Howson's strike, attempted to throw it out to his right-back, only for Beckford to leap up and deflect it into the path of Bradley Johnson with his head. That led to the goalmouth scramble that resulted in Beckford poking home to make it 2-1 and change the whole complexion. From thinking about who I'd rather us face in the play-offs, all of a sudden, we would clinch automatic promotion should we prevent Bristol Rovers from scoring in thirty minutes of football.

This is the point at which I'd like to be able to report the specific emotions that I felt in the final half an hour of the 2009/10 League One season. I'd like to tell you that I was on the edge of my seat, that I was nervous beyond reproach, and that I was in a state of uncontrollable anticipation as the final whistle drew nearer.

As everything that you've read so far attests to, I can remember the finest details about all of my most treasured sporting memories so clearly. Yet, I can't tell you a thing about what happened in the build-up to the referee ending the League One match between Leeds United and Bristol Rovers on 8th May 2010. The final score was 2-1, we'd been promoted back to the Championship after three years in League One, and thousands of fans were streaming on to the hallowed Elland Road turf.

Was this it? Was this the moment of glory that I'd dreamt about for seventeen years? Maybe I shouldn't be so surprised that I didn't know what to do after all that time, but I didn't cheer, I didn't celebrate, and I didn't smile.

I turned to my dad and hugged him, before shaking the hand of the season ticket holder next to us. Neither of the two of them smiled either. As I looked around the Kop, there was jubilation in almost every direction, absolute bedlam, euphoria on the faces of the masses, but not us three, or a few other chaps in our immediate vicinity.

My dad was known to be hyper-critical as a sports fan from time to time, but I couldn't help but agree with his assessment of 'job done'. The season ticket holder next to us tapped us both on the arm amid the chaos and said 'see you next season lads', and walked off after rolling his eyes. We'd done it, but sadly from all three of our points of view, we hadn't earned it.

My team had been so poor over the past few months that I couldn't take any pride in the promotion that we'd just won. We didn't deserve it in my eyes; there was no justice in such a modest side being able to celebrate an achievement like this. It had been dramatic, but we had lacked quality for such a long time, that I felt empty.

The first smile of the afternoon came to my face when I saw Andy and Rodney on the pitch. They both looked ecstatic, which genuinely did make me happy, but it's impossible to personally force an emotion just because you want to experience it. There's a strong argument to suggest that if I'd have been more light-hearted at the time, I'd have felt the same joy that my pals were feeling, but I'm not convinced of that at all. I'd always been a Leeds United fan first, and a football fan second, but the quality of the football that I watched had always been significant to me, and the side of the last four months had left a lot to be desired.

My dad and I left Elland Road before the additional celebrations were due to begin. The players were expected to return to the pitch once the fans had cleared off, but neither of us felt compelled to stay.

On the drive back to mine, we had a very open and frank discussion about how going to watch your football team play should make early Saturday afternoon the best time of the week. For us, we'd been happier at 5 pm on a Saturday since January, as we knew that we wouldn't have to go and witness the garbage that we'd just seen for another couple of weeks.

I learned a very harsh lesson when I saw my team achieve something for the first time during my tenure as a fan. You always feel unfulfilled when your side *fails*, while it's still possible to feel unfulfilled when your side *succeeds*. It appeared that victory wasn't enough; it would require a combination of factors for me to experience that coveted sense of euphoria that I'd waited so long for. I'd experienced it at Manchester United, yet, as incredible as that was, it remained an FA Cup third-round match. If I wanted to experience true joy from sport, there would have to be justice in the triumph of the team or individual that I was supporting.

Rodney had called me on a couple of occasions to ask me to go and meet him in town, as he, Andy, and a few other lads had got their celebrations underway in style. I told him that I'd be out in a little while; I wanted to make the most of having the house to myself to see if I was merely waiting for a feeling of joy to sink in, just as had happened after Old Trafford.

I drank four bottles of lager alone in my living room, and the feeling never came. I think I'd known deep down that it wouldn't, and that it was the solitude that I'd been craving. So many years spent waiting for this moment, how could I be feeling nothing? Even if we had been awful, surely promotion should have yielded at least some happiness?

After a slightly more aggressive call from Rodney, I reluctantly got myself together and went into town to meet the lads. I'd been watching Leeds with Rodney for fifteen years by this stage, and I could tell how important it was to him that we at least saw each other on what remained a momentous occasion.

I got into town, had one pint with the lads, before heading straight back home. As much as I tried to force the issue with myself, I couldn't get into a celebratory mood, which I could tell the lads found incredibly frustrating. I apologised to them, wished them a good night, and headed back home to be on my own.

As I tucked into a couple more solo beers later that night, I reminded myself of the substantial positive that we were back in the Championship. It may have been a positive thought, as opposed to a positive feeling, but it was a platform towards achieving something that would give me that true happiness.

Sport may not have been able to deliver for me just yet, but I felt closer to the point at which it would in the future. Besides,

I was on the brink of taking off on an adventure around the world. If that couldn't make me happy, then I might have had to accept the reality of a life without that emotion.

28

A final cry for help

Just over six months after Leeds United were promoted to the Championship, I completed the twelve-month stint of working seventy-two-hour weeks that I'd vowed to myself that I would do after receiving my inheritance. Mel, Neil and I had recently bought a one-way flight to Venezuela, having decided to start our adventure in South America, with an open mind as to where the world took us from there.

I'd done little other than work during that period, but after learning that I had to take my annual leave, I'd taken some time off over the summer; for sporting reasons of course. I took three weeks holiday from my day job between the middle of June and early July to coincide with the World Cup, Wimbledon, and the cricket season.

Although the World Cup turned out to be a bit of a disaster, I have some very fond memories of drinking on the outfield at Headingley Stadium, as they were showing England's games on the big screen there. I still haven't got over Frank Lampard's ghost goal against Germany to this day, but we were outplayed to such an extent in that second-round match that I can accept that we deserved to go out anyway.

I made up for missing all of Andy Murray's run to the Australian Open final in January by seeing the entirety of his journey to the Wimbledon semi-finals. Murray breezed through to the quarter-final, before battling past Jo-Wilfried Tsonga to reach the last four. There he faced old foe Rafael Nadal, who he had destroyed on a hard court in Melbourne. Sadly, the Spaniard remained superior on the grass and edged Murray out in three close sets. That was now two Grand Slam finals and two Wimbledon semi-finals; he was getting closer.

I also spent plenty of time at Headingley watching Yorkshire play, as we made huge strides forwards from narrowly avoiding relegation from County Championship Division One in 2009, to almost win it in 2010. We were four Kent wickets away from claiming the title on the final day, but couldn't quite get over the line as Nottinghamshire dramatically nicked it at Lancashire. It was gutting to miss out so narrowly, but that wasn't the most important thing. Cricket's role in my life was to give me a place to go to escape from the frenetic nature of the outside world, and it did that throughout the 2010 season.

The only other weekend that I took off before I went away was in September for The Ryder Cup. I had the usual plan to spend the weekend at my old man's to watch every minute of the action, but the event was badly disrupted by rain. The Sunday singles were forced back to the Monday, which meant that I missed Graeme McDowell dramatically regaining the Cup for Europe in the final match against Hunter Mahan. I resented the British weather for costing me what would have been a priceless moment and could do nothing other than hope for similar drama in Medinah, USA, in 2012.

Walking away from work for the final time after a year of seventy-two-hour weeks was a surreal feeling. I felt an incredible sense of achievement and thought of my great-grandparents as I checked out of the snooker hall for the final time to go and meet Neil in town. As he'd been working two jobs for sixteen months by this point, celebrating our last shifts together on a night out felt poignant.

When the day came for Mel, Neil and me to depart, I could barely register what I was about to do. I think I was still so exhausted from a year of running myself into the ground that I hadn't taken the time to process the fact that I was disappearing for an undefined period of time, to many places that I wasn't yet sure that I'd be going. I spent the five-hour coach journey down to Heathrow on the National Express contemplating whether I would even return to the UK; I saw every possible option as being on the table.

We spent the first week of our trip in Venezuela, and it wasn't a great start. There was nothing to do in the capital city Caracas, so we flew out to a place called Margarita Island, at a time of year in early December that is the best possible to visit. However, they were experiencing their heaviest rainfall in forty years, which made for a pretty modest island experience.

Things picked up after we travelled over land and sea for seventy hours to reach the Colombian capital of Bogota. We found a hostel, with lots of other people from all over the world staying there, and it felt more like we were travelling at that point. However, I can't say that I was enjoying myself.

The only time that I truly felt at ease was when the three of us would sit down together, without anybody else, and have a few drinks while either playing cards or watching football. We'd learned on our first weekend out there that more Premier League games were televised in South America than they were back home, and it soon became apparent that watching English football would be sacrificed for no activity.

We travelled south through Colombia and Ecuador, before reaching a small beach town in northern Peru called Mancora at the start of January. During that time, I'd found myself feeling an overbearing sense of regret about deciding to travel to South America for two reasons.

The first was that I simply wasn't enjoying myself that much. The second was because we'd chosen it over Australia, where we'd have spent the first few weeks of our trip watching The Ashes.

Although there was football everywhere in South America, there was no real surprise to find that they didn't show cricket. As a result, I'd had to spend a lot of time during the first few weeks of our trip checking the BBC Sport website to find out what was going on down under. As it was, England had been crucifying Australia and wrapped up a 3-1 series win on the day that we arrived in Mancora.

I couldn't help but feel mixed emotions about the victory. I was undoubtedly delighted that we'd won our first Ashes series away from home since I was just a few weeks old, but I couldn't help but think that I'd missed a massive trick for not having been there. I guess that any sound of mind individual would have accepted the situation for what it was, not a big deal, but I was by no means sound of mind.

The following night, Neil, Mel and I embarked on a huge night out with two decent American chaps that we'd met that day. I'd bonded with one of them over some basketball that was on the big screen at the hostel, as he watched his team, the Boston Celtics, in an NBA game. As someone that took pride in wearing his team colours when abroad, I'd enjoyed the effort that this guy had made to wear his Celtics jersey while watching them play. After chatting basketball, the five of us started drinking together, and the next thing I knew, I was stumbling into bed at 6 am.

Fortunately for me, I'd made a deal with the owner of the hostel before we'd started drinking for him to open the bar area early the next morning. I'd learned that I was in for what I knew would be a rare treat for me while I was away; Leeds United being on foreign TV.

I was aware that there was barely any chance of me seeing us play in the Championship when abroad, but twelve months on from drawing Manchester United away in the FA Cup third round, we'd been pitted against Arsenal at The Emirates at the same stage. It had been selected for South American TV coverage, and I was fired up to watch my team.

With the game kicking off at 12.30 pm back home, that meant a 7.30 am start for us, as Mancora was five hours behind the UK by way of it sitting on the most western part of the Pacific coast of South America.

After an hour's sleep, I was awoken by the two American guys, who had burst into our dorm room in excitement for 'the big game' as they put it. Initially disorientated, hazy memories of the night before started to flood back to me as I unsteadily made my way down to the bar area.

Having discussed basketball in detail with our new friends, I'd then told them that they should watch the Leeds game with us the following morning. I'd said it fairly tongue in cheek, but having been impressed by the interest that I'd taken in basketball, they agreed that they'd wake up to watch it.

As the evening had gone on, the guys had become more

and more enthusiastic about the match, and Mel and I even ended up teaching them a few Leeds chants as the drinks had really started to flow. I still hadn't thought for a second that they'd have it in them to wake up for the match, but I'd not considered the flaw in my thinking process. Waking up would have required them to have gone to sleep.

To his credit, Neil dragged himself out of bed for the game too, even though he was a Liverpool fan. We'd watched Liverpool play every weekend since we'd been away, and as Mel and I had got behind them as a show of support, he did the same with Leeds.

There was no doubt that all five of us were still absolutely pissed, but with the hostel owner requesting that we keep the noise down so as not to wake up the other guests, we kept a lid on ourselves incredibly well. We managed to keep our discussion to hushed tones, even as the American lads started to pepper me with questions as kick-off approached.

Having heard of Arsenal, but not Leeds, they had enough about them to assume that we were outsiders for the game. When they asked whether I thought we had a chance, I told them that victory was unlikely as a Championship team competing against a side that were very much in the Premier League title race at that point. However, I did instil hope by referring to events at Old Trafford twelve months before, and also drew attention to our outstanding league form.

We'd made a slightly shaky start to our first campaign back in the Championship, but a 4-1 victory at Scunthorpe United at the end of October was the catalyst for a twelve-game unbeaten streak. Our narrow loss at Cardiff City on the 4th January was the first time that we'd tasted defeat in two and half months, and there could be no doubt that we were exceeding expectations in the Championship. I didn't see why we couldn't exceed expectations against Arsenal.

As the players walked out, I felt an extraordinary kind of shiver running down my spine. All of the negativity that I'd been feeling about South America had ceased to exist. As usual, my companion sport had whisked all of my problems away, and everything seemed perfect in that exact moment.

The hostel, which was probably the best I'd ever stayed in, really was a unique setting for watching sport. With Mancora being near-thirty degrees celsius year-round, the bar was outdoors, with a thatched-roof covering it to protect people, and their view of the screen, from the sun. A huge swimming pool was directly behind where we were sitting, and as if that wasn't enough, if you turned your head ninety degrees to the right, you'd be looking out over the Pacific Ocean. It was more like a luxury Ibizan party resort than a South American hostel.

We must have looked awful, and most likely stunk of booze, but that didn't stop the barman serving us our first beers of the day as the game started. In response to mine and Mel's muted shouts of 'COME ON LEEDS', Neil and the American lads echoed us. We were all Leeds that morning.

As the half progressed, other travellers at the hostel started to wake up, and by the end of the first forty-five minutes, five or so of them had decided to join us for the game. With most of the folk of South American origin, they didn't have a clue what the match meant, so provided that the ball wasn't in and around either penalty area, I happily explained the game's significance to them. I proudly informed them that I was from Leeds (a place that none of them had heard of) and that Leeds

United were my team, pointing to the crest on my white shirt in the process.

As we reached 0-0 at half-time, I was shouted at by the hostel owner for being too loud, having instinctively clapped and shouted 'GREAT HALF LEEDS' as the referee had blown his whistle. He still served me another beer immediately after, before the American lads asked me if I'd pop up to their room with them, which I was more than happy to do.

As there hadn't been any dorm-room beds remaining when they had arrived at the hostel, they'd ended up in a private room, which they told me had suited them just fine up to that point. As I entered, and they pulled out a massive bag of cocaine, I could see why.

I'd never been much of a drug-taker. I'd had a couple of moments of experimentation back home but had always been happy enough with alcohol to feel the need to explore it any further. However, as I considered how perfect everything was in that exact moment, I couldn't have thought of a better environment in which to have a blast.

I was in South America, the source of this stuff, which I justified in my mind as 'partaking in the culture'. Add to this that I was watching my team play really well in a huge game and that these cracking chaps were making such an effort to join me in supporting Leeds, it seemed rude not to join them for a line. A few minutes later, and their decision not to go to bed the previous night made a lot more sense.

As I headed back to the bar area to re-take my seat for the second half, about fifteen people had now pulled up chairs in front of the screen. Mel and Neil were chatting to a few of them, talking in detail to these non-English people about how much football meant to us. Mel then made a point of telling them about how it meant more to me than most upon my return, and my response was to kiss my shirt with both aggression and pride. I don't know why I took Mel's comment as a compliment, but it felt strangely special to have the magnitude of my sports fandom highlighted. I hadn't felt that way since primary school.

Within a couple of minutes of the restart, I found myself feeling a lot more special as the cocaine started to take effect. Somehow, the raw euphoria that I'd been experiencing for the past hour reached a whole new level. I'd gone from feeling perfect to feeling even better than that. I wasn't finished there either.

With my focus on the game peaking due to an inexplicable intensity that had come over me, I jumped out of my seat as Max Gradel went down in the Arsenal box during a rare foray forward for Leeds. I don't know how I remembered to keep my voice down, but I found myself both whispering and shouting 'PENALTY' at the same time. The next thing I knew, referee Phil Dowd was on the screen pointing to the spot.

As I fell to the floor in both joy and fear, Neil had to explain what had happened to the people that had now joined us, as they struggled to comprehend how seriously I was taking the game. As I saw Robert Snodgrass placing the ball on the penalty spot, I re-took my seat, and raised my hands to my face, peeking through the tiny gaps that I'd created between my fingers. I had no control over what happened next.

The hostel owner had been happy with the way that we'd behaved to that point. He'd continued to remind us to keep quiet on the multiple occasions on which our noise levels had gradually increased, and we'd respected that each time. However, I had no idea how I was going to contain myself should Snodgrass put us 1-0 up at Arsenal. As the referee blew his whistle, all conscious thought vanished from my mind. Snodgrass stepped up, and struck the ball towards the bottom right corner, only for Arsenal goalkeeper Wojciech Szczesny to dive the same way. Yet, despite the Pole having guessed right, the ball nestled in the bottom corner of the net, sending an unparalleled rush of blood coursing through my veins.

Euphoric on so many levels, I jumped out of my seat, ripped off my Leeds shirt, and charged away from the bar area. Having no real control over what was happening, I couldn't even feel my legs as they carried me beyond the crowd that had gathered at what must have been the quickest speed at which I'd ever run.

The next thing I knew, the swimming pool was coming towards me, and my body wasn't trying to slow me down. It's amazing how I remember this tiny detail, but after not smiling in the immediate aftermath of the goal, I can remember a smile coming to my face as I finally came to terms with what I was about to do.

After reaching the edge of the pool, I leapt high into the air, spreading my limbs out as far as I could, releasing the explosion of energy that had just occurred inside of me. As I hit the water and sunk deep into the pool, it was as though somebody had literally thrown water in my face to snap me back to reality.

I hadn't even resurfaced before I realised that the hostel owner was going to be furious. He'd been livid about people getting into the pool in the middle of the night a couple of days earlier, and having done so well to have kept so quiet, I'd just made an enormous splash in the pool before it had even opened. Still, I can't say that I was remorseful for my actions as I resurfaced, and what followed only served to make me feel more vindicated.

As I opened my eyes, I saw three slightly blurred figures charging in my direction, which I soon identified as being Neil and the two American chaps. Just as I'd done, they took an enormous leap into the pool, creating a far louder splash than I'd done moments before, and then proceeded to start cheering and hugging me after resurfacing.

I knew that we'd done the wrong thing, but I didn't care at all as I basked in the glory of these three absolute gentlemen celebrating a monumental Leeds United goal with me in the most comical of fashions. The only thing that I regretted was not being able to hear the South American commentator's elongated 'GOOOOOOOOOOOOOOOOOOOOOOOOA AAAAAAALLLL' after Snodgrass had scored.

As we got out of the pool and re-took our seats, everyone was in hysterics about what had just happened. I instantly apologised to the hostel owner and the barman, who justifiably looked at me in disgust. It wasn't the worst thing anybody had ever done, but they'd woken up early solely to allow me to watch the football, and all they'd asked in return was for us to obey the rules. My only defence was that a multitude of factors meant that I didn't even qualify as myself in the moments after Snodgrass' goal.

Our celebration seemed to pique the interest of the other guests, and they all became as transfixed by the match as I was. In a temporary state of insanity, I started to teach the crowds Leeds chants, just as I'd been doing the previous night. One of my finest achievements to date is to engage two Chilean girls in a chorus of 'WE ARE LEEDS, WE ARE LEEDS, WE ARE LEEDS', even if we were effectively whispering it.

Arsenal stepped it up a gear when Arsene Wenger brought Cesc Fabregas on in response to them falling behind. Then, after the introduction of Theo Walcott soon after, they started causing us all kinds of problems. At Old Trafford, Manchester United had enjoyed plenty of territory but had struggled to break us down or pick holes in us. Fabregas was starting to do exactly that though, and we couldn't contain Walcott's pace in behind.

I'd sat on the edge of my seat in a state of desperate nervousness from minute fifty-four until minute ninety, as we found ourselves on the brink of another incredibly famous victory. However, with the full-time whistle looming, our left-back Ben Parker was adjudged to have felled Walcott in the penalty area, in what looked like a very harsh decision to me. However, as Arsenal should probably have had a penalty moments earlier, it didn't hurt too much.

As Fabregas stepped up and scored the penalty, I initially sunk deflatedly into my seat in total devastation. However, after we gave the ball away immediately from the restart, I was back on the edge of my seat as Arsenal almost nicked the win twice after stoppage time had ended.

When the full-time whistle confirmed a 1-1 draw, it all became a bit too much for me. The obscene amount of emotion that I'd experienced in the past couple of hours and the overwhelming pride that I felt for my team left me sobbing uncontrollably. For some reason, my fellow hostel guests started comforting me, and one of them even told me that they understood. *I* didn't even understand.

The simple explanation for my reaction was that the emotion of an outstanding performance had combined with the fact that I'd barely slept, was drunk out of my mind, and had taken some incredibly strong class 'A' drugs during the match. It was easy to rationalise when I reflected on it later that day, but the reality was that it hadn't been anything to do with those things.

How many men do you know who sob to a group of people, most of whom they don't know, without being able to cry, after their team has drawn a football match? It was ludicrous behaviour, and something that I've only recently been able to understand.

This was the one situation in which I felt comfortable to express my emotions. When watching sport, I could at least try to cry out for both help and attention. Watching Leeds United, watching football, watching sport; it was an acceptable environment in which an incredibly troubled twenty-four-year-old man could let himself go. I was pleading for these people to comfort me, for anybody to comfort me, but not just because my football team had just drawn an FA Cup third-round football match. Once again, I was pleading for somebody to help when I wasn't even aware that there was something wrong with me.

It had been over four years since I'd left Leeds to go to university, and I'd constantly struggled ever since. There'd been so many different ways in which I'd been trying to reach out for help, without ever realising that I was doing it, and I'd done some absolutely ridiculous things in the process.

Wherever I'd been looking, I'd had no idea what it was that I was looking for, and didn't even know whether I *wanted* something, or *needed* something. I'd been around so many people, in so many situations, in so many places, but nothing had been able to help.

That's just it when you have a mental health problem though; you spend all of your time looking outwardly for solutions. The last place that you find yourself searching is within, and it's so often where *your* solution lies.

29

The light

The date was 15th May 2011. I was sitting on top of a mountain in a small country on Europe's Adriatic coastline called Montenegro. It was a glorious sunny day, there was absolutely nobody around, and the whole world seemed to have stopped as I stared out at the most beautiful scene that I'd ever witnessed. Right then, in that very moment, I came to the overwhelming realisation that I'd been *depressed* for nearly five years.

After four months in South America with Mel and Neil, and five weeks staying with Rodney in New Zealand after his recent move out there, I'd finally decided that it was time for me to disappear. I came up with a plan to travel around Europe on the trains for a few months and booked a flight from Christchurch to Paris. I had no idea what my home continent had in store for me, but deep down, I knew that the most important part was for me to be on my own for a while.

I'd enjoyed elements of my time in South America with Mel and Neil, although if I'm honest with myself, the only real pleasure that I'd gained had come from drinking and watching sport with two great pals. We'd seen some spectacular things, but I'd spent most of the time feeling despondent and lost and did little other than follow my friends' lead.

My decision to fly to New Zealand had been a hasty one, but with Neil's dad living there, and the pull of spending time with Rodney always impossible to resist, it did make sense. Neil and I as good as went our separate ways upon arrival there, while Mel had headed to the USA to travel the east coast on his own; the three amigos had disbanded.

Without the two of them to motivate me, I did pretty much nothing in New Zealand. Rodney and his partner Ruth were out at work all day, and I spent four straight weeks sitting in their living room watching TV box sets and any sport that I could get my eyes on. At weekends, Rodney would always organise an activity for us, but I'd usually find myself wishing the time away until we could stay up all night to listen to Leeds United on the radio.

Overall, I found my time there to be very therapeutic, but when I realised that their housemates were sick of me being in the way, I knew that it was time to go. Besides, there's only so long that anyone should go on spending their travel-the-world experience watching American college basketball in a New Zealand living room.

Getting on the plane to Europe, totally alone, with no intention of meeting anybody, was a truly magical feeling. I couldn't help but wonder why I hadn't decided to do it earlier, as the adventurer in me had been waiting for that exact scenario for years. Better late than never though, and from the moment I landed in Paris, I didn't look back.

Everything was so exciting during my first couple of weeks there. Exploring big cities, strolling around quaint towns, and taking in the countryside on long train journeys all felt infinitely more exciting for the fact that I was on my own. It was now *my* trip, and I could do what *I* wanted to do, and be who *I* wanted to be; it was undoubtedly the most liberated that I'd ever felt.

I was about three weeks into my European adventure when I arrived in the Montenegrin coastal town of Kotor. I was recommended a walk by the lady that I was staying with from Kotor's picturesque old town, which culminates at an old fort a couple of hundred metres up one of the mountains that surrounds it. I climbed beyond the ruins for a further 100 metres or so to escape from civilisation, and it turned out to be one of the best decisions that I'd ever made.

I'm sure I'd have figured all of this stuff out at some point, but the time that I spent at that peak helped me to recognise just how much of a mess I'd been in for *years* up to that point. The turquoise waters and dramatic limestone cliffs of Kotor Bay were as spectacular as any scene that I'd ever come across, inspiring me at a time that I'd unknowingly needed it.

With the sun warming me through, not a hint of wind, and only the amazing scenery to stimulate the senses, I embarked upon a four-hour conversation with myself. It was all sparked when, impelled by the view, the most overwhelming rush of euphoria almost made me cry. It was akin to how I'd felt when the cocaine had hit me in Mancora a few months earlier, except this time, there were no artificial highs involved.

The first thing that I asked myself when I recognised that I was experiencing such a natural high was, *how long has it been since I last felt like this?*

Aside from Jermaine Beckford's goal at Old Trafford, I couldn't think of a single occasion since I'd started university that I'd felt happy around people, at least in the absence of any self-destructive behaviours. After finishing uni, the two sole periods in which I'd felt fulfilled had come when I was off work, spending my days watching sport in blissful solitude. Even as I looked back to my childhood, it had been those peaceful days on my own in my bedroom that had given me the most pleasure.

Until that day, I'd never considered how much time I'd spent on my own as a child. Yes, I'd often been out with my mates, but for the most part, I wasn't disturbed at home in the way that I so often was at university. That word, *disturbed*, was the key.

As I sat atop that mountain, my mind was able to roam more freely than it ever had before as I knew that nobody was going to disturb me. It felt like I'd waited my entire life to be in that position, totally free, and totally at peace, with no possibility of anybody interrupting me.

What makes depression so difficult, aside from the fact that most people that have it don't realise they have it, is the way that it plays into itself. The overriding feeling that you have is that things can't, and won't, get better. You feel like absolutely nothing can make you feel good, aside from artificial measures, which is why so many depressed people turn to alcohol and drugs. I'd done just that at times, but I feel incredibly blessed to have had a far more healthy companion in sport.

The reality was that I'd become almost entirely dependent upon it. For the thick end of five years, it had been the only thing that had ever got me excited, enthused or passionate. Depression leaves you almost entirely devoid of positive emotions, and I honestly don't know how I would have sought out such feelings had it not been for sport. Dependency is never healthy, though.

With the gradual deterioration of my interest in all other areas of life, such as people, education and fitness, my dependence on sport to compensate had reached an unsustainable level. I'd been so incapable of making myself happy, that I'd pinned every hope of emotional fulfilment on the success of the teams and individuals that I supported.

During this time, there'd been an endless list of near-misses and absolute failures, without any successes. I'd become so irrational during my time at university that I'd started to wonder whether I was genuinely incapable of success as a fan. However, I had eventually experienced success, and it hadn't been the answer to my depression.

Even from that mountain top, seeing things as clearly as I'd ever seen them, I stood by my reaction to Leeds United's promotion from League One. In the present day, if I saw a team or an individual that I supported undeservingly winning something as Leeds did promotion in 2009/10, I think my response would be similar. The same can't be said about Old Trafford.

If there was ever a telltale sign that sporting success was not the cure for my depression, my social media post after Leeds beat Manchester United was it. There was everything to be proud of and euphoric for after that game, yet within hours of the victory, I only felt anger.

For a football fan who supports Leeds United, there is nothing in the sport that can give you more pleasure than a victory at Old Trafford. Yet, as I reflect, even my celebrations for the goal and the final whistle were anger-fuelled. There wasn't any smiling, just screaming, shouting, grabbing and punching. Yes, it was an outpouring of overwhelming emotion, but if happiness was part of that, I had a funny way of expressing it.

The more I reflected on sport's role in what had been an incredibly difficult few years, the less I could decide whether it had been a good thing for me or not. Was my life better or worse for me being a huge sports fan, and would I have started my recovery from depression earlier had it not been the most important thing in my life? When I asked myself that question, a huge smile broke out across my face, and I can remember laughing out loud as I realised what sport was to me.

My association with sport had essentially been like a romantic relationship between two people.

As someone that had never been in a relationship, I pondered how a depressed person in an actual relationship might come to depend on their partner. I mused that they would most likely become a burden, that they would become extremely difficult when they weren't treated well, and even when they were done right by, they still wouldn't appreciate it, and might even find a way to be angry about it.

I'd been through almost five years of misery, almost five years of never being happy, and I'd just been waiting for sport to make it right. I feel like I see this a lot in everyday relationships, somebody that is deeply unhappy within themselves depending on their partner, or something in their future, to make it all better. It's not on somebody or something else to make you better though; only *you* can do that.

The philosophical place that I reached in my mind that day helped me to make sense of myself entirely. As someone that hadn't experienced happiness for so long, it was so liberating for me to be able to teach myself what I needed to do to *be* happy. I needed freedom, I needed peace, and I needed to be undisturbed. Fundamentally, I needed to be alone.

There was no guaranteeing that a couple of weeks of feeling amazing in Europe would ensure that I'd be happy for the rest of my life, of course. There were many other things that I'd need to work on for that to become a reality, but the recognition that freedom and peace were the two crucial factors in my happiness was a significant stride forward for me.

The main thing that these two pillars helped me to understand was that I would probably never want to be in an actual relationship. The way I saw it, true freedom and peace could only be achieved independently of coexistence, and I accepted with that thought that I'd likely be alone forever.

When I eventually walked back down that mountain, I felt as though I could see everything so clearly. As someone that had spent his whole life immersed in an extraverted society, I now recognised that solitude could be my default way of being; spending time with people could be done out of choice. Throughout my years of studying psychology, I must have seen the words 'extravert' and 'introvert' thousands of times, yet the incredibly obvious reality had never registered with me; I was an introvert. Awareness can be so empowering.

After all that, what was there to greet me in Kotor's old town when I arrived back to reality from my mountain-top epiphany? Sport. Pretty much the first bar that I walked past was showing English Premier League football on an outdoor screen. That oh-too unfamiliar feeling of euphoria stayed with me as I watched a couple of games over a few beers in the sun, and they weren't just any old games either. I was treated to two thrillers, as Chelsea and Newcastle United drew 2-2 and Wigan Athletic came from 2-0 down to beat West Ham United 3-2 in a relegation six-pointer. By no means was that the best sport of the day either.

At nightfall, with me having been out for nearly ten hours and in that bar for four, huge crowds started to pour in, which surprised me bearing in mind that it was a Sunday night. I couldn't help but be curious as to what was going on, and my English-speaking waiter duly informed me that Montenegrins always turned out in their droves when Novak Djokovic was playing in a big match.

Montenegro had only very recently become independent from Djokovic's native Serbia, but the Montenegrin people still very much saw him as one of their own. Djokovic had recently gatecrashed Roger Federer and Rafael Nadal's reign as the 'big two' of tennis by winning the Australian Open and embarking on an incredible thirty-six-match winning streak in 2011. That evening, Djokovic and Nadal were battling it out for the Rome Masters title on Nadal's preferred surface of clay.

I can say without any hesitation that watching that tennis match was one of the best experiences I've ever had as a sports fan. The atmosphere in that bar was electric as Djokovic edged out Nadal 6-4 6-4, with the locals cheering every point that their man won like it was a goal in a football World Cup final. By the end of it, I was a fully-fledged Djokovic fan, even though he'd beaten my beloved Andy Murray in the semi-final the previous day.

I'd never known a sport other than football to induce such emotion in people. I'd always loved tennis, but the experience of watching the utter brilliance of Djokovic and Nadal that day fundamentally changed me as a sports fan. Not only did I start to imagine how I might feel should Murray manage to win a Grand Slam, but I also contemplated whether other sports could yield the same level of emotion in me that football had always done. I'd always taken football to be the be-all and end-all, with the other sports that I passionately followed functioning as prominent support acts. Maybe they could knock football off its perch.

Regardless of all that, I would say that 15th May 2011 remains the most important day of my entire life. The day that I understood that I was an introvert was the day that I became free and at peace. It would change me as a person forever, and there's a strong argument to say that it changed me as a sports fan forever.

Above all, the most critical thing was that I was happy again. A horrific period of my life was over; I'd beaten depression.

Extra Time

30

'Aguero' moments

'AguerOOOOOOOOOOOOOOOOOOOOOOO. I SWEAR YOU'LL NEVER SEE ANYTHING LIKE THIS EVER AGAIN. SO WATCH IT; DRINK IT IN!'.

Almost exactly one year on from the day that I came out of depression, 364 days to be precise, Martin Tyler delivered my favourite ever piece of commentary. I have absolutely no affiliation with Manchester City, and not even my disdain for Manchester United was a contributing factor to the emotion that Tyler's reaction induced in me. In fact, I'd made a £50 wager with my pal Andy at the start of the 2011/12 Premier League season that the trophy would be heading to Old Trafford come what may, while he said it would end up at the Etihad Stadium. It's fair to say that Andy and I got full value for that bet, and I gladly paid up.

During stoppage time of the final game of a nine-month season, with your bitter city rivals having already won their match to move three points of clear of you, while you find yourself 2-1 down at home to the most modest of Queen's Park Rangers sides; City fans must have felt lower than they'd ever felt. All they'd needed to do was win a home match against a side battling relegation, and they'd have won the Premier League for the first time, after so many years of watching their neighbours dominate.

There they were, losing, with just 150 or so seconds of stoppage time remaining in their season. They needed an almost impossible two goals, or the outstanding season that they'd put together would mean nothing. They were effectively presenting the trophy to their enemies themselves; I suspect that every English football fan in the world was lost for an explanation as to how City had thrown it away.

Then, as Edin Dzeko scored to make it 2-2, there was hope. They only had a couple of minutes to find a still incredibly unlikely third goal, but they had one of the two that they required to snatch victory from the jaws of defeat, having appeared to have been doing their best to do the opposite with the title itself.

I can remember exactly where I was, what I was doing, and who I was with when Aguero won the league for Manchester City in the 94th minute of their 38th and final game of the season. There was actually a City fan in the York pub that I was in, and all he could do was cry uncontrollably, totally overwhelmed by a story that even the finest of creative writers couldn't have written. All that I could do was think, *I can't even imagine what it would feel like to be him right now.*

I'd only experienced one moment of sporting glory up to that point in my life, and the Leeds United team that I was supporting in the 2009/10 League One season were so undeserving of the success that they'd achieved that I'd not even enjoyed it. Sport hadn't treated me as well as I could have hoped for since I'd started my journey as a fan back in 1993, but since coming out of depression, I'd become far more accepting of my fortunes. I just hoped that maybe, one day, it would provide with me true joy.

The closest experience I'd had to what I coin as an *Aguero Moment* in any area of life up to that point, was the day that I recovered on that mountain in Montenegro. It was a life-changing event, one in which everything had seemed to fall perfectly into place. Now that I'd got my life outside of sport back on track, I just hoped that my number one interest would repay my years of loyal support with some glory. It might not be *glory in all it's glory* like those City fans had just experienced, just something that would make me feel true happiness.

In the year or so that had elapsed between that day at Kotor Bay and Aguero's divine intervention, I'd travelled for a further few months, moved home, found a new job working as a travel agent, and moved to York. The realisation that I was an introvert had left me wanting to create a life that enabled me to spend as much time on my own as possible, while also ensuring that I maintained the excellent relationships that I had with my friends and family.

I talked openly and frankly about the struggles that I'd had over the years, and all the people closest to me were incredibly supportive, while also being delighted that I'd come out of the other side. Without realising it, I'd put some strain on some of my strongest relationships due to the erratic nature of my depression, but the damage had by no means been irreparable. If anything, it only served to bring me closer to those that I cared about the most.

My new set up in a city that was far enough away from Leeds to feel removed, while also being close enough to get back with ease, couldn't have worked better. Having my own place was going to work out to be too expensive, which meant that I had to move into a shared house, but with my room having an ensuite, I barely saw my housemates. I made it clear that I didn't want anybody disturbing me, and I spent my time watching sport, writing music, and revelling in the peaceful existence that I'd created for myself.

By July 2012, I'd invested almost twenty years of time, money, effort, energy, and above all, emotion, into being a sports fan. Ultimately, I felt as though I was now deserving of some glory after such a long wait, although my newfound quality of life seemed to help ease the pressure that I'd placed on sport to provide for me. I felt myself changing.

I enjoyed watching England at Euro 2012 and was the most accepting of our exit that I'd ever been after Italy beat us on penalties in the quarter-final. We'd gone into the tournament with the weakest squad that we'd had in my lifetime, and Roy Hodgson did well with the little time that he'd had to prepare, having replaced Fabio Capello as manager just a few weeks earlier. The funny thing was that I was actually a bit relieved after we went out, as, for the first time in my life, I felt ready for a break from football. It had consumed me for such a long time, that it felt good to look forward to a summer of other sports.

I managed to get Sky TV in my room at my place in York and watched relentless amounts of sport by the week. I got back into rugby league for the first time in a long while, with Thursday and Friday night Super League matches providing outstanding entertainment. It was effortless for me to reconnect with the Leeds Rhinos, having been a season ticket holder for many years as a child, but even if the Rhinos weren't playing, I still found the sport incredibly fulfilling to watch.

When Yorkshire signed a couple of exciting overseas players specifically for the Twenty20 form of the game, I found myself consistently investing in the one-day disciplines of cricket for the first time. The combination of having South African David Miller and Australian Mitchell Starc, alongside some exciting youngsters of our own in Jonny Bairstow, Gary Ballance, and a twenty-one-year-old lad called Joe Root, made watching the more explosive formats of the game particularly enjoyable.

Wimbledon 2012 was undoubtedly the most invested I'd ever been in a tennis tournament, as Andy Murray broke down another barrier in his bid to become the first British man to win a Grand Slam in seventy-six years. Murray reached the SW19 final for the first time, and took the first set, before falling in four to sixteen-time Slam champion, and widely regarded greatest player of all time, Roger Federer.

When Murray broke down in tears as he tried to deliver his post-match speech to his home fans, an emotion came over me that I'd not felt in as long as I could remember. There was a lump in my throat, and I felt incredibly relieved to be alone, as being around other people might have caused me to shed a tear.

I found it impossible not to empathise with Murray. The raw passion, determination, and ability that he'd shown in the face of the most unforgiving era of tennis there'd ever been, made him more deserving of victory than any sportsman that I'd ever supported. He was a winner in my eyes, and the possibility that he might not win a Grand Slam in his career after what was his fourth final defeat was too unbearable to imagine.

It's funny how life works, though. For all of the pure loyalty and dedication that I'd displayed to such an array of teams and individuals over the years, it was something that I'd invested nothing whatsoever in that gave me my first ever feeling of true glory. This experience was to spark an incredible hat-trick of mini *Aguero Moments* in the space of just six weeks.

The funny thing is that I'll never know if the summer of 2012 would have made me feel the same had I still been depressed.

31

A summer of love

I was in my pal Rich's living room when Mo Farah kicked off the final bend of the 10,000m at the London 2012 Olympics. Little over a week earlier, I'd barely watched an Olympic event in my life. Yet, as the crowd at the Olympic Stadium roared Farah on as he edged clear of the field, Rich and I found ourselves within inches of his television screen screaming 'RUN MO, FUCKING RUN'.

As he crossed the finish line, and commentator Steve Cram proclaimed, 'IT'S GOLD', I lost all control of my emotions. I'd jumped on Rich as it had become clear that Farah had won the race with about thirty metres to go, but I had to remove myself from his arms soon after.

The lump-in-my-throat feeling that I'd experienced after Andy Murray's defeat to Roger Federer a few weeks earlier had returned, and tears had started to fill my eyes. I'd cried a few times in my life as a result of negative sporting experiences, but never had a victory caused such a powerful emotional response.

The feeling confused me to the point at which I felt compelled to fight it. I was embarrassed by the notion of crying in front of my friend, so I stepped away from him, composed myself, before taking in the celebratory scenes from a more balanced standpoint. I had no idea what was going on inside of me, but it felt amazing. The only regret that I have is that I didn't have the emotional maturity to allow the tears to flow.

For all the effort that I'd made over the years to book time off work specifically for sport, it had been a total coincidence that I'd taken off the two weeks of London 2012. When I'd started my job in York, my manager had asked me to put my annual leave for the year in immediately, and as I'd not been able to afford to go away, I decided to book in three weeks over the summer to spend in Leeds with the lads. It was only on Friday 27th July, the first night of my three weeks off, that I even acknowledged the UK's home Olympics.

Having not seen each other for a while, Rich and I met for a couple of beers at the pub. We'd started to settle into what I expected to be a lengthy conversation, but within a few minutes, we were distracted by the start of the opening ceremony on one of the TV screens. The bar staff had turned the music off, and the sound of a young choir's version of *Jerusalem* was now playing, which was enough to induce a few goosebumps. Suddenly transfixed, Rich and I proceeded to watch the entirety of the show, as did almost everybody in our vicinity at the pub.

Despite the immense support that I'd given to a host of English and British sports teams over the years, I'd never been a patriotic man. However, the celebration of everything British throughout the ceremony had me bursting with pride for my country in a way that I'd never imagined was possible, and more importantly, instantaneously made me an enormous Team GB fan.

I barely missed a minute of the Olympics for the two weeks that followed. Between Lizzie Armitstead claiming silver in the Women's Road Race in the cycling, right through to the moment that twenty-two-year-old boxer Anthony Joshua clinched Heavyweight gold on the final day, I essentially spent a fortnight feeling euphoric. Witnessing all of these work-a-day British people fulfilling their lifelong dreams of winning Olympic medals, in front of home crowds that displayed the kind of passionate support that we are so famous for, was special on so many levels.

There were multiple occasions on which I found myself screaming my support at the television screen, particularly in thrilling sports such as cycling, rowing, and swimming. Still, there can be no doubting that 'Super Saturday' was the defining evening. Team GB's poster girl Jessica Ennis-Hill's decimation of the field to claim Heptathlon gold, soon followed by the relatively unknown Greg Rutherford's remarkable triumph in the Long Jump had already made it one of the most memorable nights in British athletics history. Then, our long-distance superstar took centre stage.

The story of Farah fleeing his native war-torn Somalia to join his father in London as an eight-year-old is a tragic one, but his rise to stardom is one of our country's iconic tales of sporting success. His immense popularity with the British public had set the stage for something unforgettable, and the incredible drama of the 10,000m didn't disappoint.

The very fact that after twenty-four laps of the track, and nearly twenty-seven minutes, there were just metres separating eleven of these supreme athletes was enough to have you falling off the edge of your seat. To see Mo run clear of the field in front of 80,000 delirious supporters was as beautiful a sporting moment that I'd witnessed in my life up to that point. I can feel myself getting emotional as I write about it even now.

Another man to claim Olympic glory was arguably my favourite sportsman on the planet at the time. With tennis being a sport that I'd loved for as long as I could remember, having a genuinely world-class player in Andy Murray to watch had made for so many exceptional spectating occasions in the seven years up to London 2012. Seeing Murray destroy Roger Federer in the final to claim gold, having swept aside Novak Djokovic in the semis, made me overly emotional again. Murray's outpouring of feeling displayed how important the victory was to him, and although it wasn't a Grand Slam, defeating two of his main rivals to win the next best thing felt pivotal.

A few weeks later, with tennis' top stars having played at the French Open, Wimbledon, and the Olympics within the space of just a couple of months, the US Open arrived. With Djokovic having played twenty matches across those three top-level events, Murray and Federer having played nineteen apiece, and Rafael Nadal out through injury, many pundits believed that Flushing Meadows presented an opportunity for a player outside of the 'Big Four' to emerge victorious. Nothing of the sort would happen.

Although Murray looked jaded at times during the earlier rounds in New York, there was also an imperious nature about him that I'd not seen before. En route to a fifth Grand Slam final, he dismissed three very respectable opponents in straight sets, while battling back from a set down in the other three matches against dangerous players Feliciano Lopez, Marin Cilic, and Tomas Berdych. Perhaps most importantly, the latter had accounted for Federer in the quarter-finals.

Although his game wasn't always at it's best, Murray's mentality was of a man that refused to believe that any player outside of the 'Big Four' could beat him. Unsurprisingly, that man Djokovic was waiting for him in the final, and it turned out to be one of the greatest sporting spectacles that I'd ever witnessed.

The final would take place on a Monday with the weather having interrupted the tournament's schedule, and I watched through the night from my bedroom in my shared house in York, where I'd managed to get Sky Sports set up. I can distinctly recall being both frustrated and disappointed by the lack of people I knew to be tuning in, with so many apparent Murray fans having revelled in his exploits in London over the summer. I'd known very few folk that had closely followed his progress since his breakthrough back in 2005, which meant that watching the match alone in a bedroom felt sadly appropriate.

The tone was set in the sixth game of the first set when Murray and Djokovic embarked upon a fifty-four-shot rally. Djokovic took that point, but Murray nicked an astonishing eighty-seven-minute first set when he clinched a nerve-shredding tie-break 12-10. He was a set up in a Grand Slam final once again, but I barely flinched in response to him having moved ahead with that SW19 final still fresh in the memory.

The second set was always going to be huge, and I couldn't quite believe my eyes as Murray raced into a 4-0 lead. I couldn't believe my ears either as one of the commentators remarked that the match was turning in to a rout, although I knew better than to think that a titan like Djokovic was out of the set even then.

Lo and behold, he managed to battle back to level up at 5-5, but showing psychological resilience befitting of a champion,

Murray turned the tide to break the Serb and take the set 7-5. Andy Murray, two sets up in a Grand Slam final, yet more uncharted territory.

The Briton started the third set well, but there was a pivotal moment in the second game when Djokovic produced a stunning soft-touch volley at the net that sent thousands of adoring fans in the Arthur Ashe Stadium wild. In an ingenious display of opportunism, Djokovic then milked the moment for all it was worth, gesturing to the crowd to get behind him, and even from my bedroom in York, I could sense the psychological significance. My worst fears were soon realised.

Djokovic outclassed Murray for the hour that followed to bring the match level at two sets all. At 2-0 Murray, I'd dared to dream that this was going to be his time. However, with arguably the most intimidating opponent in the sport across the net, who was carrying every ounce of the match's momentum, I held no hope whatsoever, merely a wish.

If I'd have been offered this scenario at the start of the match, Murray needing just one set to claim the US Open title, I'd have bitten the hand off of whoever had presented it. However, there couldn't have been a situation that left Djokovic as more of an overwhelming favourite, with every element of the equation now suggesting that he would go on to claim his sixth Major title.

It was 1.30 am York-bedroom time, and I can remember thinking that at least I'd probably be asleep by 2 am with the fifth set unlikely to take Djokovic long to wrap up. The fifth set was over by 2 am, but to my astonishment, it was the irrepressible Murray that had dominated it.

Having looked second best for so much of the third and

fourth sets, Murray came out for the fifth rejuvenated and broke Djokovic in the first game. He then displayed some gamesmanship of his own in the second game, conducting the crowd after outlasting Djokovic at 40-30 to move to 2-0 ahead. From there, he didn't look back.

It wasn't until 1.50 am, at 5-2 ahead and with three Championship points, that I felt confident enough to say that I knew that Andy Murray was about to become a Major champion. Funnily enough, he lost the next rally to leave the score at 40-15, but when Djokovic went long with his return during the following point, the words 'Game, Set, Match, Murray' could be heard behind commentator Mark Petchey's cries of 'HISTORY IS MADE!'.

Once again, a lump emerged in the pit of my throat, and tears encompassed my eyes. As Murray dropped to his haunches, I was in no doubt that there wasn't a sportsman on this planet that deserved this more. Djokovic's comment of 'You deserve it' as the two embraced only served to reinforce that point. Four hours and fifty-four minutes of pulsating sporting action, and the British man had come out on top.

I stayed up for the half an hour that followed to see the trophy lift and went to bed feeling overcome with both relief and euphoria. Had Murray not been able to close that match out, he may never have recovered from it psychologically. With so much said of the resilience, steel, and determination of Djokovic, it was Murray that had shown more of it to halt the Serb in his tracks. I couldn't possibly have believed that I'd witness an even more dramatic sporting event a couple of weeks later in what had already become the best summer of my life.

I was twelve years and eleven months old when I first

experienced the unparalleled sporting drama of golf's Ryder Cup in September 1999. Twelve years, eleven months, and a couple of weeks later, it produced something so remarkable that I still don't think that I've fully registered it to this day.

When I'd booked my three weeks annual leave after starting my new job, the only other time off in 2012 that I'd requested had been the weekend of 28th-30th September. My dad and I had watched every Ryder Cup since my bizarre act of sensitivity back in '99, and I wasn't about to give that up because I'd started a job that involved working weekends. I'd expected to spend the entirety of Friday, Saturday, and Sunday with him, but circumstances had it that I would be elsewhere for the Sunday singles.

Between returning from my travelling trip and moving to York, I'd spent a few months working in a bookmakers in Leeds city centre. With the job involving taking bets from punters and watching Sky Sports all day, I'd loved every second of working there, and had managed to arrange a zero-hours contract with my incredibly friendly manager after I'd taken the job in York. That meant that I could go back and work the odd shift for him when required to earn a bit of extra cash for doing little other than watching sport, and when he came calling on Ryder Cup weekend, I couldn't say no to him.

Throughout the time that I'd worked with him, I'd discovered that he was probably the biggest golf fan on the planet. He'd insisted on having every minute of every tournament on in the shop, however insignificant it might have been, and when he called me in a state of panic just a couple of weeks before Medinah 2012, I couldn't turn him down.

One of his staff members had quit, and he couldn't find a

person in Leeds that would cover the Sunday 30th September shift for him. He was staring down the barrel of having to watch the Sunday singles while at work, which was just not acceptable for a fan of his magnitude. I was perfectly happy to cover, although maybe I wouldn't have been had I known what would happen.

I'd stayed up until midnight on a school-night Sunday back in '99 to watch one of the most dramatic sporting conclusions I'd ever witnessed, as Justin Leonard holed a monster putt to leave the Americans on the brink of an incredible victory. However, in one of the most controversial moments in golf history, Leonard's teammates had charged on to the green to celebrate with him, even though our man Jose Maria Olazabal still had a putt to keep the tournament alive.

Olazabal went on to miss that putt, and in an interview immediately afterwards, Europe's Sam Torrance, one of the most passionate sportsmen I've ever known, absolutely lambasted the American players for their behaviour. I'd barely watched golf in my life up to that point, but even I'd known how disgraceful their reaction had been. I'd hated them for it, and with the help of Torrance's rant, I'd felt as passionately about Europe beating the USA at golf as I had about Leeds United beating Manchester United in football.

Back in 1999, Europe had earned themselves a 10-6 lead after two fantastic days of foursomes and fourballs golf. However, a stunning Sunday singles performance from the Americans saw them stage one of the great sporting comebacks to win the Ryder Cup 14.5-13.5, with Olazabal's missed putt after that American intervention proving pivotal. Fast forward to 2012, and Davis Love III, one of the players that had stormed the green in '99, was the American captain, Olazabal was Europe's captain, and after two incredible days of golf, the USA held a 10-6 lead heading into the final day.

It had looked at one stage on the second day, or night as it was for us as we watched events in the States unfold from the UK, that we might have found ourselves as much as 12-4 down. However, as I watched the clock tick past midnight to bring in Sunday 30th September from my dad's living room, 'Mr Ryder Cup' Ian Poulter produced some phenomenal golf to help us to restrict the deficit to just four points. With the USA team the far stronger on paper, and history favouring them on home soil in the singles, we still barely had a puncher's chance as I watched play begin at 5 pm from behind the counter at the bookies.

I don't think that I'll ever work a shift that will go as fast as the four and a half hours between 5 pm and 9.30 pm did that day. Thankfully for me, barely a sole came into the shop all day, leading me to send my colleague home at 6.30 pm, and lock the doors two and a half hours early at 7 pm. I'm pretty sure that it was against the law for me to do so, but there wasn't a punter in sight during that time regardless.

By the time 9.30 pm did come around, Europe had remarkably levelled the match up at 10-10. Luke Donald, Ian Poulter, Rory McIlroy and Paul Lawrie had all won their singles matches at the top of the order, while the Americans were yet to get on the scoreboard. Then, in a moment that made European fans truly believe, Justin Rose holed a forty-foot putt on the 17th to square up his match with Phil Mickelson, just moments after the American had come tantalisingly close to chipping in.

I can remember running around the shop in delirious

celebration after Rose's putt had gone in, and as I retook my seat, I received a message from my dad merely stating, *Justin you God!!*. With the Ryder Cup heading to the wire, I contemplated getting a taxi to his flat, but couldn't bring myself to miss a second of the unbelievable golf that was unravelling before my eyes.

10-10 became 11-10 to the USA as Dustin Johnson completed a victory over Nicolas Colsaerts, which was the first point that the home side had won since the clock had turned midnight the previous night. Europe had won six in that time, which soon became seven as Rose miraculously pinched the last hole of his match with Mickelson to win 1up, making the scores 11-11.

USA's Zach Johnson and Europe's Lee Westwood then made the score 12-12 with victories for their respective sides, leaving just four matches out on the course, and four points on offer. With the USA up in one of those four, and the other three all square, the projected final score was now USA 14.5-13.5 Europe; it could barely have been tighter.

When Jim Furyk's par putt on the 18th hole somehow stayed out, Sergio Garcia had won another point for Europe, putting us into the lead for the first time all weekend at 12-13. However, Jason Dufner then sealed a comfortable victory over Peter Hanson to square things up once more at 13-13, leaving Steve Stricker vs Martin Kaymer and Tiger Woods vs Francesco Molinari as the only matches left to complete. Both were all square.

As it stood, current holders Europe were now on course to retain the Ryder Cup with a draw at 14-14, a prospect that was scarcely believable at the start of the day's play, never mind when we'd been 10-4 down at one stage the night before. Unsurprisingly, the drama was far from over.

Kaymer won the 17th hole to move 1up on Stricker, only for Woods to do the same against Molinari moments later. As Kaymer and Stricker headed towards the 18th green, with Woods and Molinari waiting at the tee, the equation was clear; a point between Kaymer and Molinari was all we needed.

By this point, I was so emotionally all over the place that I'd decided to stand up and watch. There was so much nervous energy fizzing around my body that being stationary just wasn't feasible. The delicacy of the situation started to become clear to me; this impossible weekend of golf was going to come down to the finest of margins, and would either result in pure ecstasy, or utter devastation.

With Woods hitting his drive straight down the final fairway, and Molinari finding the bunker, attention turned to their teammates at the green ahead of them. Fortunately for us, Stricker could only leave himself with a mid-range putt for par, handing Kaymer two putts with which to retain the Ryder Cup. Now, I believed it was ours.

Right on cue, as Kaymer sent his first putt on it's way, the ball seemed to gather pace as it approached the hole, while it was always missing to the right. At this point, I ran towards the screen and started shouting 'SLOW BALL, SLOW, FUCKING SLOW', somehow believing that I could influence events from 4000 miles away.

I wasn't sure how long he'd been standing there for, but as the ball eventually slowed to a stop about six feet past the hole, I turned away from the screen in dismay and saw a bloke laughing at me from the other side of the shop's front door. He had a clear view of what was happening and had undoubtedly been watching as I'd charged towards the TV screen and screamed for Martin Kaymer's golf ball to slow down. He must only have been waiting for me to see him, as in the instant that I did, he almost fell over himself in a fit of laughter, before walking off into the night. He genuinely could have been there for two hours, and I'd have had absolutely no idea.

With Stricker's par-putt slightly further away than that of Kaymer, the American was to step up first. You could have cut the tension with a knife at Medinah's 18th green, but Stricker felt none of it. He nervelessly drained his putt to leave his German counterpart having to hole his to claim the point and retain the Ryder Cup.

As Kaymer lined up his putt, the camera stopped on Olazabal. The man who'd been through such trauma in 1999 as a result of that Leonard putt, and had been through the far more real trauma of having lost his great friend and European golfing great Seve Ballesteros in 2011, couldn't watch from halfway down the fairway. He rested his chin on his chest, and pulled his cap down over his face, allowing his ears to tell him whether his team had completed a miracle. The camera then focused in on the silhouette of Ballesteros on Olazabal's shirt sleeve, and the commentators acknowledged that maybe the spirit of Seve had played a role in this incomprehensible European fightback.

Kaymer, under more pressure than he'd ever be again on a golf course, swung his putter back, before bringing it through in a smooth motion and sending the ball up the hill towards the cup. I stood there motionlessly, with my hands on my head, willing the ball to disappear with everything that I had.

'YEAAAAHHHH, FUCKING COME ON, YEEAAAAHHH!', I screamed. It was glory; total and utter, unadulterated glory. I didn't sprint around the shop on this occasion, I just stood there and stared at the screen in disbelief. We'd done it, we'd won the Ryder Cup from the most impossible of situations, against a team supposedly so far superior, in their own backyard.

There was bedlam on the 18th green, as our players sprinted towards Kaymer to celebrate with a triumphant collective embrace. As the camera panned to Olazabal, the tears had started. However, in a gesture that typified him as a man, he regathered himself to support Molinari, who was still lining up his second shot in the final match.

With the celebrations unable to truly take off until Molinari and Woods had finished their match, the European class of 2012 vacated the green, just as the American class of 1999 had. The critical difference on this occasion, of course, was that the Ryder Cup *was* over after the putt had been holed.

For me as a fan, I hadn't realised that I'd still not fully eradicated my first-ever Ryder Cup experience from my mind. Even after thirteen years, the scars of seeing that American response to Leonard's putt as a twelve-year-old boy had sat somewhere in my subconscious, unable to be entirely dispelled. It took us to come back from 10-4 down and win on American soil to lay those demons to rest, and not for the first time in 2012, tears filled my eyes as the magnitude of the achievement started to sink in.

I ran into the back of the shop and grabbed all of my things, readying myself to run down to Leeds train station to catch the last train back to York. I knew that I had until a fraction before midnight, and it looked like I just had time to see the end of the final match. The score was now 14-13 to us; there was still a very slight chance that the unthinkable could happen. Could we replicate that 1999 American team and come back from 10-6 down at the start of the singles to win the tournament outright at 14.5-13.5?

As if the dream script hadn't already been written, Woods missed his par putt on the 18th, which left Molinari with a little tester to halve the match and give Europe an unfathomable 14.5 points. Then, in a gesture befitting the memory of the great Seve, Woods told Molinari to pick up his ball, conceding the hole, in the most sportsmanlike manner possible. The point was halved, and the Ryder Cup hadn't just been retained, Europe had *won* it outright.

I only had a couple of minutes to take in the scenes from the 18th green as the European party started. It wasn't until I got back to my house in York at about 1 am that I saw the famous interview with Olazabal, who couldn't contain himself as he tried to say a few words about his friend Ballesteros. The players echoed Ollie's sentiments, all of them wondering whether there really had been an omnipotent force out there with them; the spirit of one of Europe's true greats. The emotion only served to enhance that incredible feeling of glory.

With September having become October as I'd ventured back to York, I looked back on a summer that no sports fan could ever even dream of having. I may have waited twenty years to experience the feeling, but it had been so worth the wait. The Olympics, Andy Murray's maiden Major victory, and the most dramatic Ryder Cup in history had provided such drama and quality, that Yorkshire's promotion to County

Championship Division One and Leeds Rhinos' Super League triumph had taken a backseat.

It was a two-month period that had truly taught me how to feel again, and whatever sport held for me in the future, I'd always have the summer of 2012.

32

Bleeding out

On the 8th July 2014, Leeds United sold player of the season and twenty-eight-goal striker Ross McCormack to Fulham. Before I go into more detail about the decision that I made in response to the news, I want to give you a brief rundown of what happened at my football club during the three years leading up to that moment.

After just missing out on the 2010/11 play-offs in our first season back in the Championship, an impressive performance, young midfielders Bradley Johnson and Neil Kilkenny were allowed to leave the club after not having their contracts renewed. Outstanding twenty-four-year-old goalkeeper Kasper Schmeichel was sold to Leicester City, and on the summer transfer deadline day, 10/11 player of the season, twenty-three-year-old Max Gradel, left for St. Etienne in France. A few old boys came in on free transfers or loan deals.

After a steady first half of the season, Leeds-born, lifelong fan and captain Jonny Howson was sold to Norwich City in January. A week later, lifelong fan and manager Simon Grayson was sacked by chairman Ken Bates. Promotion specialist, but long-term foe of the club, Neil Warnock, was brought in as Grayson's replacement, and we suffered a miserable second half to the 2011/12 campaign. Few results in my Leeds

United-supporting tenure embarrassed me more than the 3-7 home defeat to Nottingham Forest, and 14th place just about summed our season up.

That summer, 11/12 player of the season and Howson's replacement as captain, twenty-four-year-old winger Robert Snodgrass, was sold to Norwich while promising young midfielder Adam Clayton departed for Huddersfield Town. Ten players left the club, with twelve coming in.

After endless speculation about a protracted takeover, Middle-Eastern consortium GFH Capital completed a deal for the club in December 2012. This sparked hope and belief among our club's supporters that big money would finally be invested in the playing squad to plot a route back to the Premier League. We were sitting just outside the play-off places at the time, and I, for one, thought that a couple of January signings might be all that we needed for a promotion push.

However, the only significant development at the club that transfer window was the sale of fans' favourite Luciano Becchio, the fourth player to leave for Norwich in eighteen months. There was fury all over every online fans' forum that I read, with multiple comments labelling us as Norwich's feeder club.

Becchio's departure seemed to have a substantial impact on the field, as two wins in twelve games in the immediate aftermath culminated in Warnock leaving the club, with former Reading manager Brian McDermott replacing him. We finished the 2012/13 campaign in 13th place.

In the summer of 2013, I decided to take another travelling trip. The company that I was working for actively encouraged their employees to take big trips, on the premise that they return, and having travelled extensively across Europe, Asia,

Australia, New Zealand, and South America, I decided that I would venture to Africa, Central America, and the USA. Leeds made a solid start to the 2013/14 season and were challenging for the top six when I departed for Uganda in late October.

By the time I reached South Africa on Christmas Eve, we were sitting fifth in the Championship. From what I could follow from abroad, McDermott sounded like he was doing an excellent job with limited resources, having spent next to no money in the summer transfer window. With Ross McCormack on fire in front of goal, my take was that if McDermott was given some money to spend in January, we might have had a genuine chance of promotion. Sadly, nothing of the sort happened, and it transpired to be arguably the most embarrassing month of my Leeds United-supporting tenure.

I'd been staying at a hostel in Cape Town for ten days when I settled in at its bar for a day of sport on 4th January 2014. I'd not managed to watch as much football as I'd have liked when travelling south through Africa, even though they love their Premier League there, so after arriving in Cape Town, I committed to watching as much as I possibly could. I took in both the Boxing Day and New Year's Day games, with a full round of fixtures squeezed in between too, but the first Saturday in January brought the FA Cup third round.

As the early kick-off of Blackburn Rovers vs Manchester City was about to start, I asked the barman to check which 3 pm game was being televised, with the exciting prospect of Arsenal vs Tottenham Hotspur lying in wait at 5.15 pm UK time, or 7.15 pm Cape Town time. To my utter astonishment, the little blurb that appeared when he pressed the information button on the TV remote read *5 pm: Rochdale vs Leeds United*; why on earth was this game of football on South African television?

Although it wasn't a big game, I'd seen so little of Leeds over the three travelling trips that I'd now been on that watching us in any capacity felt like a privilege. I rushed down to my dorm room, grabbed my Leeds shirt, and readied myself to cheer on my team from 6500 miles away.

After Blackburn and City played out a 1-1 draw, a couple of Australian lads joined me for our match after seeing my shirt. They weren't huge football fans but had enough about them to reference Mark Viduka and Harry Kewell, which I, of course, enjoyed tremendously. I did have to inform them that the days of Leeds United having good players were long behind us and that the match that I was about to watch would likely be of an appalling standard. That didn't bother them, and upon hearing that Rochdale were a fourth-tier side, one of them commented that at least Leeds would be likely to win.

We were coming off the back of two league defeats, and it was easy to tell how low on confidence our players were. Rochdale looked sharper from minute one and fully deserved the lead that they took just before half-time.

We created a couple of half-chances after the break but did little other than launch the ball long to our target striker Matt Smith. I can't recall us stringing more than three passes together at any point, and when the home side made it 2-0 in the closing stages, I had no complaints.

To be fair to Rochdale, the two goals that they scored were very impressive, and they'd played far superior football than their League Two status befitted. Regardless of that, it was a pretty humiliating experience, but worse was to come the following week.

I started to wonder whether South African television was being influenced by Lucas Radebe's legendary status at our club when I discovered that our league match at Sheffield Wednesday was also on TV. I was staying at a hostel in a small town called Storm's River the following weekend when I idly checked online to see if the game would be on with it being an early kick-off. Remarkably, it was, and although the hostel only had a tiny screen behind its bar, that was more than adequate for the only English person staying there.

I was travelling with two very attractive German girls at the time, and they had a plan to go out tubing on the river that afternoon. Obviously, I turned them down to watch my team play, and when they walked back into the hostel with five minutes remaining to find that we were 5-0 down, they rightly questioned my decision. The game eventually finished 6-0, and the white shirt that I wore with such pride started to feel extremely heavy.

The strangest thing about the two defeats was that when I was frank with myself, I didn't really care. I'd become so disillusioned by my inability to identify with my football club, that results had genuinely stopped affecting me. It took the combined embarrassment of the Rochdale and Wednesday defeats for me to acknowledge that I'd been experiencing a crisis of passion for Leeds United for some time.

As frustrating as our unpredictability on the field was, there was nothing that I'd found more infuriating in recent times than the constant off-the-field speculation surrounding us. It had now been over a year since our new owners had taken over, we'd barely spent a penny on the playing squad, and rumours had even surfaced that we were struggling financially to the point at which we required fresh investment. For all the nonsense that we'd been through in my time, even I couldn't fathom how a middle-eastern consortium could take over our club without seeming to have any money.

However, after brand new takeover talks with a company called Sport Capital collapsed, an Italian bloke called Massimo Cellino had apparently agreed a deal to buy the club on the final day of January. I'd reached a point at which I was so sick of hearing about who did and didn't own Leeds United that I just felt relieved that the issue appeared resolved. The drama was only just getting started.

In a new low even for us, Cellino publicly sacked manager Brian McDermott without having yet completed his takeover. Even with an agreement in place with the current owners, the Football League still had to ratify any deal, which meant that Cellino was in no position to sack our manager whatsoever. Although we weren't in the best form, a good, honest bloke such as McDermott deserved so much better, and I couldn't help but think that the only mistake he'd made was coming to Leeds in the first place.

As if things couldn't get any more ridiculous, McDermott was reinstated as manager the following day. Cellino may or may not have realised his hastiness, but the reality was that he didn't have the jurisdiction to sack a manager of a club that he didn't yet own. McDermott wasn't in the dugout for our 5-1 victory over local rivals Huddersfield Town, but it was confirmed on leedsunited.com that day that he hadn't left the club at all. If there'd been a more shambolic sequence of events in our club's history, then I certainly wasn't aware of it.

Cellino did eventually confirm the deal with GFH Capital,

but that was far from the end of the matter. Our shirt sponsor filed a winding-up petition against us the following week over an alleged unpaid debt, while The Football League extensively investigated Cellino to see whether he passed their owners' and directors' test. Within a week of an Italian court finding Cellino guilty of not paying import duty on a yacht that he owned, The Football League refused to approve his takeover. It was yet another utterly farcical situation at Elland Road.

With our league form taking a nosedive amid all the drama, I couldn't possibly have felt less connected to Leeds United. Whilst all this had been happening, I'd been travelling through Central America with a Londoner I'd met in Panama, and I felt far more immersed in his beloved Crystal Palace's battle against Premier League relegation than I was in Leeds. I despised the situation, the whole thing was a disgrace, and I could feel my connection to my football club deteriorating.

Cellino appealed The Football League's rejection of his take-over, and a couple of weeks later, the decision was overturned. After almost three months of absolute nonsense, he finally assumed control of the club, before immediately stating that we were in financial trouble. We had an incredibly wealthy new owner, but apparently, he had a monetary mess to sort out before we could even start thinking about on-the-field progress.

We ended the season with three wins from our final five, but Cellino sacked McDermott for a second time as a result of our disappointing 15th place finish. That was 14th, 13th, and 15th from the last three seasons and yet another manager had come and gone.

I was sad to see McDermott go, as I had time for him as a man and a manager. He'd seemed like a cool head in the middle of this total shit storm, and his ability to connect with the fans had not gone unnoticed throughout his time in charge. All I knew from there was that Cellino's first managerial appointment was going to have to be a good one to keep me from totally falling out of love with my beloved club.

Two days before I was due to fly back to the UK from what had been a truly incredible trip through Africa, Central America and the USA, a bloke called Dave Hockaday was announced as our new manager. Hockaday's managerial resume included just one previous club, non-league Forest Green Rovers, where he had overseen two near-misses from relegation, and two mid-table finishes. He'd eventually departed Rovers by mutual consent the previous October after an awful run of form. From what I know, he'd been out of work since.

At this point, I started to feel as though I couldn't take any more of the embarrassment that was Leeds United. My opinion was that all those fans that turned up to Elland Road week in and week out deserved the very best, and they were getting the absolute worst. I actually felt grateful for the fact that I'd been living in York for the eighteen months or so before my travelling trip, and that my working Saturdays had prevented me from being able to get to games. I felt truly awful for the tens of thousands of people that quite simply live for that team, and I reached the point at which I knew that one more incident might just push me over the edge.

On the 8th July 2014, Leeds United sold captain, player of the season, and twenty-eight-goal striker Ross McCormack to Fulham. White blood had been pumping through my veins for over twenty years, but having suffered so many cuts at the hands of my football club, I felt the final drop bleed out of me when I saw that news.

At that very moment, I made the biggest decision of my entire life. I quit as a supporter of Leeds United Football Club.

33

The rebound

I was nearly twenty-eight-years-old when I broke up with my football club. I use this terminology because there can be absolutely no doubt that I'd essentially been in a relationship with Leeds United throughout my twenty-one years as a supporter. The funny thing about this is that I'd not managed a single romantic relationship with another person during my life up to that point, which might explain why I'd poured such a ludicrous amount of emotion into being a football fan.

After the sale of Ross McCormack, I felt that there was literally nothing left at Elland Road with which I could identify. It was as though the heart and soul of our football club had been ripped out each time a transfer window had come along over the previous three years, with every connection disappearing with it. With both that and the off-the-field issues in mind, I felt completely vindicated in my decision to quit. I was intuitive enough to recognise that it can't just have been about the club though, it must also have had something to do with me.

There were just over three years between me coming out of depression and quitting Leeds. In my personal life during that time, I'd travelled the world extensively, found a job that I loved, moved to a new city, embraced my introversion, and found true happiness in solitude. Most importantly, as far as

Leeds were concerned, I'd experienced glory across several sports other than football.

When I thought in more detail about the concept of me having had a relationship with Leeds United, I contemplated the notion that I might not need them any more. I felt so fulfilled in other areas of my life that the time seemed right to escape from the constant drama of being associated with the club. After all, drama only gets you so far without quality.

The sport during the summer of 2012 had been so special because the performance levels of the Team GB Olympians, Andy Murray, and the European Ryder Cup team had been so high, while the drama of the events that they were involved in had also been incredible.

In reality, 2009, with which I'll include 3rd January 2010, had been the only year in which I'd seen Leeds show any quality between 1st January 2002 and 8th July 2014. Twelve and a half years of vociferous support with only twelve months of quality to show for it is a dour return, and I can't imagine that I'd have been anywhere near as committed had it not been for the drama.

Between 2001/02, when we collapsed from the Premiership's summit, and 2010/11, we battled relegation or challenged for promotion during every season apart from one. That was 2004/05, in which we finished 14th in our first season in the Championship, although my first experience of us being outside the top tier as a fan, and Ken Bates coming in to save us from the brink of liquidation, had been more than enough to keep me interested.

2011/12, 2012/13, and 2013/14 had yielded yet more awful football, and we hadn't even had the drama to go with it.

Honestly, even had there been the drama of a relegation battle or a promotion push, I still think that there's a good chance that I'd have quit due to the desperate lack of entertainment on display.

I know extremely little about relationships, but I suspect that healthy ones centre around the qualities that two people see in each other. It seems to me that the idea behind being with someone is that you are attracted to them for what great company they are, and are likely to stay with them for as long as they remain that way.

From the outside looking in, an unhealthy relationship looks like one that is consumed by drama. Some couples seem to live off the concept of breaking up and making up, with the emotional rollercoaster being the element that keeps them interested. The reality is that a lot of people appear to enter relationships because they are trying to mask insecurities or personal issues. Realistically, that's only sustainable for so long.

As I reflect, I recognise that my relationship with my football team centred around drama from the instant that David O'Leary's team fell apart. I'd not enjoyed watching us play for twelve and a half years, but had stuck with it because of the emotional attachment that I'd developed to my side. I'd spent large parts of that time feeling unfulfilled in my personal life, and the drama that Leeds United provided was what kept me coming back.

With no sign of any expansive football on the horizon, my interest faded once I found happiness back in 2011, which was confounded by the lack of drama. I tried and tried over those three years to rediscover the passion, but after so long of pouring so much in, I just felt that I was getting nothing other than frustration out. Just like an unhealthy relationship, or how I imagine one, eventually there comes a time at which you have to say *no more*. My relationship with Leeds United had been an unhealthy one, which is why I walked away.

Had I not had such a strong base of other sports through which to devote my fandom, I suspect that the transition from being an enormous fan of my club to not being one at all would have been more complicated. As it was, I merely stopped checking the news online, and by the time that the 2014/15 season came around, it was as though the previous twenty-one years had never happened. As I reflect, it makes me quite sad that I was able to cast away my most treasured interest so suddenly, but I can't deny that my quality of life improved henceforth.

From there, I threw myself into every other sport that I'd ever followed. I moved back to the Leeds office of the company that I'd been working for in York, found my own place just outside of town, and invested in both Sky Sports and BT Sport. For the first time in twenty-eight years, it felt like everything was in it's right place.

I spent more time than ever down at Headingley watching cricket and even made it down to Nottingham to see Yorkshire win the County Championship Division One title that September. Soon after, I revelled in Europe retaining golf's Ryder Cup at Gleneagles in Scotland. It may not have been as incomprehensible as Medinah two years earlier, but the drama and quality on display did reaffirm it as my favourite tournament across any sport.

During my time in the States earlier that year, I'd spent most evenings sitting in bars watching the basketball play-offs. With the NBA having both an Eastern Conference and a Western

Conference, each with it's own time zone, the trend was to watch the East between 6 pm and 9 pm, and then the west between 9 pm and midnight. The frenetic and athletic nature of the sport engrossed me, and when the new season started in October, Sunday night became NBA night.

When 2015 arrived, I watched rugby union's Six Nations in it's entirety, including an incredible final round in which all three of England, Ireland, and Wales had been in with a chance of winning it. With England having beaten Wales, Wales having beaten Ireland, and Ireland having beaten England, the tournament came down to points difference, with Ireland eventually nicking the title with +63, in comparison to England's +57 and Wales' +53. There were an incredible twenty-seven tries across Italy vs Wales, Scotland vs Ireland, and England vs France that day; it was truly sensational viewing.

It wasn't all great sport though, as I regularly woke up at ridiculous times to follow England's 2015 Cricket World Cup campaign down in Australia and New Zealand. We were ripped apart by the Aussies, the Kiwis, and Sri Lanka, before crashing out in humiliating fashion at the hands of Bangladesh, and talk after the tournament was that there would be a thorough review of our One-Day cricket setup. Apparently, a four-year journey to becoming a competitive side for a home World Cup in 2019 started there and then.

Having followed up his maiden Grand Slam victory at the US Open back in 2012 by winning Wimbledon in 2013, Andy Murray suffered a challenging, injury-hit year in 2014. However, he bounced back in 2015, reaching another Australian Open final, and semi-finals at the French Open and SW19. It had looked like it would be a year without glory for Murray though after a fourth-round loss at the US Open, before he pretty much single-handedly guided Great Britain to a first Davis Cup triumph in seventy-nine years. He later took the 2015 Sports Personality Of The Year award, with calls for a knighthood coming in from high places.

My favourite ever rugby league moment came in late September of the same year. A dramatic Ryan Hall try, with the last play of the regular season at Huddersfield Giants, won the Leeds Rhinos the league leaders shield. Having already claimed the Challenge Cup in August, the Rhinos then went on to beat old foes Wigan Warriors in the Grand Final to secure a historic treble. Club legends Kevin Sinfield, Jamie Peacock, and Kylie Leuluai had all announced that they would retire at the end of the season, and the treble represented a perfect way for them to say goodbye.

Despite all that, the most prominent sporting moment in the eighteen months since I'd quit Leeds United came from an unexpected source. It was only the night before a planned weekend away in Sheffield at the end of November 2015 that I realised that we would have a showpiece event to enjoy on the Saturday night. My pal Rich, the boxing fan of our group, had proposed a plan for a day out in the pub watching football, followed by a few pre-night out drinks at our apartment. From there, he wanted to head out for about 9 pm to get to a sports bar, as Wladimir Klitschko was defending his World Heavyweight titles against Briton Tyson Fury.

Boxing was a sport that I'd always enjoyed watching, without ever having developed a love for it. Earlier in the year, a group of us had made the effort to stay up all night for the highly anticipated Floyd Mayweather Jr vs Manny Pacquiao bout, which I'd found to be one of the biggest disappointments in all my time as a sports fan. I hadn't even known what I was hoping for going into that fight, but whatever it was, my expectations certainly weren't met. That was part of the reason that I approached Klitschko-Fury with indifference.

Bearing in mind how much time I'd spent with Rich over the years, I'd not watched anywhere near enough boxing with him. I loved sport, and this was his sport of choice, which really should have meant that we'd enjoyed many a huge fight together by then. That wasn't the case, but how fired up he was as we watched the end of the undercard at a Sheffield sports bar was hugely infectious.

I'd only seen Fury fight once before and had found him rather underwhelming in his defeat of Steve Cunningham a couple of years earlier. Videos of him punching himself in the face against Lee Swaby had been doing the rounds on social media too, and bearing in mind that Klitschko hadn't lost in eleven and a half years, it was hard to see anything other than Ukrainian dominance.

Rich was equally dismissive of Fury's chances but did say that he'd always found something curious about the Mancunian. His unbeaten record added an extra dimension to the occasion, and Rich was keen to stress that a Briton fighting for a World Heavyweight belt should never be understated.

What fascinated me most about the first few rounds was that although neither fighter seemed to land a punch, Klitschko looked visibly uncomfortable in the ring. I'd seen him defeat David Haye a few years earlier, and it had been front foot domination from the off that night. However, I felt as though I could see it in his eyes that he didn't know what to do about

Fury's impressive head and foot movement, and it was the challenger who was displaying far more intent.

Rich went into detail about how impressive Fury's ability to switch between orthodox and southpaw stances was, and whichever style he took on, you'd have thought that it was he who had owned the belts for nine years.

Klitschko started to work his way into the bout in the middle rounds, although Fury took any punch that his opponent landed well, while also being sure to land in response. I can remember one of the commentary team stating that this hadn't been in the script, which is the point at which I knew that we had a fight on our hands.

With there being little in the way of eye-catching moments, a lot of our fellow punters started to get impatient, and cries of 'FUCKING DO SOMETHING' and 'KNOCK HIM OUT' began to ring out around the bar. I think that I knew that boxing was having it's first profound effect on me right then, as I was captivated by the fight despite it's steady tempo.

It felt like Fury was playing a game of chess, and always seemed to be one move ahead of the champion, despite his vastly inferior experience. I can remember commenting on the state of Klitschko's face after the eighth round, to which Rich replied that he now truly believed that Fury could win the fight.

Things opened up a little in the next couple of rounds, with Fury landing the cleaner shots to leave Klitschko in yet more peril, and it was impossible to see how the Brit couldn't be ahead on the scorecards as we entered the final two rounds. However, disaster struck in the 11th, as Fury was docked a point for repeatedly punching Klitschko on the back of the head, and I thought that his hopes might have gone with it.

Something that I did know about boxing, which Rich reemphasised after the deduction, is that getting a decision on points in the back yard of any champion is hard enough, never mind a heavyweight who has reigned for nine years. Even as Fury gave as good as he got in the final round, I couldn't see the judges scoring it in his favour.

Having had no faith in him whatsoever pre-fight, Rich and I both affirmed that regardless of how the decision went, Tyson Fury had won two fans after his performance. I was so taken aback by how engrossed I'd become throughout those twelve rounds that I felt compelled to acknowledge that boxing itself had won a new fan. Then, everything went silent, as legendary announcer Michael Buffer prepared to declare the winner.

'From the UNITED KINGDOM'. As soon as Rich and I heard the words, we went wild. I can remember feeling like I was a real boxing fan, having been one of only two people in the place that had been able to deduce that Fury had won from the words 'United Kingdom'. I think we took some of the people around us aback a little with our ecstatic celebrations, and I surprised myself with how happy it made me.

The copious amount of alcohol that I'd consumed undoubtedly accentuated the feeling, but I could tell from my years of fandom experience that it wasn't just that. The fight had felt like a journey, with Fury taking us on a ride that none of us had anticipated we'd be going on beforehand.

I think that part of the disappointment about Mayweather-Pacquiao for me as a sports fan had been the lack of investment that I'd had in either fighter. The simple fact that Fury was British had drawn me in, and his utterly outstanding performance had done the rest. I couldn't shut up about it for hours afterwards, and I think that Rich felt grateful that he now had somebody else with whom to share his passion.

I can remember watching Fury's post-fight press conference in bed the following morning, disgracefully hungover, but still buzzing about what had happened the previous night. As I'm not a religious man, I'll never forget feeling a keen urge to dismiss Fury's claim that God had planned this journey for him. He genuinely believed that his path to glory had been predetermined, that it was his *destiny* to become the Heavyweight champion of the world.

A year or so later, when it became apparent that Fury was suffering with severe mental health issues, his post-fight words did ring true with me, but for a very different reason.

34

The football facade

If 2015 had been a year of rebounding from my break up with my football team, 2016 was a year of coming to terms with it.

Since returning to Leeds in the summer of 2014, I'd started to believe that I had well and truly cracked life. I felt like I had everything that I'd ever wanted; a job that I loved, my own place, watching every bit of sport that was going, and the freedom and peace to know that I could do as I pleased at all times. Yet, as the summer of 2016 approached, some of my behaviours indicated that there was something still not quite right with me, not that I could see it at the time.

On the surface, the first few months of the year had been unbelievable. I'd taken the trip of a lifetime to Antarctica with my grandad, I'd booked yet another round-the-world adventure to go away for six months over the winter of 2016/17, my sister had got engaged, stag do's and weddings had just started among the lads, and sport was serving up more quality and drama than ever.

Andy Murray put together another fantastic tournament at the Australian Open, only to lose in the final at Melbourne for a record fifth time. Despite his straight-sets defeat to Novak Djokovic, Murray had looked imperious throughout, and he would go on to reach a first French Open final in May, before claiming his second Wimbledon title in July.

England made major strides in white-ball cricket by reaching the final of the Twenty20 World Cup in India, less than eleven months after the humiliation of the 2015 fifty-over World Cup. Only six of the fifteen-man squad that had capitulated in Australia and New Zealand made the cut less than a year on, and I spent many a working lunch break at my local sports bar following our explosive young side in India.

The likes of Jason Roy, Ben Stokes, Jos Buttler, and Yorkshiremen Joe Root and Adil Rashid, all displayed the kind of skills that I'd only dreamed of seeing from English players in One-Day cricket, and there can be no doubts that we really should have won the final. For anyone who's not seen Carlos Brathwaite's four straight sixes off Stokes' last over that day, I'd recommend watching it, as difficult as it was to stomach.

Having dismissed his chances of pursuing a professional career in the sport after the London 2012 Olympics, Anthony Joshua completed an incredible rise to boxing glory by destroying Charles Martin to claim the IBF World Heavyweight title. I'd loosely followed Joshua's progress before that, but I'd only significantly invested in the Martin fight and his dramatic bout with Dillian Whyte a few months earlier. Both fights had come in the aftermath of Tyson Fury's victory over Wladimir Klitschko, and with every Heavyweight strap now in British hands, there were bound to be some spectacular nights to look forward to in the future.

I found myself regularly staying up until 4 am to watch basketball in April and May, as my adopted team, the Oklahoma City Thunder, made it to the NBA Western Conference Finals. Coming up against reigning NBA champions the Golden State

Warriors, we took a 3-1 lead in the best-of-seven series, but lost three straight games to miss out on the chance to face the Cleveland Cavaliers in the overall Finals. Losing genuinely hurt, even if I'd only been a fan for two years, but both the quality and drama on display throughout the play-offs had made the late nights more than worth the while.

While all this had been happening, a quite incredible story had been unfolding in football. Having been 5000/1 to win the Premier League at the start of the season, Leicester City had found themselves top of the pile at Christmas. Although they ceded their lead to Arsenal in the weeks that followed, they did what Leeds United could not manage back in 2001/02 and recovered to reclaim pole position in late January.

When the ten-man Foxes suffered a stoppage-time defeat *at* Arsenal in February, which left both the Gunners and Tottenham Hotspur just two points adrift, I suspect that most football fans assumed that their entirely unexpected challenge was about to come to an end. However, they brushed themselves down, and finished the season with eight wins and four draws from their last twelve games, completing the most astonishing story in English football history with two matches to spare.

The whole nation rightly got swept up in what was one of the great sporting fairytales. It was the most remarkable of achievements, and the Leicester players and manager Claudio Ranieri deserved every last bit of praise that came their way. However, as happy as I was for everyone associated with the new champions, I couldn't help but see the bigger picture; it was a damning indictment of the state of English football.

As well as Leicester had done, the quality on display

throughout the 2015/16 Premier League season had been absolutely awful, in my opinion at least. It had been little better in 2014/15 when a solid but unspectacular Chelsea side had cruised to the title, and since Manchester City's and Liverpool's battle to the death in 2013/14, the pinnacle of English football had produced little in the way of drama either.

I couldn't help but have a pop at the big football fans among my mates, by claiming that the sport had been terrible to watch for some time. As I reflect, it's likely that I was going through a phase of resenting it, possibly as I still had some hang-ups after my break-up with Leeds, but there was undoubtedly some logic to my argument. With so many other sports displaying such quality and drama, I wanted the lads to see that there was more to sport than football, even if it was about to provide the centrepiece for our summer.

In June 2016, I fulfilled a lifelong dream to go to a major international football tournament, as seven of the lads and I took a road trip to France for the European Championships. Never in my life had I been as excited as I was on the drive down to London, and I felt endlessly euphoric as we cruised south through France knowing that we were going to see England vs Russia in Marseille that night.

We blared out all the classic England football songs in the eight-seater van that we'd hired and drank lager after lager while chanting out of the windows. The overwhelming feeling of excitement and anticipation that encompassed me was even better than I'd dreamt it would be.

I can remember being a bit *underwhelmed* by the atmosphere on the subway as we approached the Stade Velodrome. There were a few England fans on there, but everything was a bit subdued as we pulled in to the stadium's station. Then, as we climbed the stairs back to ground level, the noise started to pick up, until I felt as though I'd walked into a wall of sound as we exited the station.

It was like being at a festival. There was music playing, people dancing, delirious fans charging around all over the place, and most importantly, everyone was *so* happy. It was the opening game of the Euros for both England and Russia, and the atmosphere in Marseille was irrepressibly optimistic.

On a personal note, the occasion represented the first opportunity for me to support a football team since the 2014 World Cup. England had been terrible in Brazil, and I'd quit my club team just a couple of weeks later; I'd waited two years to experience that burning pre-match passion, and it had come on an occasion of which I'd spent my life dreaming.

The stadium was rocking as Wayne Rooney led England's players out, twelve years on from the European Championships at which he'd announced himself on the international stage. I don't know if this was partially down to the personal affection that I'd had for Rooney over the years, but I'd desperately hoped that manager Roy Hodgson would pick him to play in a holding midfield role, and was elated when I saw that he had.

To the onlooking eye, we played well throughout the ninety minutes, but little did I know about how poor this Russian team were at the time. We dominated the first half and should have been ahead, but as the game reached seventy minutes at 0-0, I feared that I wasn't even going to get to celebrate a goal.

Then, when we won a free-kick on the edge of the area, which must only have been about forty yards away from where we were standing behind the goal, I braced myself.

I didn't even see the ball leave Eric Dier's boot, just Russian' keeper Igor Akinfeev spectacularly diving in vain, as the ball almost burst the back of the net. Had the net not been there, I honestly think that the ball might have hit me in the face, such was the ferocity of Dier's strike, and the bedlam that ensued felt almost as special as Jermaine Beckford's goal at Old Trafford.

As much as I'll never forget that moment, the whole occasion was effectively ruined for me when Vasili Berezutski headed in a stoppage-time equaliser. It would have been considerably worse after the game had I been in the opposite stand, where Russian hooligans charged at the English supporters, punching, kicking, and stamping on anyone unfortunate enough to be in their way. I'd bought our tickets from a random Russian bloke online, which made me feel even luckier not to have been in amongst it all.

The lads were disappointed, but in good spirits after the game, as we swiftly made our way back into central Marseille to avoid any more potential trouble. I, on the other hand, was utterly miserable, and typically resenting football for disappointing me like it so often did. I'd been through enough pain as a football fan to know that I always needed an hour or so after a bad result to recover, and I eventually came around.

We stayed in France for a week after that, living the dream of watching football every day in the sunshine. In keeping with my current opinion, the standard of football was dreadful, but drinking beer every day and watching sport while in another country with my mates is about as good as it gets for me.

We didn't manage to get tickets for England's second group match with Wales but stocked up the house that we'd rented just outside Lille with barbecue food and beer. We'd already had a fantastic day by the time the match started, and it came as no surprise to me when the football destroyed my mood through a Gareth Bale free-kick. Goalkeeper Joe Hart should undoubtedly have done better, but we deserved to be behind, we'd been awful.

Credit to Roy Hodgson, he made a bold move by throwing on strikers Daniel Sturridge and Jamie Vardy at half-time, and although neither team seemed to be able to string two passes together, the move paid off. Vardy equalised about ten minutes into the second half before Sturridge poked home a winner in added time to spark pandemonium among eight Englishmen in a French country house.

The quality may have been desperately lacking, but the drama went some way to making up for it, which it invariably does when it goes in your favour. We had a huge party to celebrate what had been a wonderful week, before taking the long journey back to Leeds by road the following day.

We put in another disappointing performance in our final game against Slovakia, with the six changes that Hodgson made to the starting line-up failing to pay off. A 0-0 draw, coupled with Wales' 3-0 victory over Russia, meant that we finished second in the group, which likely meant that we'd face a tough second-round match.

As it was, we ended up facing Iceland, a match-up rightfully seen as an easy passage into the quarter-finals. There was no doubt that the smallest nation in the tournament, with a population of just 330,000, had done brilliantly to finish above Portugal in their group to snatch second spot, but this would be the equivalent of seeing a Premier League team face a League One team. I refused to believe that the equivalent of

Leeds United beating Manchester United in the FA Cup third round could possibly happen again.

We went 1-0 up through a Rooney penalty after only four minutes, although Iceland immediately replied through a goal that came from one of their now-famous long throws. Just over ten minutes later, the unthinkable happened, as the minnows took the lead through a tame Kolbeinn Sigporsson strike that Hart couldn't keep out. If falling behind was just a bit embarrassing, the remainder of the match was as bad as anything I'd witnessed during my time as a football fan.

Iceland deserved tremendous credit for how hard they worked, but it would be wrong to detract from just how bad England were that night. We could barely pass the ball, were brittle at the back, looked clueless going forward, and couldn't have deserved to lose a game more when the final whistle went. The only thing that Hodgson deserved praise for was throwing on eighteen-year-old Marcus Rashford with five minutes to go, who offered more in that time than our entire team had throughout the tournament.

I made a point of storming out of the bar that I was in bang on full-time. I didn't want to talk to anybody after such a humiliation, although I undoubtedly overreacted. If I'm perfectly honest, there was a degree of calculation in it, as I wanted the people that I was with to know that I was lashing out at football. Two years on from abandoning my club, my country had found a way to take me to a new low.

When I got back to my flat that evening, I drank nearly half a bottle of whiskey, almost entirely because I *wanted* to be dramatic. Don't get me wrong, I was so, so angry at the fact that Iceland had knocked us out of Euro 2016, but I felt like milking the situation for all it was worth. As much as I believed that I'd become an emotionally well-rounded individual since beating depression, football still had a way of provoking hugely irrational behaviours in me.

A month or so later, it was rumoured that Gareth Southgate would be given the England job, with Hodgson having resigned immediately after the Iceland debacle. Southgate had managed one club team before, guiding Middlesbrough to Premier League relegation, before being sacked a couple of months into their first Championship campaign down. He'd then taken over as England Under-21's manager, overseeing the team's elimination in the group stage of the U21 European Championships; a considerable underachievement.

Put simply, as I saw it at least, both of Southgate's jobs in management had ended in abject failure. Yet, there was a chance that the Football Association were going to reward him with one of the biggest jobs in world football. I was so disillusioned and so unable to control my emotions that I told the lads that if he were appointed, I would quit as an England supporter just as I had Leeds. As it was, Sam Allardyce was the eventual choice, and my England-supporting career lived to fight another day.

My disdain for football was making me want the whole world to abandon the sport. I saw it as a total injustice that fans had an unconditional relationship with football while ignoring so many sports that provided a superior fandom experience. I wanted to shake people into reevaluating their loyalties, which actually said a lot more about me than it did about them.

35

The process

A few months on from my infuriation at the football facade, I had an epiphany akin to the one that I'd had on that mountain in Montenegro back in 2011. I'd decided to start my latest travelling trip by flying to India to watch England play Test cricket abroad for the first time, and I experienced an overwhelming feeling of euphoria while watching us bat in the glorious Punjabi sun.

I was so overawed by the very fact that I was watching England play cricket in another country, another lifelong dream of mine, that I almost started crying. Essentially, I was so surprised by how good my life could be, that my emotions completely and utterly overwhelmed me. In that moment, whatever happened on the cricket field didn't matter, as I found that the *process* of watching the sport was so good, that it was now more important than the *prize* of the result.

As my mind raced with curious excitement, I started to think about all the amazing sporting events that I could potentially travel to in the future, while also contemplating all the great moments that I'd experienced in the last couple of years. As I did, Tyson Fury's comments about destiny popped into my head.

While the lads and I had been at the Euros, we'd heard that

Fury had also travelled out to follow the football. Apparently, he'd been buying huge rounds of drinks for fellow fans in French bars, while hitting the booze pretty hard himself. Soon after, it transpired that he was suffering from mental health issues, with the fulfilment of his apparent destiny to become World Heavyweight champion having tipped him over the edge. The relevant boxing boards stripped him of his belts due to his inability to fulfil his duties, and I couldn't help but empathise with his psychological decline.

It would later transpire that becoming world champion had been the equivalent of him conquering Everest. It was as though he'd completed his journey, and reached the place at which he'd assumed would provide him with permanent inner peace and contentment. As I saw it at the time, his realisation that the feeling of achievement had a shelf life had been too much for him to take, and he hadn't known what to do with himself moving forwards.

When I thought about it in more detail, I realised how similar my journey as a football fan had been to Fury's journey to the ultimate Heavyweight prize.

The reality was that I'd spent extremely little time enjoying the process of watching football over the years, but had stuck with it so steadfastly as I'd been chasing a prize that I unwaveringly believed would fulfil me. The mere thought of Leeds United winning a trophy, or England winning a major tournament, had been the reason that I'd poured so much time, money, effort, energy, and emotion into being a football fan.

On the one occasion that Leeds had achieved something, promotion from League One, it had been so unfulfilling that I'd not even enjoyed it. When I thought about it, it didn't surprise me that I'd started to lose the passion only a year later, although I thought it likely that my coming out of depression had played a significant role in that too.

Just as Fury must have done during his pursuit of Heavyweight glory, I'd put so much pressure on football to provide me with one enormous life-defining moment, that had it happened, it would have been a total anticlimax. If one of my teams would have achieved something while playing outstanding football, it may have fulfilled me to an extent, but it was madness to have even considered it to be the route to true happiness. Fortunately, I'd managed to create that for myself through hard work over the previous few years, and now the process of watching sport could provide the fulfilment, without an eventual prize being the mitigating factor.

That's the real beauty of watching Test cricket for me; it's played at such a slow pace that it allows my mind to wander wherever it pleases, while still keeping me entertained. There is no other form of sport that, while watching, I could have figured out the absolute truth behind why I quit Leeds United. It was an answer for which I'd subconsciously been searching for years.

Two conscious reasons had dictated my decision. The first, as I'd always explained to my fellow Leeds United fans when they'd questioned me, was that I felt so ashamed by the off-field issues and the treatment of the fans that I couldn't bring myself to be associated with the club any longer. The second, was that the total lack of quality and drama on the field had seen my passion gradually decline to the point at which I'd had literally nothing left to give. However, only at Mohali Cricket Ground did I realise the subconscious motivator that had defined the biggest decision that I'd ever made.

During my dark days of depression, I'd come to depend on the perceived life-changing prospect of experiencing glory with Leeds United to such an extent, that the enjoyment of watching us had become redundant. When I came out of depression, that prize of glory subconsciously became infinitely less important to me, as I had so many other things in my life to be happy about and pour my passion in to.

With my fandom now depending so much less on what *might* be, the *prize*, I was left to try and enjoy what *was*, the *process*. Sadly, the process of watching and following Leeds United became so unenjoyable that I hadn't wanted to do it anymore. If you're partaking in something that you're not enjoying, and you're not even interested in the potential reward at the end of it, it's unlikely that you're going to want to continue doing it.

I'd spent so many years following Leeds so passionately that I started to experience genuine guilt as I found myself losing interest. I was attached to my club, and like a romantic relationship, it had hurt when things had started to become stale.

Quite simply, Leeds had meant too much to me for me to be able to go on feeling like a half-hearted fan. When things became as embarrassing as they did, I saw an opportunity to get out of the relationship, as not only was I getting nothing out of it anymore, I felt too guilty for not having had anything left in me to give. So, I left my football team, and if I come to regret the emotional decision that I made in the future, I'll have to deal with it.

As a result of all this, I couldn't help but feel a little relieved that Gareth Southgate hadn't taken over at England when I'd threatened to quit if he had. I'd have made that decision based on the irrational anger that I still felt towards football, even if my belief that it would have been an unfathomable appointment was rational.

Ironically, only a few days after my enlightenment in India, Southgate *was* appointed as permanent England manager after the sacking of Sam Allardyce. I didn't quit as a fan.

As I made sense of it all and recognised how much I was enjoying watching cricket in India for what it was, I learned that there was more to life than the prize. I'd experienced so much happiness since coming out of depression because I'd stopped putting pressure on the end result.

During my darker days, I'd believed that a future life that I envisaged for myself would change everything, and give me total emotional fulfilment. As it was, I'd had to work to find happiness, and the key to it was to relish the process itself, as opposed to treating the process as a pursuit of a prize.

I took great pleasure in contemplating just how much I'd enjoyed so many sporting events in the moment since quitting Leeds United. However, I could barely recall a single football match that had entertained me in that time, with the odd bit of drama the only thing that had kept me interested. Nothing summed this up more than Portugal winning Euro 2016 having won just one of their seven matches. They finished third in their group after three draws with Austria, Hungary and Iceland, and needed extra time or penalties to win all but one of their knockout games. Credit to them for winning it despite all that, but as far as I was concerned, it epitomised how shambolic the sport had become.

By no means was I abandoning football altogether, I desperately hoped that I would start enjoying it again at some point.

I was sure that I would, but until then, I wanted to do nothing other than pour my fandom into enjoying the sports that did provide the quality that I craved, preferably with some drama thrown in for good measure.

If a prize came at the end of that, then I'm sure that I'd be utterly ecstatic, but it was an incredibly liberating feeling to be able to let go of the need for one. Whatever happened moving forward, I just felt grateful that there was more to my sports fandom than football, and there was more to my life than the pursuit of a prize.

36

The elements

The fundamental nature of my sports fandom changed for the better once I became conscious of the fact that the prize wasn't everything. There were so many factors involved that could bring me joy when watching sport, and although the prize was one of them, I found peace once it became a bonus exclusively.

After my epiphany in Mohali, I started to contemplate the specific elements of the fandom experience that had yielded the most powerful emotional responses in me over the years. As much as football had influenced me, I'd learned that other sports had drawn different kinds of reactions, which made me wonder if these feelings were somehow quantifiable.

I came up with six elements, with three of them relevant in any sport-watching capacity, and the other three only applying if a fan is supporting a specific team or individual. I recognised that some might have been more important than others, but perceived each of them to be significant in their own right.

The only stipulation that I found for applying these elements was that a previous understanding of the specific sport that I was watching was required. There were few sports that I hadn't previously invested in at this point of course, but I recognised that if anybody else were to apply them to a sport-watching experience of their own, they'd have to bear that in mind.

The first element was *quality*, which referred to the standard of the specific sport that I'd been watching. When it came to this, I could look no further than tennis, as watching the incomprehensible ability levels of the 'Big Four' of Roger Federer, Rafael Nadal, Novak Djokovic, and Andy Murray, had been a privilege to experience.

The second was *drama*, which referenced the events that I'd not been able to take my eyes off due to how closely contested they were. Golf's Ryder Cup was this element exemplified, as every single hole of every single match, as well as the tournament as a whole, felt like it was on the finest of knife-edges at all times.

The third was *culture*, which represented the influence of an environment on how I acted as a fan. Football was undoubtedly the winner here, as the raw passion, aggression, and unity had been more influential on my behaviours than all the other sports combined.

The fourth was *odds*, which is the first of the elements that could only apply when supporting a team or individual. The greater the *odds* that your charge has of winning, the lower that your expectation will be, which in turn means the more powerful the emotional experience that you're likely to have if they do. This was why Tyson Fury's defeat of Wladimir Klitschko had been so special.

The fifth was *connection*, which referred to how much I felt that I could relate to or *connect* with a specific player. There'd been many examples of this, with Wayne Rooney in football, Andy Murray in tennis, and Ian Poulter in golf all displaying the raw British passion that had given my sport-watching experience an extra edge. The 2012 Team GB Olympians also applied here but by way of me feeling as though I could have a pint at the pub with almost every one of them.

The sixth and final element was *journey*, which could mean several things, but on the whole, represented how much I perceived that I'd been through with a team or an individual as I'd supported them. The most substantial journey that I'd embarked upon as a sports fan had undoubtedly been with Leeds United. Although I can only look back on former experiences now, it's a fascinating adventure to recall.

The equation for my six elements was simple; the more of them that are present, and the greater that each one is, the more intense and engaging that the sporting experience would be. It didn't matter if there was a prize of sorts at the end of it all, what really mattered was how engrossing the process was.

Soon after I'd left India, I watched Roger Federer and Rafael Nadal in the 2017 Australian Open final. The *quality* was about as impressive as is possible in sport, and the *drama* of Federer coming back from a break down in the fifth set to win his 20th Grand Slam was incredible. It didn't involve any of the other four elements, but the *quality* and the *drama* were at such a high level that I could barely have enjoyed watching alone from a flat in Kuala Lumpur more.

A few months later, on the weekend that I'd returned from my travels, I watched Anthony Joshua defeat Klitschko in what was undoubtedly the best fight I'd ever seen. Both fighters displayed great physicality, mentality and technicality for the *quality*, and the *drama* of them each making full recoveries after hitting the canvas was astounding. The betting pre-fight suggested that the fight was too close to call, but it was how long the in-play *odds* must have been that ended up making Joshua's victory so wonderful. He had all but lost the fight after being knocked down in the sixth round, only to stop the veteran Ukrainian after a thunderous uppercut in the 11th.

In the summer of 2017, a few of the lads, my dad, and I got together for the British and Irish Lions tour of New Zealand. The first two Tests saw rugby of the highest *quality*, and the very fact that the third Test was a draw displayed just how *dramatic* the series was. The *odds* on us were long as we'd been expected to lose comfortably, which made it all the better when we competed so well, and I felt a strong *connection* with a number of the Lions due to the passion and unity that the English, Irish, Scottish, and Welsh players displayed during battle.

With so much sport providing so much entertainment, I wasn't remotely bothered by the return of the Premier League for 2017/18. It had been over three years since I'd enjoyed anything related to English football, and I'd effectively switched off from the sport altogether, aside from a weekly bet and the thrill that fantasy football provided. What I hadn't accounted for was the fact that Pep Guardiola had now had a year to adapt to the English game.

Within a few weeks of the season's start, I found myself scrambling to put as many of Manchester City's attacking players into my fantasy team as possible, as they won 5-0 twice, 6-0, and 7-2 in their first eight games. For the first time in as long as I could remember, I was tuning in for *Match Of The Day* every Saturday night, solely to watch the City highlights.

Guardiola's City team single-handedly helped me to rediscover my love for football throughout 2017/18, entirely because of the incredible *quality* that they displayed as a team.

There was barely a hint of the other elements throughout the season, with Liverpool's 4-3 defeat of City being the one notable *dramatic* affair, but Pep's men were that good to watch that nothing else was required. English football had been crying out for someone like him, and with Jurgen Klopp building something similar at Anfield, I could tell that the good times were returning to the Premier League.

Had City not been so brilliant, I genuinely don't know if the footballing summer of 2018 would have ended up being the best summer of my entire life. If I hadn't rediscovered my love for the beautiful game by then, I don't think that I'd have approached it with the immense enthusiasm that I did. The feel-good factor of the best weather in living memory played a big part too, of course.

Above all, it was the *culture* that made Russia 2018 as special as it was. If I'd been in any doubt about this before, then that World Cup unequivocally confirmed that sitting in my favourite Headingley beer garden, in the twenty-five-degree cloudless skied heat, amid scores of die-hard England fans, is when I'm the happiest that I can be.

The fact that everybody's expectations for England were so low, and the *odds* on us winning the tournament were as long as they'd been in my lifetime, made watching us show genuine *quality* en route to a semi-final wonderful to behold. We were no City, but the 6-1 destruction of Panama was one of the highlights of my entire England-supporting tenure, regardless of how substandard our opponents were. We might have lost to them had it been a couple of years earlier after all.

I'd thought that beating Tunisia with a stoppage-time strike from Harry Kane was *dramatic* enough, but then there was the penalty shootout with Colombia. It had been twenty years and three days since I'd first cried after an England game when Eric Dier stood over his penalty on 3rd July 2018. Back on 30th June 1998, David Batty's missed spot-kick had left me shedding tears of despair, but when Dier beat David Ospina to send us into the quarter-finals in Russia, I wept with joy.

The fact that I'd seen England lose on penalties in 1998, 2004, 2006, and 2012, while never winning a shootout in that time, made that Colombia victory better than I could ever have imagined. It was as though I'd waited my entire life for that moment, and there could be no doubting that such a painful *journey* as an England fan made it that much sweeter.

Our defeat of Sweden in the quarters was flawless, and I could scarcely believe my ears when the words 'England are in a World Cup semi-final' were uttered. Yes, we ended up going out to Croatia, but nobody will ever be able to take the raw emotion of Kieran Tripper's free-kick away from me. It was the World Cup that had it all, and I'll cherish it for as long as I have a functioning memory.

On the subject of *journeys*, there were none more inspiring than the one that Tyson Fury had been on in the three years since defeating Wladimir Klitschko. Two and a half years on from that famous night in Dusseldorf, Fury returned to the ring having recovered from the mental health issues with which I could so acutely *connect*. He dispatched a couple of modest opponents in the UK, before diving headfirst into another World Heavyweight title fight, this time against unbeaten American Deontay Wilder. Once again, the *odds* were heavily against him.

If anybody had thought that Fury's Klitschko victory had

been a one-off, he proved them wrong in Los Angeles. He oozed *quality*, absolutely dominating Wilder for the vast majority of the first eleven rounds, although he had to come through a knockdown in the ninth after a slightly sloppy moment. Then, in a moment of astonishing *drama*, Wilder caught Fury with a huge shot in the 12th, sending him crashing to the canvas. The Brit appeared to be out cold, but somehow rose from the dead and held out to send the outcome to the cards. If it weren't incredible enough for me that the judges scored the fight a draw, I'd put £5 on it at 25/1 pre-fight.

In February 2019, I flew out to St Lucia to watch England play cricket in the West Indies. By the time that I arrived, we were already 2-0 down in the three-match series, meaning that the Test match that I was flying out for had absolutely nothing riding on it.

As I took in the cricket with my old man and Rodney, there was little in the way of quality or drama throughout the five days. As I'd first started following international cricket by watching Ceefax's live score updates of England's 1994 tour of the Windies with my brother, there was a degree of *journey* involved, but the absence of having something to play for rendered odds and connection redundant.

However, the party *culture* of drinking beer with vast swathes of England fans in the Caribbean sun was so spectacular that it made for one of the best sport-watching experiences of my life. I can only imagine what the atmosphere would have been like had the match been of critical importance; it was sports fandom paradise.

I could go on forever about the incredible experiences that I had watching sport over the eight years from May 2011.

Football may have provided me with some ups and downs during that time, but once I learned to enjoy the process in the absence of a pursuit of the prize, I became as close to total emotional fulfilment as I perceived that I could get as a sports fan. Everything became about the moment, the occasion, the present; what might be in the future was no longer defining.

If I needed any further affirmation as to what a good place I was in, then how much I wanted to see Leeds United gain promotion to the Premier League at the end of the 2018/19 season was it. Little did I know that over twenty-five years on, I'd have a life-defining moment back where my *journey* as a sports fan had begun.

37

Back where it all started

After over twenty-five intense years as a sports fan, it took me to step into the shoes of another to come up with the idea of writing this book. It was the night of Wednesday 15th May 2019, and I'd just watched an incredible game of football at Elland Road with my pals Andy, Bill, and Bentley. I could empathise with their experience that night to such an extent, that I felt compelled to write about it.

Before I go into detail about the night itself, I want to rewind to the start of the 2018/19 season. After a record-breaking 2017/18 campaign, Manchester City were widely expected to win the Premier League at a canter once more. However, Jurgen Klopp's Liverpool had proven that they could beat the champions on their day, having turned them over in both the league and the Champions League the previous season. There was also a consensus that Jose Mourinho's Manchester United may have it in them to push City closer in 18/19, having claimed second spot in 17/18.

The hype surrounding the red half of Manchester was quickly vanquished, as they lost two of their first three games, and only managed seven wins from their first seventeen. After a 3-1 defeat at Liverpool, who were every bit as good as their billing with fourteen wins and three draws at the same stage,

Mourinho was sacked. City meanwhile, were just a point behind Liverpool with fourteen wins, two draws and a single defeat, and the two sides were producing football the likes of which I'd never seen in England.

The mentality of Guardiola and Klopp was to play total football; passing out from the goalkeeper, refusing to waste possession at any moment, and working relentlessly to get the ball back from the instant that they lost it. The two teams were in a league of their own when it came to keeping the ball, while also seeming to be far more determined to win it back than any opponent they faced. It was as close to footballing perfection that I'd seen, aside from Guardiola's classic Barcelona team that is, but funnily enough, they weren't the only teams in England playing such an attractive brand of football.

Although he'd been in charge of Argentina when England had faced them at the 2002 World Cup, I hadn't heard the name Marcelo Bielsa until 2015. I'd seen an interview with Mauricio Pochettino, who was doing an excellent job as manager at Tottenham Hostpur at the time, who'd described Bielsa as one of the best managers in the world. I'd later learn that Guardiola had spoken even more highly of him, and rumour had it that Bielsa was the originator of the high-pressing, possession-based style that I now so adored watching City and Liverpool play.

I went to my local in town after a 10 am-4 pm shift at work on Sunday 5th August 2018 to find it to be far more busy than usual. I'd had no idea that Leeds United's opening game of the season against Stoke City was being televised, but I was glad to have something to watch while I sank a couple of pints.

I'd followed Leeds' progress loosely since quitting as a fan back in 2014 and had always wanted to see them do well for the sake of my friends and family who remained big supporters. They'd had a couple of false dawns in that time, but had never really threatened to be promoted or relegated, and were now entering their ninth successive season in the Championship. From what I'd heard, the team had done little on the pitch to enthuse the fans.

There had been cause for optimism off-the-field though, as Italian businessman Andrea Radrizzani had purchased the club from the unpredictable Massimo Cellino. One of his first moves had been to buy back Elland Road from the lease agreement that had been in place since the financial peril of 2004. It was the perfect way to get the fans on side, and when £7m was paid for Patrick Bamford a year later, the highest transfer fee splashed out since 2001, the city held a collective breath.

As I'd heard so much about Bielsa before his appointment, I'd told Andy and Bill that I thought that Leeds had a real chance of winning promotion when he took the job. I'd long been a believer that the manager was by far the most important person at a football club, and although I'd barely seen any of his teams play, I couldn't ignore endorsements from Pochettino and Guardiola.

Despite all this, I was still hugely surprised by how impressive Leeds were in their 3-1 defeat of Stoke City that day. They were passing the ball brilliantly, working their socks off, individual players looked too good for the standard, and the team as a whole were unrecognisably cohesive.

The following week, I saw the second half of their 4-1 win at Derby County, with the same style of football on display; it was an absolute pleasure to watch. I could already sense the optimism growing among the fans, and I was of the firm belief that they were right to feel that way.

Just before Christmas, I had a day out with my one of my old work pals, who is a huge Sheffield Wednesday fan. Even though neither of us were Leeds fans, we couldn't help but be swept up in the atmosphere at my local, as Leeds came from two goals down to beat Aston Villa 3-2 in stoppage time at Villa Park. Villa had been on a great run under new manager Dean Smith and had looked to be on course for a comfortable victory at 2-0 at half-time, but Leeds were outstanding in the second half; I couldn't help but imagine how I'd have celebrated the win had I still been a fan.

The victory left Leeds top of the Championship at Christmas, six points clear of third-placed West Bromwich Albion, and there was a sense that Premier League football could be returning in 2019/20. It wasn't just the league position that the fans were excited by though, Elland Road regulars were telling me that what I'd seen in the second half at Villa was happening every week. Leeds United were a genuinely good football team for the first time in what I believed to be seventeen years, and I couldn't have been happier for every single supporter that had stuck with them.

After the turn of the year, City and Liverpool went on to play out a scarcely believable title race, with City's 2-1 victory over their rivals on 3rd January turning out to be critical. Liverpool were still four points clear after what would be their only defeat of the season, but dropping just eight points from their final seventeen games proved too costly to claim their maiden Premier League crown. City's 2-1 loss at Newcastle United at the end of January sparked an astonishing fourteen-match winning streak, and although Liverpool won their final nine, the champions retained their trophy by a single point.

If the Premier League title race was quality of the highest order, then the drama of the 18/19 Champions League was even more astounding. There'd already been some incredible matches before the semi-finals, but what Liverpool and Spurs produced in the last four was unforgettable.

After losing their first leg with Barcelona 3-0 at the Nou Camp, Liverpool managed the most unlikely of 4-0 triumphs at Anfield to book their place in the final in Madrid. Tottenham's comeback was arguably even more spectacular, as three Lucas Moura goals saw them come back from 2-0 down on aggregate at half-time of their second leg at Ajax, to win 3-2 with the last kick of the game. I was with my pal Sam, a Liverpool fan, for the Spurs match, and all that we could do was shout 'FOOTBALL, FOOTBALL, FOOTBALL' after Moura's decisive third goal.

Sadly, while City and Liverpool had maintained their brilliance for an entire season, Leeds hadn't quite been able to do the same. After a Boxing Day victory over Blackburn Rovers, the gap between them and fourth-placed Sheffield United was ten points. However, five defeats from the ten games that followed saw the Blades wipe out that deficit, and when the two teams faced off at Elland Road in mid-March, it was the epitome of a six-pointer in the battle for promotion.

Norwich City were comfortably top and looked set to be champions, leaving the clash between the two Yorkshire sides billed as a potential second-place decider. It was Sheffield United who came out on top, nicking a 1-0 victory, although there was plenty of drama to come in the promotion race yet.

During the next round of fixtures, Leeds came from behind

to beat Millwall, while Sheffield United were beaten 3-2 at home to Bristol City. Advantage Leeds. A week later, the Blades won at Preston North-End while the Whites lost at Birmingham City. Advantage Sheffield United. There were two matches for each team during the week that followed, which saw Leeds win twice and Sheffield United draw twice, and all of a sudden, Leeds had a three-point advantage going into the final four games. Then, my old club managed something that only they could.

Relegation-threatened Wigan Athletic travelled to Elland Road without having registered an away victory all season. It certainly didn't look like they would get that elusive win at second-placed Leeds, especially when they found themselves both a man and a goal down after just seventeen minutes. However, in typically unfathomable Leeds United style, they managed to lose the game 2-1, despite having seventy-seven percent possession, thirty-six shots, and ten on target to Wigan's two. I messaged Bill after the game to tell him how sorry I was about the result, and he said that he'd never seen anything like what he'd just witnessed.

Sheffield United had, of course, won their match, taking them back into second place on goal difference, and when they took six points from their next two fixtures with Leeds only managing one, it was the Blades who had clinched automatic promotion. Thirteen years on from the harrowing 3-0 defeat to Watford, Leeds United would face the Championship play-offs once more.

I chatted to Andy and Bill a lot between the end of the regular season and Leeds' play-off semi-final first leg at Derby County. Although I wasn't entirely neutral because I was desperate for

Leeds to go up for their sake, I was able to provide a rational, mostly impartial view of the team's chances based on what I'd seen of each side in footballing terms.

I reminded them that Leeds had beaten Derby twice already that season and that there was a reason that they'd finished third and sixth respectively. Leeds were an outstanding football team, at this level at least, while Derby looked exactly like the majority of Championship teams that I'd seen over the years; a few decent individual players, but incongruous as a unit. Most importantly, Leeds had a manager in Marcelo Bielsa who had a true footballing philosophy and decades of experience. In contrast, Derby had Frank Lampard, who was in his first season as a boss.

The day after Leeds won the first leg at Pride Park 1-0 to take control of the tie, Bill messaged me to tell me that he'd got me a ticket for the second leg at Elland Road. He said that after everything that we'd been through together as fans before 2014, he wanted me to be there with him, even though I'd long since abandoned him and the other lads. I couldn't have been more honoured by his gesture, and was delighted to accept, even if I felt a little uncertain about returning to a place at which I'd been through so much.

It had been over twenty-five years since I'd made my way down Beeston Hill to watch Leeds United vs Manchester United with my dad as a seven-year-old. I'd had absolutely no idea what being a football fan would have in store for me at that point, but I don't think that even my sports-mad father could have predicted how huge a role it would play in my life.

Something I'd never contemplated during my twenty-one-year Leeds United-supporting tenure was that I would one day watch them play at Elland Road without being a fan.

I met up with Andy, Bill, and Bentley in town after work on Wednesday 15th May 2019, and sat on a rooftop bar sinking pints of lager in the sun. As much as I enjoy that environment on any given day, I find it unbeatable when I'm exposed to it before a huge sporting occasion.

The lads were all conflicted bundles of confidence and nerves, and I tried to ease their fears by explaining that there was only one football team that would be going to Wembley, provided that something remarkable didn't happen. They asked me a few questions in regards to *my* emotions, to which I told them with total honesty that I felt nothing other than excitement on their behalf.

I was genuinely surprised that there wasn't at least a little regret or jealousy underlying about not being able to experience what might be one of the great Leeds United nights as a supporter. Somehow, it felt natural to be heading to Elland Road as an honorary fan.

As I wasn't feeling crippled by anxiety, I was able to enjoy the pre-match experience immensely, and even partook in some of the nostalgia. We reflected on the various play-off campaigns that Leeds had been through, imagined where the club might be had that 2006 match against Watford been different, and ventured some of our favourite top-tier moments from before relegation fifteen years earlier.

When the clock reached 7 pm, we left the pub and swung by the nearest supermarket to pick up a large bottle of beer apiece for the stroll. I could feel the excitement and anticipation in the city centre as we walked south through town, and more and more white shirts surrounded us as we drew closer and closer to Elland Road.

As heartbreaking as it had been to have missed out on the Championship's top two, Bill still had the pragmatism to recognise that the *odds* had been long for Leeds to win promotion at the start of the 2018/19 season. He was aware that his football club had experienced more than their fair share of ups and downs throughout the campaign, but it had been one hell of a *journey*, that he only hoped would continue on to Wembley. The bigger picture was that if Leeds could simply avoid defeat that night, and win one more game of football, they would reach the end of what had been as windy a fifteen-year road back to the Premier League as could ever have been anticipated.

We climbed the steps and walked over the motorway bridge, taking in a first view of the stadium as we did, and strode the final 100 yards amid a sea of white, yellow and blue. There were fans all around us in full voice already, and they were ready to play their part in yet another critical night in this football club's history.

Since my days as a Premiership season ticket holder, I'd almost exclusively been in the Kop, with the odd occasion in the west or south stands and one solitary game in the east stand upper. I'd not been back in the east stand itself since I was a child, so as we headed through the turnstiles, so many memories came flooding back to me.

Mark Viduka 4-3 Liverpool. Leeds 1-1 Manchester United, Wes Brown's own goal that wasn't. Leeds 3-3 Lazio in the Champions League. Leeds 3-0 West Ham United to send us top of the Premiership on 01/01/02. Leeds 0-2 Manchester United, 27/04/94. It was overwhelming to have all of these moments flashing before my eyes, but felt genuinely amazing at the same time.

As we walked through the gangway and out to our seats, it was like I'd been sucked into another world. The atmosphere was astonishing, with noise reverberating all around us; Elland Road is such a special place to be on a big night. There was a different aura about the place though; I could tell that the fans sensed that this was their time. A goal up from the first leg, and a knowledge that their team was superior to their opponents, it was now a matter of getting the job done.

When the two sides took to the field, I felt as though I'd rewound the clock to the David O'Leary days. The *connection* between the fans and the players reminded me of New Year's Day 2002, with the Kop having a personalised chant for each of the starting eleven players. It didn't end there either, Leeds United was now connected from fan to player to manager to chairman. At last, the club was United again.

From the minute the game kicked off, I was so impressed by Leeds' *quality*. Yes, I'd seen them play on TV a few times that season, but seeing the whole pitch gave me a different perspective of what was a special Bielsa operation. Not only was every player comfortable on the ball, but they all offered themselves whenever a teammate needed help. The way that they hunted in packs after losing it was far superior to anything I'd seen from a Leeds team back in the Premiership days, and Derby barely had a kick in the first twenty minutes. With that goal advantage in mind, I could only see this game going one way.

I may have reacted more wildly to goals in the past, but there was something so, so special about watching my friends celebrate Stuart Dallas putting Leeds 1-0 up after twenty-four minutes. Don't get me wrong, I was jumping around like a madman too, but being able to feel their ecstasy instead of indulging in my own was extraordinary. I didn't stop at the lads either.

In what was as close to an out of body experience as I could imagine having, I found myself looking around the whole stadium while the delirious celebrations were happening. Without realising I was doing it, I raised my arms out in front of me and felt like I was literally soaking up the emotion of every fan in the ground. I was completely overcome by euphoria, and not because of the sport itself, but because of the euphoria that the sport had induced in thousands of other people.

That was the moment, right there, that I truly understood what being a football fan was all about. For all my years of obsessing over the prize, I'd never actually taken a moment to appreciate what the *culture* of football fandom gives a man during the process of supporting his team. It is a time at which he can be a part of himself that he can't otherwise be.

Whatever is going on with a man behind a football fan doesn't matter when a goal is scored, as he is free of his fear of emotion. Whatever deep-rooted issues he may have, he can explode without judgement, and can feel as strongly as he wants or needs to feel without trepidation. He can hug and kiss his fellow man without retribution, and embrace his instincts without dread. He can be at one with his tribe in a way that isn't possible in any other environment. Essentially, as a football fan, a man doesn't fear love.

That is why the *culture* of football fandom is unique. From all my experience, no other sport can even come close in terms of raw passion and emotion, and it's precisely why I was so obsessed with it for so long. Football gave me something that no other sport could; a place in which I could comfortably express my emotions.

If I'd only had the emotional maturity to recognise this a few years earlier, then maybe I wouldn't have given up on Leeds United. Paradoxically, I most likely wouldn't have realised this had I not given up on Leeds United, as that epiphanic moment after Dallas' goal would never have occurred. It was a moment that I never wanted to end, but alas, there was a football match to watch.

Everything that I'd experienced inside Elland Road up to that point told me that it was finally this football club's time. The *quality*, the *connection*, the *odds*, and the *culture* were all in their favour, with the *prize* at the end of the *journey* in clear sight. As long as there was no *drama*, then they would reach their destination of Wembley. Sadly, Leeds United and *drama* can never be mutually exclusive.

After dominating the remainder of the first half, Leeds conceded on the stroke of half-time. It was a horrendous equaliser to lose, with Derby's Jack Marriott taking advantage of a defensive catastrophe to change the complexion of Lampard's half-time team-talk. If Leeds had reached the break 2-0 up on aggregate, that probably would have been that. It was all to play for at 2-1.

There'd been a party atmosphere between minutes twenty-four and forty-five, but I could have cut the tension with a knife during the break as I sank my half-time pint. I could see the anxiety on people's faces and understood why they looked so concerned; I knew as well as anyone what they'd been through over the past couple of decades. Based on the football that I'd seen, I was still sure that their team would have enough, but rarely does logic prevail at Elland Road.

I hadn't even made it back to my seat by the time that Mason Mount had put Derby ahead on the night. Leeds had totally and utterly bossed the first three-quarters of the tie, but a goal seconds before half-time, and another seconds after, meant that it was all square on aggregate. I tried to tell the lads to keep calm, as their superior team, on their home ground, still had forty-five minutes to find a winner. After that goal, though, the home side were no longer superior.

Leeds completely fell apart after Mount's goal and should have been 3-1 down *before* Liam Cooper blatantly fouled Mason Bennett inside the penalty area. Harry Wilson fired past Leeds' keeper Kiko Casilla from the spot, and it was Derby who were heading to Wembley as it stood.

Scores of Leeds fans were too disbelieving to be able to sing, but there were thousands of others doing everything that they could to be the 12th man that their team needed them to be. These supporters had amazed me too often during dark times, but finally, they got what their loyalty deserved.

Four minutes after falling 3-1 behind, that man Dallas cut inside from the left before firing an unstoppable strike past Derby stopper Kelle Roos. It was 2-3, 3-3 on aggregate, and it felt like every emotion that is possible for human beings to experience was circulating the stadium.

The contrast between the first 135 minutes of the tie and the thirty-five minutes that followed was immeasurable. Leeds had looked so accomplished, so in control, yet one defensive error had turned it into a footballing free for all. The game was so open, and it now felt like it was there to be taken for whichever team wanted it more. The beauty was that both teams seemed to want it equally, but only one could triumph.

Just before the eighty-minute mark, Whites defender Gaetano Berardi lunged in on former Leeds man Bradley Johnson and was shown a yellow card. Amid the chaos that was this match, I'd failed to notice that Berardi had already been booked, and when the referee brandished the red, everybody knew that it was now Derby's to lose.

With just five minutes remaining, Derby poured forward in numbers, before defender Richard Keogh slid Marriott in on goal. The striker brilliantly dinked the ball over the onrushing Casilla, and as the ball nestled in the back of the net, I couldn't help but put my hands on my head in dismay. I wasn't even a Leeds United fan, but that awful sinking feeling that I'd experienced so many times as a supporter made me fall back into my seat.

Leeds fought valiantly to find an equaliser, and they received faint hope when Derby lost a man of their own in stoppage time. However, that turned out to be the last significant moment of an incomprehensible game of football, and as the final whistle went, Elland Road was left to wonder how on earth it was yet again grieving.

Bentley and I lost Andy and Bill in the aftermath of the game's end, but I felt it important to stay and applaud the distraught Leeds players as they showed their appreciation for the support. Fans' favourites Kalvin Phillips and Pablo Hernandez were in tears, but based on the little that I'd seen of them that year, it was hard not to feel as though they deserved better. On this occasion, it felt like everyone at Leeds United deserved better, yet still, it was pain for those in white.

Bentley and I said little on our stroll back into the city,

where we found an inconsolable Andy and Bill in a takeaway by the train station. As much as I felt for Andy in his state of disbelieving anger, it was Bill's comments that concerned me far more. He said that he didn't know if he could do it any more. He said that he thought that I'd made the right decision by getting out when I did.

When your feelings govern you, you sometimes act without considering how you could influence others. When I quit supporting my football team, I did it without truly knowing what I was doing, as although it was a decision based on logic, I made it when at my most emotional. I have no problem if a decision that I make is to my detriment, but it would mortify me if it were to impact somebody else negatively.

If I hadn't have set the example of quitting Leeds, then there is no way that Bill would have even contemplated the idea. Hearing him say it sent a shiver down my spine, and I was desperate to try and talk him round. It wasn't the right time for rationale, though, so I attempted to comfort him by letting him know how much I felt his pain. What I wanted to say to him was that now was the worst possible time to quit Leeds United, as even though they had lost, Elland Road was a more special place than I'd ever known it to be.

That night, I'd been living proof of how wonderful football can be when the *prize* doesn't define a fandom experience. It had been heartbreaking to see Leeds lose, but as a sports fan, I'd just lived something more powerful than any victory could be. It was the experience that'd had everything; *quality, drama, culture, odds, connection, journey*.

When I'd quit Leeds United, the only thing that was present for me as a fan was the *journey*, and of the six elements, that is the one that suffers the most in the absence of all of the others. Now, although the *odds* would likely shorten, the club had everything else in abundance, which is why I couldn't bear the thought of Bill jumping ship.

As we ate our filthy kebabs, I realised that part of the reason that I wanted to get through to Bill was that I could see so much of my former self in him. I could see the man that had poured everything that he had into his football club, that had received barely anything other than pain in return and had reached a point at which he felt he could give no more.

In the height of my emotion back in 2014, I found an answer that I knew would make me feel better in that very moment, and it was to run away from what had felt like an abusive relationship. The reality was that I'd spent so long chasing something that I didn't have, that I never stopped to appreciate what I did. I'd been so obsessed by the idea of the prize, which was nothing more than a feeling that I'd never experienced, that I hadn't realised how good the process of supporting a football club could be.

That night at Elland Road, it became clear to me how difficult the prize is to obtain in sport. What's more, even when you win the prize, sometimes it doesn't even feel that good, as the Liverpool fans with whom I watched their Champions League final victory over Spurs a few weeks later attested. The match itself had been such an underwhelming affair, that they said that winning the biggest club competition in world football had undoubtedly been anticlimactic.

That was what made me want to write this book. I wanted to tell any sports fan across the world that is desperately waiting for a prize at the end of their journey to stop thinking about it.

Just concentrate on enjoying the journey itself, because what's the point in working towards a moment that might be, when you can make the most of the moment that is.

My take was that I could write a book that explained my twenty-five-year journey as a sports fan, and how I learned the importance of enjoying the elements of the process, as opposed to the pursuit of the prize. Then, with a bit of luck, I might be able to write another book twenty-five years later, in which I'd not only experienced the glory of the process but also landed a prize to go with it.

38

The golden goal (part one)

Here comes Archer, running in for one last time with those long, languid strides. He releases the ball, and it flies in towards Guptill's pads. The Kiwi flicks it into the on side, and as soon as he hits it, he knows that he's not found a gap for the ball to reach the boundary.

Famed for being lightning quick, Guptill immediately charges down the wicket towards the bowler's end. He knows that if he's going to win the World Cup for his country, he's going to have to rely on that pace and make it back down to the striker's end for two.

The camera pans out towards the boundary, where who else but Jason Roy is tearing in from the rope to collect the ball. It's only moments after he's made two errors in judgement to gift New Zealand valuable runs, but the hopes of England now lie in the hands of his fielding.

Just as Guptill is turning at the non-striker's end to start the twenty-two-yard journey back from whence he came, Roy, under unimaginable amounts of pressure, picks up the ball seamlessly. With Guptill having taken two or three strides back down the wicket, Roy completes one perfect fluid movement to release the ball towards wicketkeeper Buttler, who looks desperate as he waits to receive the ball by the stumps at the striker's end.

The ball flies through the air, and it is now a race between it and Martin Guptill to see who can reach their intended destination first. Buttler collects the ball about two yards to the right of the stumps, with Guptill only about five yards from home and moving at incredible pace. In the space of what must only have been a tenth of a second, Buttler destroys the stumps, and Guptill makes his ground.

For the briefest of moments, I have absolutely no idea who has won the 2019 Cricket World Cup. Is it England, or New Zealand?

Although my father has unquestionably been the most substantial influence on the development of the fan that I've become, there is one sport that my maternal family introduced me to.

I've been going to Headingley Stadium to watch cricket for longer than I can remember. I grew up about 500 metres from the ground, and my maternal grandmother, who lived just down the road from us, would take my brother Matt and me to watch Yorkshire play when she was looking after us. As we grew up, we'd head down for the final session after finishing school from time to time, and although football was becoming my sport of choice at this point, cricket was Matt's true passion.

Throughout the 1990s, I spent vast amounts of time with Matt watching Test cricket. The two of us would always tune in when England were on TV, but he was so captivated by the sport as a whole that he'd sometimes sit on the couch and stare at the Ceefax scorecard as it ever so slowly updated. If you think that Test cricket is boring enough as it is, try watching a digital screen that only refreshes every couple of minutes. Even when it did refresh, there'd usually have been no change in score at all.

As he was my big brother, and I had a tendency to follow him in whatever he did, I adopted many of his cricketing habits. We'd often use his scorebook to keep score of whatever match we were watching for ourselves, and when playing a bit of garden cricket, we'd take it in turns to impersonate the bowling actions of many of our Yorkshire and England heroes.

Although I played for a local team throughout high school, I was always far more interested in spectating and spent many a Sunday morning watching Matt play at a decent standard. I'd sometimes go out for walks on my own at weekends around the same time, and if there were ever a match going on at a local club, I'd take real pleasure in sitting and watching for an hour or two.

On the far grander stage, I was lucky enough to get down to Headingley to watch the Ashes in both 1997 and 2001, and as England started to rise from the depths of Test cricket in the mid-2000s, my love for the game grew deeper than ever. There can be no doubt that the 2005 series against the Australians was seminal, and my horizons were broadened to all forms from there.

Even though we were an awful One-Day side at this point, I have fond memories of watching the 2007 World Cup alone in my university halls. In the summers between university years, I spent many a sunny day watching Yorkshire across every discipline, and Headingley became a bit of a sanctuary for me when I returned from Newcastle to save for travelling. It was the perfect sport for me to relax to in solitude amid the chaos of working seventy-two hours per week across two jobs.

Due to travel commitments and my move to York, I saw far

less cricket than I'd have liked in the first half of the 2010s, but once I returned to Leeds in 2014, it fast became my number one sport. Being at Trent Bridge to see Yorkshire lift the 2014 County Championship trophy remains one of the greatest moments of my time as a sports fan, but while I revelled in our defence of the title in 2015, something more significant had happened earlier that year.

I still don't know to this day whether I'd have thrown myself into the 2015 Cricket World Cup in Australia and New Zealand had I not so recently quit Leeds United. I experienced a bit of a rebound from the end of my relationship with my football club, and the incredible effort that I put in to wake up at all hours to follow us was undoubtedly abnormal.

Had we been a top fifty-over side at this point, it might have made more sense, but setting my alarm for 4 am to watch Australia, New Zealand, and Sri Lanka maul us couldn't have been more fruitless. The loss to Bangladesh to send us tumbling out at the first hurdle was seen as one of the darkest days in English cricket at the time, although it didn't come as that big a surprise to me. I'd never known us to be a good One-Day International (ODI) side in over twenty years of supporting us.

With a home World Cup to come in 2019, there could be no doubting that if we didn't make a conscious effort to address our white-ball cricket limitations now, then we never would. We'd spent so many years selecting players from the Test setup that had never been good enough in the shorter forms of the game, and not once had it paid off for us. Finally, the England and Wales Cricket Board (ECB) changed tack.

In the immediate aftermath of Australia and New Zealand 2015, recently appointed captain Eoin Morgan led a revolution in the way that we treated white-ball cricket. In our very first innings since the 2015 shambles, we posted our maiden score of 400 or more in a fifty-over match, hammering World Cup-finalists New Zealand by 210 runs in the process. A new-look squad that included the likes of Ben Stokes, Jason Roy, Jonny Bairstow, Adil Rashid, and Liam Plunkett, nicked the series 3-2, while playing the most exciting cricket I'd ever seen from an England ODI team.

We made astonishing progress in the months that followed, and by April 2016, we were competing in a T20 World Cup final. Having been such a substandard short-form batting side for such a long time, I suddenly found myself overcome with excitement at the mere thought of watching us go after teams. I nipped out on my lunch breaks to watch our matches throughout the tournament, and the likes of Roy, Joe Root, Morgan, Stokes, and Jos Buttler took it in turn to destroy the bowling attacks of opposition teams. As devastating as it was to see us lose in the final to the West Indies, it had been groundbreaking to see us play such a fearless brand of cricket.

A few months later we broke the world record for the highest ever fifty-over score, as Alex Hales smashed 171 from 122 balls to help us to 444/3. We then demolished our own record a couple of years later with a staggering 481-6 against Australia, and managed another score of 400+ in the West Indies in early 2019. That performance wasn't the most prominent news to come out of the Caribbean during that tour though.

Up until 2018, the ECB's rules dictated that any player that had moved to England later than their 18th birthday, who also had a British passport, would only be eligible to play for us seven years after their arrival. However, I was surprised to see the ECB make another bold decision, changing their rules just weeks before the start of a World Cup year, which meant that only three years of residence was required to qualify for England duty. That stipulated that one of the most exciting young bowlers in world cricket, British passport-holding and Barbados-born Jofra Archer, would be eligible to play for us at England and Wales 2019, with him having moved to England in early 2016. With the addition of Archer, our squad now looked imperious.

In the aftermath of being knocked out at the first hurdle by Bangladesh in 2015, there can't have been a cricket fan in the world that would have believed that England would begin their 2019 World Cup campaign as favourites to win the tournament.

I was so proud to have followed such a remarkable journey that I booked every one of our group games off work. I say that, I'd have probably done the same had we made no on-field progress from 2015 at all.

39

The golden goal (part two)

It's Sunday 14th July 2019. I'm standing outside the Original Oak pub in Headingley at 9.30 am. I know the exact bench at which I want to spend the day sitting. The one that has a perfect view of the big screen, is the closest to the speakers for the commentary, and has the sun on it for longer than any other bench in the pub's outstanding beer garden. I want everything to be perfect, simply because it can be.

I know the pub doesn't open until 10 am, but I gladly sacrifice half an hour of my morning in the knowledge that it is a small price to pay. I have my brother Matt, who is the biggest cricket fan I know, and my pals Rich, Rout, Wilko, and George coming to join me. I struggle to comprehend how I can care so little about Roger Federer and Novak Djokovic facing off in the Wimbledon final that afternoon.

I'm the first person to enter the pub, and a surge of adrenaline rushes through me as I take a seat at my desired bench. As my brother arrives, I head to the bar to grab a mug for the 99p unlimited coffee, exchanging pleasantries with the bar staff that I've seen a lot of over the previous few weeks in the process. I sit back down next to my brother, and any lingering anxieties ease. Now the day can really begin.

Since England's Cricket World Cup campaign had begun

against South Africa on 30th May, all roads had led to that moment, and I hadn't missed a second of the action. I was fortunate enough to get to three of our group matches, while I'd watched the other six, and our semi-final match, from the exact spot that I found myself sitting that morning.

Reaching the final of our home World Cup hadn't come easily for us. Group stage defeats to Pakistan, Sri Lanka, and Australia had left us needing to win our final two round-robin games against top-quality India and New Zealand sides to qualify for the semi-finals. Fortunately, opening batsman Jason Roy returned to the side after a three-match injury absence to help inspire the team to two comfortable victories, which sent us through to face the Aussies in the last four.

The Australia match was one of those glorious days of sport that only occur once in a blue moon. We destroyed our biggest rivals in every aspect of the game, skittling them for a modest 223, before knocking off the runs with eight wickets and eighteen overs to spare. With New Zealand having upset India the previous day in the other semi-final, we knew that we were going into the final as comprehensive favourites.

Although they were world-renowned for dominating the sport of rugby union, New Zealand were the perennial dark horses of fifty-over cricket. They'd reached the final four years earlier, and had entered the 2019 edition as rank outsiders, with some of their most dangerous batsmen having either retired or now considered past their best. However, spearheaded by one of the world's best batsmen in captain Kane Williamson and an outstanding seam bowling attack, they'd unassumingly gone all the way again. They were not to be underestimated.

Watching England's bowlers restrict the Black Caps to 241-8

in a World Cup final, on a big screen in my favourite beer garden in the world, in glorious sunshine, with my brother and a load of my mates, was as close to perfection as I could have hoped for from the first half of the day. Even if the ball was likely to nip around for New Zealand's dangerous opening pair of Trent Boult and Matt Henry, our batting line-up was far too good not to knock off 242 runs in fifty overs. The ease at which we'd chased down the 224 against the Aussies was all the proof that I needed.

With Roy and Jonny Bairstow regarded as the most explosive opening batting partnership in ODI cricket, and the world-class Joe Root, Eoin Morgan, Ben Stokes, and Jos Buttler following, it seemed impossible that we would fall short of our target. However, I'd been conscious of underestimating the Kiwis pre-match for a reason, and they set the tone for our innings with the very first delivery.

Left-armer Boult steamed in and got the brand new ball to swing from outside off stump and back into Roy's pads. Somehow, it was given not out by the umpire, and although New Zealand appealed, an Umpire's Call verdict on the Decision Review System led to Matt and me sharing the biggest sigh of relief of our cricket-watching lives. The relief wouldn't last long.

The superb Boult and Henry, backed up by Lockie Ferguson and Colin de Grandhomme, reduced us to 86/4, 156 runs short of our target. The batting conditions had dumbfounded each of our apparent superstars, and the Kiwis' 241 suddenly looked like a very respectable total. With only two recognised batsmen remaining in Stokes and Buttler, both of whom had just arrived at the crease, our opponents knew that it would be theirs to lose should they snare one more wicket. I lost all interest in the social aspect of the occasion at that point.

The group of us had all been very relaxed throughout the day, drinking our beers and chatting away merrily as we casually watched our team steadily work towards a presumed inevitable glory. It took the loss of four wickets for me to register that everything that this team had done since exiting the 2015 World Cup had come down to half an innings of cricket, and most likely the batting capabilities of Ben Stokes and Jos Buttler.

I didn't know if it was the ball losing a bit of its movement, or the conditions slightly improving for batting, but I was amazed by how comfortable Buttler looked from ball one of his innings. He tucked his first two deliveries away for two and one respectively, and did so with the confidence of a bloke that had been out there all day. Stokes, on the other hand, was having to dig in and battle to keep every delivery out, so hard were the bowlers making it for him.

By this point, we'd fallen comfortably behind the required scoring rate, but as the cricket expert among us, Matt insisted that this would not be an issue provided that these two could stay out there for the rest of the innings. He also acknowledged that it would be no mean feat for Stokes and Buttler to do that, everything considered.

After nearly an hour of gritty, determined batting, there was a critical moment in the 34th over when Stokes knocked three consecutive Henry deliveries for two. The crowd responded with a roar of encouragement, as they sensed for the first time that we were still very much in with a chance.

Meanwhile, Wilko, who was tennis mad, had moved on to

another pub that he knew was showing both the World Cup final and the Wimbledon final. As England and New Zealand had moved into the last ten overs at Lord's, Djokovic and Federer had entered a deciding fifth set on the other side of London, which had left Wilko in a state of crippling sports fandom conflict. My opinion was that he should have been prioritising England, but deep down, I couldn't help but enjoy how much stress the situation was causing him.

When both Buttler and Stokes passed fifty in the 44th over, we found ourselves needing fifty-three runs from thirty-six balls. I still thought this looked like a tall order, but Matt reminded me that this was Jos Buttler territory. The reality was that there was only former India captain MS Dhoni in world cricket that could compare to Buttler when it came to completing a run chase for his team. As long as he was there, we were just about favourites to win this match. *As long as he was there.*

Sensing that it was now time to make his big move, Buttler went after a wider delivery from Ferguson the very next over, and sent the ball looping high in the air towards the off-side boundary. Substitute fielder Tim Southee came hurtling in from the rope and stooped low to take a brilliant catch. We now needed forty-six runs from thirty-one balls, with only five wickets remaining, and with no Jos Buttler. 'It's all on Stokes', I can implicitly remember Matt stating.

We could only manage seven runs from the next over, to leave thirty-nine required from twenty-four deliveries, and when Chris Woakes fell to Ferguson the next ball, things were looking bleak. Liam Plunkett was next in and managed to plunder a four, but at the end of the 47th over, only eighteen balls remained, with thirty-four runs still required. New Zealand were favourites, but hope remained as long as Ben Stokes was out in the middle.

At the start of the day, there'd been quite a few fans that had turned up specifically for the cricket, but the beer garden hadn't been close to being full. However, a sunny Sunday afternoon brought plenty of people that had no interest in the sport with it, and the chatter and the noise around the place had picked up considerably.

Never in my life did I think that cricket would have the capacity to do this, but as we entered the final three overs of the 2019 World Cup final, a beer garden full of people fell silent before every delivery. It was a totally unfamiliar sports fandom environment for me, and although I only had a tiny plot of Headingley grass to go by, it felt like the whole country had come to a standstill for cricket for the first time ever.

Bowling was Boult, and Stokes hit his first delivery for four. He and Plunkett then managed six more runs from the remaining five balls of the over, and we now required twenty-four runs to win from the final two. If we thought that it was dramatic enough that the biggest of all cricketing occasions could end up being so close, it's no surprise that we genuinely couldn't believe what those final twelve deliveries produced.

It was the solid but unspectacular Jimmy Neesham to bowl the penultimate over, but he did brilliantly with his first two balls to restrict Plunkett and Stokes to singles. From his third ball, he went one better, as Plunkett was caught in the deep by Boult when attempting a big shot. We needed twenty-two to win from nine deliveries, but the one saving grace from Plunkett's dismissal was that the batsmen had crossed before Boult had taken the catch. Stokes would face Neesham's next ball.

As Neesham sent down the 592nd legitimate delivery of the day, our sole hope Stokes got plenty of bat on it, but not quite out of the middle. The ball flew high in to the air and out towards the boundary, but didn't appear to have the momentum to clear the rope. The camera focused in as the ball fell back towards the surface, but to our absolute horror, Boult was waiting underneath it. The ball nestled in his hands just inside the boundary rope, and that, surely, was that. The whole journey that this team had been on, ending by the *barest of margins* on the Lord's boundary-edge.

However, in a truly astonishing turn of events, the off-balance Boult took a step backwards and planted his foot on to the rope. He released the ball a split second later, throwing it into the hands of Guptill, who was standing just a few yards away. As it was, he'd not released the ball before stepping on the rope, which meant that not only was Stokes not out, it was six runs. It couldn't have been a more polarised moment, and we now needed sixteen to win from eight, with Ben Stokes still at the crease.

Stokes could only manage a single from the next ball, and off the final delivery of the over, Neesham rearranged new batsman Jofra Archer's stumps. Not only had we not managed a run, but we now only had two wickets remaining.

That left one of the world's best batsmen in Stokes, to face one over from one of the world's best bowlers in Boult, with fourteen runs separating the two teams. It was probably part of how I'd become hard-wired from sporting pain, but at that point, I had no faith.

First ball, Boult to Stokes, no run. Stokes could have taken a single, but it would have taken him off strike. Fifteen runs required to win from five balls.

Second ball, Boult to Stokes, no run. Stokes gets bat on ball again, but it rolls straight towards a fielder, giving him no option but to stay where he is. Fifteen runs required from four balls, it was going to take a miracle.

Third ball, Boult to Stokes, SIX! Boult sends it down well outside off stump, but Stokes gets down on one knee and slaps it over midwicket for a maximum. Nine runs from three balls.

Fourth ball, Boult to Stokes… SIX??

In the most inconceivable moment that I'd ever seen on a cricket field, Stokes got enough on the ball to send it rolling, *rolling*, down to deep midwicket. It looked like it would be a close run out call if Stokes was to come back for two, but in the circumstances, he absolutely had to try.

As Stokes desperately sprinted back down the wicket to try and make his ground, fielder Martin Guptill launched the ball towards wicketkeeper Tom Latham and the stumps at the striker's end. As the ball flew through the air, there was no doubt that it was going to be close, but if Stokes could get there, England would still have a chance with seven runs required from two balls.

Incredibly, not only did Stokes get there with a despairing dive, but Guptill's sixty-yard throw landed flush on the England man's outstretched bat. The pace on the ball saw it fly off towards the boundary, and what's more, Stokes had inadvertently found a perfect gap between the fielders. It raced away to the rope, and I had no idea what that meant.

Every single one of the other guys there did the same thing in that moment. Overcome with both excitement and confusion, we all turned to Matt, who we were aware was one of the world's biggest cricket geeks. To our utter delight, he was jumping up and down and shouting 'IT'S SIX, IT'S SIX, IT'S SIX'.

It was almost impossible that what had just happened could have happened, but it was another six runs to Stokes, and another six runs to England. We were now 239/8 from 49.4 overs, attempting to surpass our opponents' 241/8 from fifty. Out of absolutely nowhere, we needed three runs to win from two balls.

We all had to take a moment to settle ourselves down after such incredible drama, which was aided by Boult taking his time to plan his next delivery in light of what had just happened. He and Williamson were trying to arrange the field, now knowing that they had a lot more to consider than simply trying to stop Stokes clearing the rope. Two balls to go, two balls to win a World Cup.

The first of those was a brilliant yorker from Boult, which Stokes could only dig out from underneath him. He then set off down the wicket as the ball rolled off through the outfield once more, before turning in an attempt to get back for two. As it was, the second run was never on, and Adil Rashid, who hadn't even faced a delivery, was run out by miles at the non-striker's end. That barely made a difference, as Stokes was back on strike, with two runs required from the 600th and final ball of the day's cricket. Or so we thought.

Matt's latest assignment was to inform us that if we were only to score one run from the last ball, the match would go to a 'Super Over'. As much cricket as I'd watched in my time, I had no idea what a 'Super Over' constituted, as the only manner in which I knew that a tie could be settled was through a 'Bowl-Off'. Still, we all hoped that it wouldn't have to come to that, as the fate of this remarkable cricketing journey lay in the hands of Ben Stokes and Trent Boult.

Mark Wood had readied himself at the non-striker's end as our final batsman, as Boult strode into bowl for one last time. It was a full toss, there for the hitting, but Stokes feathered it away into the on-side, knowing that a single run would result in a tie. If he could get back for a second, his country would be world champions.

As the cameras panned out to follow the ball down to long-on, it was clear that it had reached the fielder too quickly, as far as we were concerned at least.

Handling the pressure brilliantly, Neesham picked up the ball and hurled it into Boult. The pace bowler, who had been so involved in the previous couple of overs, seamlessly took in the throw and whipped the bails off the stumps. Wood was comfortably out of his ground.

After facing 300 balls apiece, the score had ended up at New Zealand 241, England 241. Of everything that I'd imagined might happen in a game of cricket that day, it would all come down to a concept that I'd never even known existed.

40

The golden goal (part three)

When Sergio Aguero scored in the 94th minute of the final game of the 2011/12 Premier League season, to snatch the title for his team, from their biggest rivals, on goal difference, I never thought I'd see anything like it ever again. Those were the words of legendary commentator Martin Tyler, 'I SWEAR YOU'LL NEVER SEE ANYTHING LIKE THIS EVER AGAIN'.

I didn't think I'd witness anything remotely as dramatic across any sport, anywhere, at any time, for the rest of my life. I didn't even think I'd hear about anything like it that I might be able to go back and learn about or watch online retrospectively. It was a once-in-a-lifetime event as far as I was concerned.

It had the *quality* of the play, it had the *culture* of the celebrations, it had the *connection* between the fans and the players, it had the *odds* that were piled against them at 2-1 down, and it had the *journey* that the football club had been on; all the way from the third tier of English football in just thirteen years. Above all, it had the *drama*, which undoubtedly is the decisive factor when it comes to what the fandom experience is about for those who love sport the most; emotion.

With all the elements having fallen in to place, the biggest *prize* of all for an English club football team had lain in wait at the end of that particular journey for Manchester City; the Premier League title. As I saw that City fan crying his eyes out in the York pub that I was in, all I could do was imagine what it must feel like to experience something like that as a sports fan. I never thought I'd see anything like it ever again, and I certainly didn't think something similar might happen to a team of mine.

I've never been as grateful for my brother Matt's cricket obsession than I was after Ben Stokes had tied the 2019 Cricket World Cup final for England. I wouldn't have even been the cricket fan that I was had it not been for him, and I knew that I owed him a lot for that bearing in mind how many amazing experiences the sport had given me throughout my life. However, when he explained exactly how a Super Over worked to the lads and me as the dust attempted to settle on what had been the most remarkable hour of cricket, I wanted to present him with a medallion.

Each team would have to face one over from the other, and whoever scored the highest number of runs in their mini-innings out of England and New Zealand would win the World Cup. Only one bowler could be selected to bowl his team's six deliveries, and the captains were to choose two players to go out and bat. When batting, a team could lose one wicket, but would be all out if they lost two before the end of their over, rendering any remaining balls redundant. One critical rule that I couldn't believe that Matt knew, was that the team that had scored the most boundaries in their regulation fifty overs would win in the event of the Super Over itself being a tie. We'd hit more boundaries.

As we'd batted second of the two teams, we were to bat first in the Super Over. Captain Morgan decided to send out Stokes and Buttler first, the two players whose quality had carried us into this position in the first place. Stokes had looked absolutely out on his feet when walking from the field after Boult's final over, but no captain in their right mind would deny such an astonishing character another chance to win a World Cup for his country.

There was far too much chaos and commotion for anybody to be able to hear the commentary as New Zealand's players returned to the outfield. Then, as the camera panned to Stokes and Buttler as they strode out towards the wicket, every man and woman in the Original Oak beer garden let out a massive roar in support of our heroic pair.

In that moment, I recognised that this incredible four-year journey, a spectacular seven-week tournament that had come with so many ups and downs, and a World Cup final was all going to be decided by a game of one-over cricket! Unsurprisingly, it was that man Boult that was readying himself to bowl the Super Over for his country, and as he prepared to start his run-up for the first delivery, the pub fell silent once more.

First ball, Stokes goes for the big shot, and doesn't quite catch it. The ball loops up in the air, but lands safely short of third man, and two New Zealand fielders chase the ball down to prevent a boundary. However, Buttler is lightning quick between the wickets, and gets back for a third run. 3-0 off 0.1.

Second ball, Buttler doesn't quite catch it, and the ball runs down towards the onside boundary. The fielder collects it with ease, and throws it in to ensure that England only get a single. 4-0 off 0.2.

Third ball, Stokes gets hold of it, and finds the gap on the on side boundary. A fielder charges around from deep midwicket, but his despairing dive is in vain, as the ball crosses the rope for four. 8-0 off 0.3.

Fourth ball, Stokes gets some bat on a wide one, and slices it out to a fielder on the off-side. Nothing more than a single is on offer there, and Stokes races through to the non-striker's end looking totally and utterly exhausted. 9-0 off 0.4.

Fifth ball, brilliant ball from Boult, but Buttler digs it out and heads off down the wicket sensing a chance of running two. Kiwi fielder Henry Nicholls dramatically loses sight of the ball in the early-evening sun, allowing Buttler and Stokes to make their ground with ease. 11-0 off 0.5.

Sixth ball, Boult almost gets the yorker in, but not quite, and Buttler picks it up before it lands. The ball flies off towards the onside boundary, and just like with Stokes' shot from the third delivery, he finds the gap between the fielders. Four runs, 15-0 off 1.0.

When that final Boult delivery crossed the boundary rope for four, I thought that it would take a miracle for New Zealand to chase us down from there. In a final that had seen the pendulum swing more prominently than anybody could have imagined, it was now comfortably back on the side of England. Having scored fewer boundaries than us in their fifty-over innings, the Black Caps now needed sixteen from one over if they were to win their maiden World Cup, and deny us from winning ours.

I remember almost nothing about what happened between the Super Over innings. I must have been so all over the place by this point emotionally, not to mention the fact that I'd had about eight pints, that I couldn't process my surroundings. All

I can recall is staring at the big screen silently, with my hands on my head, as England's players made their way through the Lord's Long Room to take to a cricket field for one last time in this utterly astonishing game, tournament, and journey.

It was Martin Guptill and Jimmy Neesham to bat for the Kiwis, and that man Jofra Archer to bowl the Super Over for us. Archer had been cut a controversial figure in the build-up to the tournament, with West Indian cricket fans disappointed that he'd decided to represent his father's home nation, as opposed to the country in which he'd spent the first twenty years of his life. There'd even been some critique in England surrounding his selection for our World Cup squad with him having played so little international cricket. However, he'd silenced everybody with his supreme bowling performances, and here he was with the fate of English cricket in his hands; what pressure for a twenty-four-year-old from Barbados.

First ball, Archer appears to be feeling that pressure, as the umpire signals for a wide, meaning a run for New Zealand, with all six deliveries still intact. It's incredibly close to the mark, but the decision stands, and the Black Caps now only have to score fifteen from their six balls to win. 1-0 off 0.0.

Second ball, brilliant from Archer, but dugout by Neesham, who manages to scramble back for two after the ball rolls steadily down to long-off. Had he caught more of the ball, it would likely only have been a single. 3-0 off 0.1.

Third ball, SIX! Archer just misses his length this time, and Neesham middles the ball on the half-volley to send it flying over the onside boundary. It's an astonishing shot in the circumstances, and it's very much advantage New Zealand. 9-0 off 0.2.

Fourth ball, Neesham doesn't quite catch this one, and sends the ball in a similar direction to his previous shot, but crawling along the ground on this occasion. The Kiwi pair sense the chance to run two, although it's going to be very close with a good throw. BUT NO! England fielder Jason Roy fumbles the ball in the outfield, and Neesham easily makes his ground. It's an error from Roy at the worst possible time, and New Zealand now only need five to win from three balls. 11-0 off 0.3.

Fifth ball, almost exactly the same outcome, and this time Roy throws the ball to the wrong end! If he sends it to Buttler at the striker's end, Neesham is likely run out, but instead he throws it to Archer at the bowler's end, where Guptill is comfortably making his ground. Now only three to win from two balls, New Zealand are so close. 13-0 off 0.4.

Sixth ball, Archer bangs it into the pitch, and Neesham swipes but doesn't get hold of it. Archer runs down the wicket and grabs the ball, but there is enough time for both Kiwi batsmen to make their ground for one run. It will be Guptill on strike for the final ball of the World Cup, with New Zealand needing two to win from it, and England needing to restrict them to one or less.

By 7.30 pm on 14th July 2019, I'd spent over twenty-five years as a sports fanatic wondering what it would feel like to experience true glory. I'd had moments of utter euphoria as a result of sporting victories, none more so than in the summer of 2012 during the London Olympics, when Andy Murray won his first tennis Grand Slam, and when Europe battled back from the abyss to win the Ryder Cup at Medinah, USA. As I reflect, they were all indeed moments of glory, but I'd been waiting for something more than that. I'd been waiting for *glory in all it's glory.*

This is it, one Jofra Archer delivery to decide an almost nine-hour long cricket match, a World Cup final, at the end of an incredible seven-week tournament in our own country, after the most sensational four-year journey from the base of a mountain too big even to imagine summiting.

Here comes Archer, running in for one last time with those long, languid strides. He releases the ball, and it flies in towards Guptill's pads. The Kiwi flicks it into the on side, and as soon as he hits it, he knows that he's not found a gap for the ball to reach the boundary.

Famed for being lightning quick, Guptill immediately charges down the wicket towards the bowler's end. He knows that if he's going to win the World Cup for his country, he's going to have to rely on that pace, and make it back down to the striker's end for two.

The camera pans out towards the boundary, where who else but Jason Roy is tearing in from the rope to collect the ball. It's only moments after he's made two errors in judgement to gift New Zealand valuable runs, but the hopes of England now lie in the hands of his fielding.

Just as Guptill is turning at the non-striker's end to start the twenty-two-yard journey back from whence he came, Roy, under unimaginable amounts of pressure, picks up the ball seamlessly. With Guptill having taken two or three strides back down the wicket, Roy completes one perfect fluid movement to release the ball towards wicketkeeper Buttler, who looks desperate as he waits to receive the ball by the stumps at the striker's end.

The ball flies through the air, and it is now a race between it and Martin Guptill to see who can reach their intended destination first. Buttler collects the ball about two yards to the right of the stumps, with Guptill only about five yards from home and moving at incredible pace. In the space of what must only have been a tenth of a second, Buttler destroys the stumps, and Guptill makes his ground.

For the briefest of moments, I have absolutely no idea who has won the 2019 Cricket World Cup. Is it England, or New Zealand?

As wicketkeeper Jos Buttler ecstatically sprinted away from the cricket stumps that he'd just smashed to pieces, it all became clear. It was England. We'd done it, in the most dramatic circumstances imaginable, we'd won this most astonishing game of sport.

I'd like to see a figure of how many times in my life I've lost all control of myself. There really can't have been many, and I don't think that I've ever lost my mind in the way that I did right then.

I took off in an unplanned direction, sprinting wherever my legs decided to take me. I was screaming deliriously, jumping on strangers, while charging around a beer garden in which I'd spent so many sporting occasions. I was completely out of control, but eventually managed to find my way back to the lads. The emotion of the situation was far, far too much for me to be able to handle, and as I embraced my big brother, I burst into tears on his shoulder.

Having just written about twenty-five years of sport-related feelings, I can't think of any words that can suitably express how that moment felt. It was ecstasy, euphoria, the pinnacle of existence. It was far better than I'd ever dreamed it could be, but I can't fathom a sentence that adequately explains what was happening inside of me. It just didn't seem real that after all that time, one of my sporting teams had won the ultimate *prize*, and every single element had come together during the *process*.

The *journey* that we'd been on since 2015, throughout the tournament, and during the match, had been scarcely believable. The *quality* that every single one of those eleven players had displayed had been unparalleled to that of any other England cricket team. The *connection* that I felt with the players in that moment, particularly to the three Yorkshire lads and the heroic, teary-eyed Ben Stokes, was so powerful. I only wish that I could have seen what the *odds* had been for us to win this World Cup after the 2015 debacle, as well as at the various points at which we'd looked down and out during our epic Lord's battle with the Black Caps. Celebrating with the hundreds of people packed into the pub enveloped the pure passion that makes British sports fandom *culture* the best in the world to be immersed in during a moment of glory.

That was just it though. With all of this having come together, and the ultimate *prize* having been attained, the emotion of the situation would have been nominal without the one other element. Glory in all it's glory can only be achieved in the face of unimaginable *drama*.

That is why I call the 2019 Cricket World Cup final my *Aguero Moment*. All the elements had fallen in to place, and then the most *dramatic* of knife-edge situations had somehow landed in my favour after looking so unlikely to across so many moments. When Boult had stepped on the boundary rope after catching Stokes; when Guptill had launched the ball in from the boundary to try and run Stokes out, only for the ball to deflect off our man's bat and run away for six; when Roy had charged in from the boundary having just made two fielding errors to pick up and throw under the most extreme of pressure; when Guptill had dived in and got his bat past the crease just a fraction of a second after Buttler had destroyed the stumps.

I'd like to tell you that I was able to take a second amid the chaos in that beer garden to *experience* the moment, just as I had done at Elland Road a couple of months earlier. However, this, quite simply, had not been an option. I'd been too engulfed with delirium to have a clue as to what was happening. The events of that day are proof to me that it's not possible to stop and *experience* a moment when you are totally and utterly *lost* in one.

That, for me, is why the act of being a sports fan is incomparable to anything else in life. You can become so consumed by emotion as you support, that you become devoid of the capacity to remove yourself from the moment. It is about being so engrossed in what you are feeling that the ability to consciously consider anything else in your life becomes wholly redundant. Maybe it is different for other sports fans, but for me, only *drama* can make this happen. Add to that the ultimate *prize* lying in wait at the end of the most incredible *journey*, and there are so few things that can yield a more powerful emotional response.

After withdrawing my face from my brother's shoulder, I hugged each friend with whom I'd just experienced the greatest moment of my entire life. I then let out another scream of joy, as the magnitude of what had just happened started to sink in.

I made my way to the bar to get the most celebratory of rounds in, and continued to wipe the tears from my cheeks as

I joined the queue. I was standing behind an enormous bald bloke, who turned around immediately after I'd got there. He caught a quick glimpse of my expression before turning back to face the bar, but having clearly picked up on the tears in my eyes, he turned straight back around to take a closer look.

As he did, I could see that this absolute beast of a chap had slightly red eyes himself. He then said 'Have you been fucking crying too?', before giving me an enormous bear hug. As glorious as that was, and as much as I enjoyed his embrace, it was what he said afterwards that most resonated with me.

'Enjoy this while it lasts mate, who knows when we'll be here again.'

41

The destination

I feel like my whole life has been a story of chasing a pot of gold at the end of a rainbow. Sometimes it's been a good thing, sometimes it's been a bad thing, but having learned how to make the most of it as a personality trait, I wouldn't change it for the world.

In sporting terms, I'd been chasing that pot of gold for nearly twenty-five years by the time I took my seat at Mohali Cricket Ground in India to watch England play Test cricket in 2016. I had experienced some special sporting moments by then, but the need to keep chasing glory as a fan faded when the process of watching sport became a pot of gold in itself.

After England won that most unbelievable 2019 Cricket World Cup final, I learned a valuable lesson about sporting glory. When a total stranger implied that we didn't know when we'd be 'here' again, I realised that the best sporting journeys for a fan don't end with the winning of a *prize*. That day, the England team, and all of their fans, reached a *destination*.

When I was depressed, I essentially spent four and a half years chasing the future. I was so miserable in the present that I started to create ideas of happiness in my head, which only served to act as a distraction from my current unhappiness. I kept believing that a sporting victory of some kind, or a travelling trip, or some other concept that I'd not yet imagined, would come along and provide me with total personal fulfilment. The problem was that I saw all of these things as *prizes* that would deliver permanent contentment, as opposed to *destinations* that I should embrace while temporarily there.

That bald bloke in the Original Oak pub inadvertently helped me to see that moments of total euphoria should be seen as a *place in time*. Each one is a pot of gold that you discover at the end of a rainbow, and the key is to enjoy it's riches before the moment passes. When you view a moment in time as a place though, you recognise that you can revisit it in your mind whenever you feel like doing so. I learned that if you chase a rainbow, and find a pot of gold there, it's riches can be endless.

During the couple of days that followed the 2019 Cricket World Cup final, I watched every interview going, took in each different broadcaster's highlights show, and read pundits' perspectives from all around the world. There was so much more to that glorious day than just my personal experience; I wanted to know how it affected every cricket fan across the globe.

I've gained immeasurable pleasure from revisiting that place, and all the others in my sporting memory during the writing of my story. I may not have reached too many *final destinations* at the end of my various sports fandom journeys, but any journey that I've embarked upon has had temporary stop-offs along the way. As I've revisited each one of those *destinations*, I feel like I've been able to experience it with a slightly different perspective, and gain something new from it each time. Each one of those pots of gold seems to have fresh coins in it whenever I return.

Back at that Test match in Mohali, I recognised that reaching the destination wasn't the be-all and end-all, as I became conscious of how good the journey could be. It was as though the journey itself became the destination, as the freedom and peace of sitting in the glorious Indian sunshine watching elite level sport made me feel about as happy as I could imagine feeling. It felt like I was walking towards a rainbow with a sherpa carrying a pot of gold for me, all the while knowing that there might just be an even bigger pot waiting for me at the end.

That was the problem for me with Leeds United. I wasn't enjoying the journey at all, and not only could I no longer envisage there being a pot of gold at the end of it, I couldn't even see a rainbow. Everything about my football club was in such a bad place that I stopped believing that there was even a destination for me to walk towards, which made the journey pointless as I saw it then. If I'd had the foresight to recognise that I would eventually find the path again, I might not have abandoned the journey altogether.

Ultimately, I can't help but feel partially glad for having quit Leeds though, as the passion that I developed for all the other sports that I threw myself in to probably wouldn't have reached the same level had I not. Having lost sight of the Leeds United rainbow, I couldn't help but look out for other ones, as the very nature of my personality dictates that I can't enjoy a journey without one.

One day, I hope to return to the mountain in Montenegro on which I came out of depression. It's an example of a highly significant literal destination that I can revisit, and although I'm unlikely to feel exactly as I did back on that day in 2011, I'm sure that it will provide a different kind of joy. The incredible view of Kotor Bay might not seem quite *as* spectacular as it looked back then, but maybe I'll see a part of the landscape that I missed.

I feel as though the privilege of a sports fan, particularly one that has been on an epic journey, is that they can revisit the destinations that they so rarely reach whenever they wish to. For the rest of my life, I can go back and experience the 2012 Olympics, Andy Murray winning the US Open, the Medinah miracle, and above all, the 2019 Cricket World Cup final. I can think back to these events and gain tremendous pleasure, or better yet watch them back thanks to the technological age in which I've grown up. Each time I do, I gain something from the slightly different perspective that I have, which occurs both from new details that I pick up on, and based on how I change as an individual over time.

Moving forward, I can't wait to chase some more sporting rainbows, now that I realise how much I enjoy the journey towards them that is. If I reach one and discover a new pot of gold in the process, then I will delight in it's riches at the time, all the while knowing that I can revisit it whenever I feel like in the future. Should I not reach that coveted destination, then I'm sure that I'll have enjoyed the journey so much that it won't even matter.

What I know for sure is that the sight of a rainbow, and the knowledge of a potential pot of gold at the end of it, will encourage me to embark upon many more journeys as a sports fan yet.

42

A man behind a sports fan

I have a confession to make. When I came up with the idea of writing this book, I had no idea how I intended for it to end. The 2019 Cricket World Cup hadn't yet started, and I didn't foresee that it's final would turn out to be the best day of my life. Once it did, I knew that I had the perfect conclusion, and didn't think for a second that I would change it.

I set out writing back then to try and understand why men are so obsessed with sport. I'd just witnessed three of my best pals going through fandom hell after Leeds United were beaten in that dramatic play-off semi-final second leg with Derby County. More than anything, I wanted to understand why sports fans put themselves through it.

From a social media post I'd read, Leeds' price to reach Wembley had been cut to 1/40 with one bookmaker when Stuart Dallas had scored his first goal of the night. His team were 2-0 up on aggregate, they were playing at home, and had dominated the tie; it would seemingly have taken a miracle for them to lose from there. Somehow, they managed it, and it was yet more devastation for the Elland Road faithful.

The defeat, and Bill's contemplation as to whether he would join me in quitting as a supporter of the club, got me thinking about whether being a sports fan was worth it in emotional terms. As much as you can enjoy a journey as a fan, there are only so many times that you can take the crippling pain of a crushing defeat, and Leeds supporters have experienced that feeling more than most.

Ultimately, the odds are against any team to achieve success in a season. There were twenty-four sides in the 2018/19 Championship, with only three teams going up, with anything other than promotion likely to leave most fans unfulfilled. There's always the chance of relegation too, which really is an awful experience.

The funniest thing about all this is that promotion, or the reaching of a fan's desired destination, doesn't always fulfil you either. On the one occasion that I witnessed Leeds United achieve something during my twenty-one years as a fan, which came by way of us finishing second I should add, I barely celebrated. We were such a poor team that there was scarcely an atom of me that enjoyed a moment for which I'd waited my whole life.

With all this considered, I asked myself why sports fans as a collective are so obsessed and decided to set out on a mission to discover the answer by chronicling my fandom experiences. The way I saw it, by discussing how sport has affected me emotionally over the years, I might have been able to figure out why *I* have been so obsessed, which in turn might help me to understand why so many other people are. I hadn't realised that not only had my sports fandom affected me as a person in the past; who I was as a person had affected my sports fandom too.

I realised that I needed to write about my relationship with sport, as opposed to just writing about the sport itself, which changed the question that I'd asked myself when I'd first come up with the idea. It wasn't about why *men* are so obsessed with sport, but why *I* am so obsessed.

Upon figuring this out, the process became a far more personal one than I'd ever imagined. I found that I was delving into areas of my past that I'd not revisited, with certain parts being very challenging to face.

As I was writing about my depression, I started to experience these incredibly overwhelming pangs of emotion, as I recognised that although I'd both thought and talked about that period of my life, I'd never actually *felt* about it.

When I started to relive how I felt during the most difficult period of my life, I opened up an almighty can of worms to my entire childhood too. I started to think back to specific times and thought about how certain incidents had made me feel, which prompted more of these emotional pangs. It was as though I'd buried those feelings deep inside of myself, and they all started to come flooding out at once.

Discovering that I'd repressed large parts of my past was one of the most overwhelming experiences of my life. I barely slept over the couple of weeks that followed and was all over the place emotionally and psychologically, which led to me taking a break from my writing process. As someone that had been through mental health issues before, I held genuine fears that I might be on the brink of going down the wrong path again.

I decided to take a different approach to the one that I'd previously taken and talked to my friends and family about what I was going through. I spent four and a half years depressed, and who knows how much more quickly I could have recognised the issue had I just opened up and spoken to someone about it.

Throughout that time, I allowed myself to feel, both when on my own and in the company of others. I even shed a few tears in the process. As a result, not only did I come out of the other side feeling better than ever, I also managed to understand some of the psychology behind why I'd historically been so obsessed with sport.

Before I go into detail about it, I want to make it abundantly clear that this is all just theory. I've always had a fascination with psychology, even if I didn't enjoy my degree, but by no means do I consider myself to be a self-styled counsellor or therapist. What I can say is that I've done a lot of research, and have come up with a model that explains the vast majority of my past behaviours. It makes sense to me at least, but I'm open to the fact that it could all be off the mark. I feel as though only now that I know more about myself than I've ever known, am I aware of how much I might not know.

There are a few personality traits of mine that I perceive must be natural, as I was displaying them from very early in my life. From what my mum tells me, my brother was the most chilled out baby imaginable. He was happy to play with anything that was within reach, and if nothing was close enough, he'd just sit there placidly without a care in the world. I, on the other hand, was the direct opposite, always looking out for new things to discover, and desperate to try and go after something that I knew was out of reach. I had this ridiculous curiosity for the world and an *intuition* that helped me to recognise patterns and see how things fitted together. If I saw something interesting, I had no choice but to pursue it, as whatever it was, I *had* to give it a try.

Although I had this abnormal curiosity, I was always

perfectly happy to play on my own. I was far more interested in interacting with the world and it's contents, as opposed to interacting with other people, which displayed early tendencies of an *introverted* personality. Apparently, I was always taking off on my own, as my excitement to discover how everything worked didn't require me to play with other kids.

Another aspect of my nature caused me problems when it came to this though, as even though I was 100 percent dependent at that age, I couldn't understand why I couldn't do whatever I wanted at all times. The instant that my parents or a carer prevented me from being able to go off on my own and interact with all the things that I could see, I'd throw the wildest tantrums. Even at such a young age, I'd become so overwhelmed by a perceived loss of *control* that I'd scream relentlessly, and lurch my body to try and escape the clutches of whoever was holding me. I'd sometimes go as far as to bang my head on the concrete repeatedly, such was my despair at not being able to do what I wanted. Neither my brother nor my sister displayed anything remotely similar to this.

Finally, and arguably most importantly, I was an extremely *sensitive* child. I had multiple allergies on a physiological level, but on a psychological level, I experienced emotions very strongly, and could also detect the feelings of others seamlessly. That sensitivity was clearly on display during my tantrums, but an example of it's positive effects occurred when I'd just started at nursery, where my friend would cry every time his mum would leave him there for the day. My reaction, as a toddler, was to run to the bathroom to fetch some tissues, which I would then bring back for him to use to wipe his tears. I believe that a combination of my intuition, introversion, need for control, and sensitivity, have played a significant role in my sports fandom, alongside some of my childhood experiences.

When I was sixteen months old, my mum went through a traumatic life event that undoubtedly changed her, just as it would change anybody. Despite it, she was amazing for ninety percent of my childhood and gave me everything that I needed to ensure that I was fit and healthy. As she did so well for the most part, in such challenging circumstances, I've always considered myself to have been very fortunate to have had the childhood that I had, which I still believe to be the case.

However, things weren't always perfect, and there were times at which things became too much for her. She had a very erratic temper, and as a sensitive child, I was terrified of her when she was angry. I still received huge amounts of love from her, but until I started delving deep into my past feelings, I hadn't ever dealt with how the inconsistency and the unpredictability affected me emotionally. I didn't recognise until I wrote this book that the fact that things could have been a lot worse for me doesn't mean that I didn't experience a degree of trauma.

I have fond memories of my interactions with my dad when he still lived at home with us, and there was a lot of love and warmth between us, as there was with my mum. He very much guided me in a sporting sense and taught me how to play multiple games, which was a hugely beneficial thing for me throughout primary school and high school, but deep down, I think I found the pressure of trying to be the best that I could be quite challenging at times. He was always very encouraging, but I think that I perceived that if I wasn't doing something to the absolute best of my ability, it wasn't good enough.

Things were pretty chaotic at home after my dad moved

out, and after he left, I started to withdraw a lot. I'd spent a lot of my childhood with my brother up to that point too, but he'd reached an age at which he was out a lot more with his mates or playing cricket, and I can remember feeling a bit lost. I had a temperamental relationship with my mum, and with my dad and my brother not around as much, I didn't know where to turn.

Soon after, when I started high school, I found that I'd make a considerable effort with other kids to try and develop secure friendships, while also feeling genuinely fearful of conflict. Although I always felt like I could fit in easily, I couldn't bear the thought of falling out with anyone, which meant that the easiest thing for me to do was to adapt to be whatever the situation required me to be. The constant process of adaptation was an exhausting one, particularly bearing in mind that as an introvert, merely talking to people was energy-sapping.

The reality was that whether it was with my family members, or with my friends, I didn't always feel secure in my relationships with other people. I didn't understand how to reach out to try and fulfil my own emotional needs and found myself in a near-constant survival mode state. I was so sensitive to how people perceived me, that I became hyper-vigilant in almost all situations to ensure that I behaved in a way that wouldn't result in my exposure to criticism or conflict. I took everything personally, even piss-taking among the lads at school, and if it weren't for my ability to adapt and survive, I'd have probably spent all my time feeling emotionally traumatised.

I had a couple of friends that I felt completely comfortable with, but high school is a place in which you are constantly interacting with a whole host of other kids. As I didn't feel 100 percent comfortable at school, and I didn't feel 100 percent comfortable at home, I started to look for a place in which I would feel 100 percent comfortable, and for someone or something with which I felt 100 percent comfortable.

About halfway through high school, when I got cable TV in my bedroom after moving house, and Leeds United started their rise towards the top of English football, I had found both of these things. I'd not had the ability to develop relationships with other people in such a way that made me feel as though I was both accepted, and that I wasn't having to try hard. I struggled to fully relax and be myself, and feel as though I was in control of who I was, but I'd always had this in abundance when watching sport.

At that point, I became attached to my football club. I found that I could gain all the emotional gratification that I needed through a relationship with a sports team, without having to deal with the potential fear and shame that interactions with people brought due to my high sensitivity. I could watch sport on my own, which played into the hands of my introversion, my intuition had me imagining how amazing it might feel should I experience glory as a fan, and although I wasn't in control of the outcome, I was in total control of how much I had to give to the relationship.

Ultimately, I only really felt as though I was truly myself when I was on my own, or in a tranquil setting with one or two of my closest mates. Then, alcohol came along and helped me to enjoy previously overwhelming social environments, and gave me the confidence and desire to be out socialising. Its primary role was to suppress my sensitivity, which made interacting with other people a whole lot easier, and a whole lot more enjoyable.

I found that I started to develop closer friendships as I reached sixth-form college, as it was considerably less chaotic than high school, and I was able to spend more time in smaller crowds, which suited my personality. Still, I wasn't sure of who I was and continued to feel very sensitive to criticism and conflict, even on a jovial level.

After I turned eighteen, I started to understand that being sensitive or emotional did absolutely nothing for a young man, and it must have been around then that I began to suppress that side of myself even without the alcohol. Suppression or repression on any level only serves to cause internal conflict though, which I think is why my mental health declined once I got to university.

I'd known how sensitive I was for a long time before I went to Newcastle, but it had caused me so many problems over the years that I started to pretend that it wasn't there. By doing that, it was as though I switched off a whole chamber of feelings inside of myself, and I didn't have the external stimulation to rebalance emotionally. I felt trapped in a university environment over which I had no real control and reached a default mindset in which I permanently wanted to escape.

The classic move of a depressed person is to look out to the world for happiness, as you don't have the rational mindset through which you can look inward, which is where the problem almost always lies. Subconsciously, I felt so much self-loathing for the fact that I didn't know how to find interpersonal relationships emotionally gratifying that I blamed everything about the university experience itself for my unhappiness.

It was everybody else's fault for being boring, uninteresting, and having nothing about them, not my fault for being terrified of my vulnerabilities and insecurities. As a result, if I had to be around people, I plied myself with alcohol and spent the rest of the time pouring everything that I had into my relationship with sport.

Above all, my sports fandom was a safe environment in which for me to express my emotion. As a very emotional man, I was desperate to unleash everything that I was feeling but also felt critically ashamed that I was naturally that way. Sport was the one release for me, and although I had a horrible time in terms of my teams' success, having that entity that I knew could provide me with emotional fulfilment, while also asking nothing from me in return, was huge for me at the time.

I battled through university, half-killed myself working my seventy-two-hour weeks, and spent six months travelling without feeling happy. Then, at the end of all that, I discovered that being on my own was the solution for me, as, after years and years of being surrounded by people, I understood that I was introverted. When I returned from my travels, I created a world for myself in which I was on my own as my default way of being, choosing only to engage with people at a time that suited me. As happy as this made me, some of my behaviours still suggested that something wasn't quite right.

Having beaten depression on my own, and put the whole experience down to the simple fact that I was an introvert that had lived an extroverted existence, I became arrogant. Without realising it, the me-against-the-world mentality that I'd developed during my depression had engrained itself within me, and I became very dismissive of other people's views. The same old sensitivity issues that I had with criticism were still there, but

I'd developed what I thought was a resilience to it, which was just an extreme stubbornness. I believed that I didn't need to listen to what anybody else had to say, as I could now survive anything on my own, just as I'd perceived myself to have done when I was younger.

Critically, I've been happier than ever during the eight years between coming out of depression and beginning the writing of my story. However, I didn't realise until I started writing that I'd never actually felt for my depressed former self, or for the child that had a much more difficult experience than I'd allowed myself to think that he had. When those pangs of emotion started occurring, and I couldn't sleep, I began to recognise that I'd completely ignored the highly sensitive person inside me, and been in denial about my need for control.

Deep down, I think that I've been using my introversion as a mask to hide my sensitivity and need for control, as I've perceived them to be weaknesses. I've never been able to feel vulnerable around other people, as I was so ashamed of how vulnerable I felt as a child. After discovering such happiness in solitude in recent years, I found a box to place myself in that made me feel good about myself.

Even having been in such a healthy place in recent years, my recent revelations have made me realise that there is a perfectionist streak in me that I've been trying to satisfy for my entire adult life. The shame that I've felt about my emotional and sensitive nature has made me strive to become a master of my feelings, and I can now see how judgemental that I've been about other people's behaviour as a result.

That perfectionist streak transferred itself into my sports fandom, and it took until five years after I came out of depression to recognise that chasing that perfect moment isn't the most important thing. I feel the same about the writing of this book; the important thing isn't how it turns out, it's how much I've enjoyed the journey of writing it, which I have done endlessly. I genuinely believe that this journey of self-discovery is going to change me for the better forever too, and hopefully, I can learn to enjoy sport for what it is to an even greater extent.

The beauty of having discovered all of these repressed feelings is that for the first time in my life, I feel able to accept myself for who I am. By no means am I going to start using language like *sensitive and need control and proud*, but I can see that there are a lot of positives that I can take from these traits.

The upside to being sensitive has been that although I've felt easily hurt on an emotional level over the years, I've also been susceptible to the incredible feelings of euphoria that I've discussed throughout this book. The positive to having a desire for control is that I've taken total control of my own life, and done some of the most amazing things over the past few years. Without it, I don't know if I'd have travelled to the Euros in France, headed out to India and the West Indies to watch the cricket, or become the sports fan that I love being today.

A big lesson that I've learned from this writing experience is how different a solution is from an answer. Creating a world in which I can do as I please all the time has been the perfect solution to the various issues that I had when I was younger, but the fact that I am introverted is only a fraction of the answer. My intuitive nature, my sensitivity, and my desire for control are all factors too, but I believe the real answers run even deeper than that. If there are any counsellors, therapists, or psychologists reading this, I'd love to hear your thoughts.

I believe that as a result of both my nature and nurture, I have a dismissive-avoidant attachment style. The most prominent signs of this style of insecure attachment are for someone to have a near compulsive need for independence, and a strong preference not to depend on others, or have others depend on them. They view themselves as being invulnerable to feelings and find serious difficulty in forming close, intimate relationships with other people. They tend to dismiss any views that contrast with their opinions of themselves, and in some instances, avoid attaching to others at all costs.

I can't guarantee this is the case, of course. Still, it would explain why I essentially attached myself to my football club, and other sporting teams and individuals, while actively avoiding relationships with other people in my adult life. From what I've read, it tends to occur when there have been inconsistent emotional experiences in childhood, and although I'd buried those deep within my subconscious, I've come to terms with the fact that things weren't always perfect for me. People with this attachment style are also particularly susceptible to depression, which is something about which I know all too much.

Alongside this, I think I fall into a category of individual known as the Highly Sensitive Person. I recently read a book by Dr Elaine Aron that detailed substantial scientific research into this type of person, and I tick almost every box. I experience high levels of empathy and compassion, I'm a very emotional and intuitive individual, and I'm easily overwhelmed in highly stimulating social situations.

Ultimately, I think this explains why I have been such an extreme sports fan in my time. Although I may have poured more in to sport as a way of compensating for the lack of intimacy in my life, I can't help but believe that the magnitude of my fandom has come as a result of how strongly I feel things. My friend George once said to me, 'I've never known somebody to be as happy as you are when you're happy', which just about sums being highly sensitive up on a good day. Sadly, the same applies to the darker emotions, but since coming out of depression, I've managed to create a life for myself that allows the maximisation of the positive feelings, and the minimisation of the negative ones.

As overwhelming as discovering these repressed feelings was, it's been incredibly liberating for me to be able to accept myself for who I am after all this time. I've been fortunate that my parents have been so open and willing to discuss some of this stuff with me, and have been instrumental in me being able to figure out some of the things that I have. I've also been able to open up to the lads about it, who have provided invaluable support while also challenging me on my theories to ensure that I keep an open mind.

I feel as though I've been able to let go of the perfectionist in me, and don't feel such a need to be as good as I possibly can be at everything that I do. I have my strengths, and I have my weaknesses, and I feel OK with being able to confront those weaknesses without feeling a tremendous sense of shame.

You might be wondering why I'm telling you all this. Well, I set out writing this book to try and understand why men are so obsessed with sport. I can't tell you that; I can only tell you why *I* am so obsessed with sport. I've tried to provide an answer that is as honest, and accurate, as I can give you, although I'm aware that I may not have got it all right.

The reality is that I was born with a lot of advantages in

life, and had a great upbringing for the most part. However, a couple of small details in regards to my nature and my nurture were just a little bit off-centre, which was enough for me to go through some very challenging experiences.

With that in mind, I hope people are less shallow than I've been over the years. I want the world to understand that there will be *a man behind a sports fan*, or a person behind every unhealthy behaviour that we so mercilessly judge. If I can be so privileged and still end up going down a difficult path, I can't imagine what people with far more complicated predispositions and life experiences might go through. If nothing else, I hope my story can open more minds up to all the factors that are involved in making every one of us different.

I've essentially spent my life addicted to sport. I've depended on it in both the good times and the bad, yet only after writing about my twenty-five-year relationship with it has that become clear. It seems to me that any dependency stems from an addiction that we have to our emotions. We are all emotional beings and spend our lives looking to feel as good as we can wherever possible. As part of my view of emotion, I was too ashamed to be able to see that, but now I can accept myself for the sensitive man that I am, I'm hopeful that I can create an even better life for myself than the one that I already have.

More importantly, I'm hopeful that I'll be able to use my experiences and the knowledge of self that I've developed to help other sports fans. I know that my story is an extreme example, but I've known too many men over the years who have visibly had an unhealthy relationship with their fandom. With all the fantastic work that's happening around the mental health of sports professionals themselves, I hope this can raise awareness about the struggles that fans across the world face too.

For now, though, there's only one fan that I feel a degree of direct responsibility for, and I'll be keeping a very close eye on his development. If his journey so far with his football club is anything to go by though, I think he'll be just fine.

43

Marching on together

On Sunday 21st October 2001, a couple of weeks before my 15th birthday, my little brother James was born. I went down to the hospital to meet him and see my mum, before rushing off to get down to Elland Road. After earning a point in an entertaining 0-0 draw with Chelsea, it was confirmed that James would end his first day on Earth with Leeds United atop the Premiership.

As my stepdad was a Manchester United fan, I can remember having a few jokes with him and my older brother Matt about who James would support. The consensus was that it would be left to James to decide, which left me scheming as to how I could subtly go about persuading him to become a Leeds fan once he was old enough to understand what football was.

Three years later, I revisited the conversation with my stepdad with a very different mindset. Leeds had since been relegated to the Championship, there was a lot of talk about the club potentially being liquidated due to our financial implosion, while Manchester United continued to win trophies on all fronts. Having become more educated about the psychological impact that your football team can have on you as a fan, I started to consider James' long-term interests.

As much as it pained me to say it, I suggested to my stepdad that it might be a good idea for my little brother to follow in his father's footsteps, not his brother's. His response was to say that the only thing that mattered was what made James happy, which although I respected, was the exact point around which I was attempting to future pace. My stepdad then acknowledged that we had no idea where either team would be when it was time for James to decide anyway, and the discussion was shelved once more.

On 6th September 2008, with my stepdad's permission, I took James to his first football match, a few weeks shy of his seventh birthday. Due to a combination of factors, James had started to express an interest in Leeds United, not Manchester United, and although I genuinely had my doubts as to whether it was good for him, we headed off to Elland Road to watch Leeds' League One match against Crewe Alexandra. At the time, Leeds were sitting in mid-table in League One, while Manchester United had just confirmed their status as the best team in world football by winning the Champions League. They would go on to win a third straight Premier League title that season.

Despite all that, James didn't look back after Leeds' 5-2 victory that day. He was able to understand the significance of our play-off semi-final defeat to Millwall at the end of his first season as a fan, our victory over his father's team at just eight years old in January 2010, and our promotion from League One a few months later. During the first half of the 2010s, he was a regular at Elland Road to watch Leeds play Championship football, and by the time that he got his first season ticket in 2017/18, his decision to choose his home-town team was starting to look like a good one.

Italian businessman Andrea Radrizzani had just assumed 100 percent control of the club, and he acted immediately to buy back Elland Road, making it the property of Leeds United for the first time in thirteen years. I can remember hearing about it and thinking that it was the first piece of positive off-the-field news that I'd heard about Leeds in decades. Meanwhile, Manchester United had limped to sixth in the Premier League and hadn't even threatened to challenge for years. Sir Alex Ferguson's departure had signalled the end of their dominance of English football, and they were having all sorts of difficulties plotting a route back to the top.

Although James' first campaign as a season ticket holder ended modestly, Marcelo Bielsa was appointed as manager a few weeks later. The multi-million-pound signing of Patrick Bamford provided further proof of the club's positive intent, and soon after, Elland Road was hosting some of the most entertaining football from a Leeds United team in it's history.

Not only did James attend every home game of the 2018/19 season, but he also followed in his big brother's footsteps by travelling around the country to away games in support of his team. When we watched a televised fixture together on one of the few occasions that he wasn't at the match, his behaviours as a fan while in the act of supporting Leeds reminded me a lot of myself. Although he's a little quieter than I am and was therefore not as overt, there was a natural passion and aggression about him that brought a smile to my face, while also registering with my warier side.

He was there on that desperate night against Derby County as Leeds crashed out of the play-offs, which I found heartbreaking. As a man who experienced so much pain as a Leeds United fan, the thought of my seventeen-year-old brother suffering the dark side of football fandom was hard to process. James was not to be deterred though and renewed his season ticket the following day.

When he asked me whether I'd like to go to an away game with him early in the 2019/20 season, I bit his hand off. It felt entirely natural for me to go to a Leeds game with him, and as away-days had been the undoubted highlight of supporting my team back in the day, I couldn't wait for the occasion. We went to Preston North End, and his ballistic celebration when Eddie Nketiah equalised for Leeds in the dying embers of the match only served to reiterate my opinion that James was not just a Leeds United supporter, he was a *fanatic*.

As Bielsa guided the club to the top of the Championship table by March 2020, everything appeared to be in place for Leeds to make their long-awaited return to the Premier League. They were playing the best football in the league, had overcome a mid-season blip, and looked as united as any group of players I'd ever seen at the club. Even with everything that had happened at Elland Road in the eighteen years since the beginning of Leeds' fall from grace, it appeared that it would take something unprecedented to stop this particular promotion charge.

Although there were far more important things to consider at the start of the Covid-19 crisis, James, Andy, Bill, Rodney, and all the other Leeds fans that I spoke to couldn't help but have one thought at the forefront of their mind. *Everything that feasibly could have happened at Leeds United since Premiership relegation in 2004 appeared to have happened, leaving nothing other than a global pandemic to prevent top-flight football from returning to the city for 2020/21.*

After a couple of months of desperate uncertainty, it was finally announced that the 2019/20 Championship season would be completed. However, even with this being considerably better news than the distinct possibility of a voided season, all those battle-weary fans that had experienced so much hurt couldn't help but fear the worst. When Cardiff City beat Leeds 2-0 in the first game back, their fears appeared to be vindicated.

However, with everything about this new model of Leeds United Football Club being so much improved, it didn't surprise me to see the Whites turn over promotion rivals Fulham in their next game. A slight blip of a 1-1 draw followed against Luton Town three days later, but a 3-1 victory at Blackburn Rovers was the perfect response, particularly with West Bromwich Albion and Brentford breathing down their necks at the top of the table.

I believe that the moment that every Leeds fan truly felt that promotion back to the Premier League was going to happen came with the 5-0 demolition of Stoke City at Elland Road. Although I didn't watch the game with James or any of the lads, it was an absolute privilege to see a Leeds team play in such a way, in the exact fixture in which they'd started their journey under Bielsa the previous season. If it wasn't all but wrapped up by then, the last-gasp winning strike from Pablo Hernandez at his old club Swansea City was the cue to get the champagne on ice.

With West Brom and Brentford refusing to give up on a top-two spot without a fight, nothing short of three points was required against Barnsley in the antepenultimate game of the season. I went to the pub to meet Andy, Bill, Mel, and a total fanatic pal of ours called Liam for the game, and it took a battling 1-0 victory over an impressive Tykes side to leave Leeds requiring just a point to secure promotion. After the game, I messaged James to ask him how he was feeling, and he told me that he finally felt ready to celebrate. Had he been through the trauma that some of his more senior fans had been through, he may not have been so confident. It turned out that he was right to be.

On Friday 17th July 2020, 5920 days on from relegation on 2nd May 2004, Leeds United were promoted back to the Premier League. West Bromwich Albion couldn't beat Huddersfield Town in their penultimate Championship fixture of the season, which left Leeds an unassailable five points ahead of their closest rivals, who now only had one game to play.

I was out for dinner at the time, but my immediate response upon hearing the news was to message James, my older brother Matt, my dad, and the lads to congratulate them. I can't deny that I felt a degree of sadness for the former fanatic in me, as it would have been one of the greatest moments of my life. However, the adaptation that I'd undertaken over in recent times, by which I'd essentially come to support the club through a desire to want nothing but good for it's fans, left me feeling overwhelmingly happy for the city as a whole.

The following day, Brentford lost at Stoke, which confirmed Leeds as champions. In a beautifully poetic moment, I was walking through Headingley that Sunday afternoon when I heard cries of 'CHAMPIONE CHAMPIONE OLE OLE OLE' coming from every pub in the vicinity. Leeds had just beaten old foes Derby County, and a city-wide celebration that had started on the Friday looked like it would go on long into the Sunday night.

In another life, I'd have been in and amongst the party. However, the smile of satisfaction that came to my face suggested to me that I was perfectly content with the once-removed supporter of the club that I'd become, as opposed to the fanatic (fan) that I might have been. When I saw the Leeds players lift the Championship trophy after a 4-0 pummelling of Charlton Athletic a few days later, that feeling was reaffirmed.

Despite the various lockdown restrictions that had been put in place by the government to prevent mass gatherings during the Covid-19 crisis, I received a couple of videos from James during that week. He'd been right in amongst thousands of fans as they'd celebrated Leeds' promotion in the city centre and outside Elland Road, and I certainly couldn't bring myself to take on the responsible older brother role by asking him why he wasn't socially distancing. That would have been pretty rich coming from a fan that had kicked doors off their hinges and nearly burned pubs to the ground, and in reality, I wanted nothing more than for him to celebrate however the fanatic in him saw fit.

From here, I intend to support James, and all of the other Leeds United fanatics that I know, as they begin their march on a whole new journey together. I hope that the next twenty-six years in Leeds' history will replicate the drama of the last twenty-six, with the caveat that the level of quality displayed by Marcelo Bielsa's class of 2019-20 goes with it. Who knows what the next few years hold, maybe I'll end up writing a book about my little brother's experiences following his football team's rise to the top of the English game, the exact position that they were in at the end of his first day on Earth.

Above all, I'm grateful for the fact that I foresee few issues to come for the man behind that particular sports fan. He seems far more well-rounded, mature, and responsible than his older brother was at his age, not that I would change a thing about the journey that I've been on had I the option. After all, how many fans have experiences such that they feel compelled to write a book about them?

It's been pretty exhausting to chronicle it all if I'm honest, so part of me is hoping that the next chapter in my life is a little less dramatic. I'd like to say that's up to me, but I think we both know that it's for sport to decide.